AMERICAN TERRORISM:
A BRIEF LEGAL HISTORY OF THE LYNCHING OF BLACK FOLK IN THE UNITED STATES

Farria Law Group
Haslet, TX
www.farrialaw.com

©2020 by the Farria Law Group
All Rights Reserved.

Any references to Internet websites (URL's) were accurate at the time of drafting; neither the Farria Law Group nor Garrick A. Farria is responsible for inaccurate information or broken URL links.

Library of Congress Cataloging-in-Publication Data is available upon request
Library of Congress Control Number: 2020917243

Farria, Garrick Arthur

Cover photo: Tallahatchie River Photo Credits: M. Susan Orr-Klopfer / Public domain
Emmett Till's watery grave in Sumner County, MS on August 31, 1955

Includes bibliographical references and endnotes
ISBN: 978-0-578-75855-8

1. Legal History—African-Americans—Lynching—15th century--16th century—17th century—18th century—19th century—20th century—21st century
2. Legal history—4th Amendment-5th Amendment-10th Amendment—13th Amendment—14rh-Amendment—15th Amendment—1964 Civil Rights Act—1965 Voting Rights Act—1968 Civil Rights Act Expansion
3. Africana Studies—African-American Studies—Black Studies
4. Civil Rights—Enfranchisement—Race Relations—Political Participation

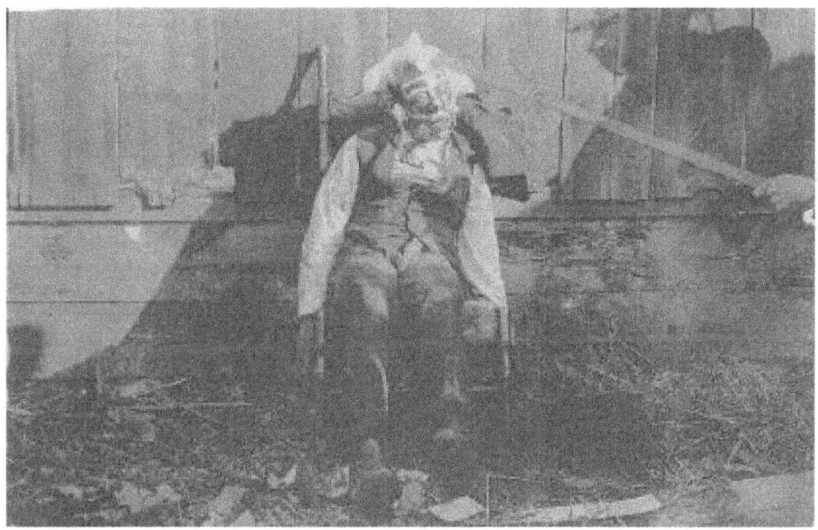
Anonymous African man propped up in a chair to show off the desecration of his body post lynching, notice the glued cotton to his face, and the stick holding his head up. The unknown location around 1900 (Public Domain).

The United States Supreme Court is the highest Court in the land. The phrase "equal justice under the law" is etched into Western Pediment and right about above the main entrance to the Court. (Public Domain)

About the Author

Garrick A. Farria, born in New Orleans, LA, grew up in Cincinnati, OH. He attended several area high schools including, Walnut Hills High School and Cincinnati Country Day School and, received a post-graduate diploma at Blair Academy (Blairstown, NJ). His story could have ended right there after a fateful night in Cincinnati, OH, during the Summer of 1993, however.

Garrick and his high school buddy Eugene Anderson were hanging out in the Short Vine section of town near the University of Cincinnati (not far from where Sam DuBose got lynched by gunshot decades later). Garrick and Eugene got accosted by a couple of White women CPD officers who forced Garrick to place his hands on the scorching hood of a cop car that was left running in the summer heat.

One of the cops had her hand on her holstered service weapon the whole time her partner ran his identification. Garrick was lucky that night. The cops merely threw his I.D. at his feet after coming back "clean" and scolded him about "fitting some description of someone they were looking for." Garrick could have been stopped by Ray Tensing that night, or Brian Encina, or Betty Shelby, or Tim Loehmann, or Joseph Pantaleo, or any other member of the law enforcement lynch unit, and things may have turned out drastically different.

The Creator and ancestors had different plans. Eugene eventually went on to get a Ph.D. from the University of Virginia.

Garrick received a Bachelor of Arts degree in African and African American Studies from Temple University, a Master of Arts degree in African American and African Studies from The Ohio State University (with a thesis titled "*A Historiography of Pan-Africanism and its Relationship to the Emigrationist Movement from 1829-1908*"), and received a Juris Doctorate from Texas Wesleyan University School of Law (now TAMU School of Law).

Garrick has been a member of the State Bar of Texas since 2011 and is admitted to practice in the Northern District of Texas. Garrick focuses his law practice primarily in the areas of Employment and Labor Law, Civil Rights, and Criminal Defense.

Garrick has over fifteen years' experience working in the American Labor Movement with two of the oldest industrial and service-based unions in North America, namely UNITE! (and UNITE-HERE) and the Service Employees International Union. Garrick and his family were stuck in Hurricane Katrina. At the same time, he served

as the UNITE-HERE Louisiana District Manager representing union members at the Ernest N. Morial Convention Center, the Louisiana Superdome, the old Fairmont Hotel, and the Loews Hotel.

Garrick and his wife Denita Singh have been married for seventeen years and have been living in Tarrant County, Texas, since their post-Katrina relocation. They have a son they are incredibly proud of named Demitrius. His parents, parents-in-law, siblings, and countless nieces, nephews, aunties, uncles, cousins, and friends along the way have been tremendous blessings.

Garrick A. Farria at the Lorraine Motel Historical Preservation Site and National Civil Rights Monument, Memphis, TN.
A gunman lynched Dr. Martin Luther King, Jr. on April 4, 1968, at this location.

Photo Credits/ Garrick A. Farria February 17, 2016

Rosewood, FL Massacre 1923 Levy County, FL (Public Domain)

New York Times Headline on Rosewood Massacre, January 8, 1923 (Public Domain)

Acknowledgments:

My wife Denita gets the lion share of credit for her love, support, and patience as I have been slowly rebuilding my library that washed away during Hurricane Katrina. She also served as an early editor of this work in the preliminary stages.

My mom, Rhodia Farria Charlton, who's passion for our people and story of her experience at LSUNO (now UNO) after the lynching of various Black leaders and how that was met by cheering and clapping by White classmates, lit a burning fire under me. She also helped by serving as one of my proofreaders.

My Dad, Arthur Farria, Jr., who always made sure we stayed connected to New Orleans, no matter how far away we were and, always taught us that hard work and dedication pay off.

My Siblings Jerren Farria and Ronita Farria Dean, your undying love and support have been incredible, and thank ya'll for raising such beautiful families; my nieces and nephews are amazing.

My aunts Lenthia Rolling and Cabrenthia Rolling, and my cousin Doncelyn Johnson also deserve special acknowledgment for their assistance with preparing the final manuscript, proofreading, and editing.

My crew from the 8th Floor of Gladfelter Hall at Temple University: Kelly Harris, Nate Thompson, Norman Bayard, John King, Brian Ekundayo Jones, Dave Norment, Faith Washington, and Dana King—thanks for the challenge, inspiration, motivation, and love.

My O-State crew: Tanya Devaughn, Jelani Favors, Derrick White, Michael Johnson, and Alvin "Killah" Conteh; thank you all for the friendship, support, and brotherhood over the years. And thank you for your contributions to this work.

The older folks that took us under their collective wings back in the day at Temple and had been guiding students through critical information ever since: Sam Livingston, Eddie Becton, Valethia Watkins, Mario Beatty, Troy Allen (maa kheru), and Greg Carr.

I am eternally grateful to Nathaniel "Pop" Norment, Sonia Petersen Lewis, Theophile Obenga, Molefi K. Asante, William E. "Nick" Nelson (maa kheru), James Upton, Lupenga Mphande, Carla Pratt, Neal Newman, Michael Green, Tonya Pierce, and Neil Sobol.

The good brothers and sisters I connected with over the years: Brandon Monroe, Eugene Anderson, Christian Hill, John Hudson, Treigg Turner, David Williams, Jim Johnson, Renea Overstreet, Ivette Melgarejo, Pascal Lee, Jean Hervey, Bruce Raynor, Mark Fleischman, Edgar Romney, Clayola Brown, Lynne Fox, Noel Beasley, Lynn Talbot, Chris Chafe, Ahmer Qadeer, Keith Mestrich, Ed Vargas, John Lacey, Wade Rathke, Louis Jamerson, Moricka Burgess, Andrew Shirley, Bill Covington, Toya Barnes-Teamer, Danneal Jones, Christina Vasquez, Ezekiel Tyson, Christina Fuentes, and Martin Miller, thank you all for the assistance, guidance, and opportunities to learn and grow.

Special Acknowledgements to Greg, Pop, Sam, John, Dana, and Norm. As educators, I understand how busy you all are. I appreciate the time you took to read early drafts, the suggestions you made, and the guidance you all offered in steering this work; your contributions are very much appreciated.

Special Acknowledgements go to the online curators at the Digital Collections at the Cornell University Library—Rare Collections Department and their posting of the public domain works from the Loewnthall Collection of African-American Photographs.

Special Acknowledgements also go to the Birmingham Civil Rights Institute, Birmingham, Alabama. Klu Klux Klan Exhibit Credit: The George F. Landegger Collection of Alabama of Photographs in Carol M. Highsmith's America, Library of Congress, Prints and Photographs Division [LC-DIG-highsm-05074]

Special Acknowledgements to the good folks at the Southern Poverty Law Center, the Peace and Justice Museum and Memorial, the American Black Holocaust Memorial, and the Ida B. Wells Museum. Thank you all for all the essential work that you do in preserving the historical record around the brutal practice of the lynching of African people in this country.

There is no way this project would have reached completion without the love and support of so many folks; hopefully, the universe is pleased I alone own all the mistakes.

This book is dedicated to Demitrius, Ja'nae, Pierre, Tre', Christina, Roman, Ryanne, and Langston; prayerfully, you all can shape a different world with different outcomes.

Table of Contents

Prologue

Chapter 1 Introduction—American Terrorism as a Concept

Chapter 2 Historical Uses of Lynching against African People in the Western Diaspora—American Terrorism in Practice

Chapter 3 Early Colonial Attitudes towards Enslaved Africans—American Terrorism before There Was an America

Chapter 4 American Law and American Terrorism through Reconstruction

Chapter 5 American Law and American Terrorism from Jim Crow through the Civil Rights Movement of the 1960s

Chapter 6 American Law and Modern-Day American Terrorism

Chapter 7 American Law and American Terrorism in the Twenty-First Century

Chapter 8 Confronting American Jurisprudence, American Law, and American Terrorism—Conclusion and Solutions

Works Cited

Prologue

This book was incredibly challenging to write. Not so much creatively or even in the technical sense, but the subject matter can be a bit overwhelming. African people in this country have been brutalized Century after Century after Century in often gruesome and gut-wrenching ways. The gristly details are not being shared for shock value but rather to honor the terrorized and provide a fulsome account of the historical record.

This book presents a brief historical and legal analysis of the continued lynching of Black people in the United States. It is not an exhaustive text at all. It does not cover each decision handed down from the U.S. Supreme Court, or other cases from the federal or state judiciary that addressed African people in America. It analyzes cases that played crucial roles in setting the stage for the brutal practice of lynching to occur.

This book also examines some statutory laws passed on the federal, state, and local level intended to control the handling and movement of the sons and daughters of Africa on these shores. Close attention is paid to some of the laws that led to the rise of *American Terrorism* meted out against Black women, men, and children over the long arc of our short history in this land.

There is also an analysis of an international case and the use of international law by African American freedom fighters and the vast amount of evidence they presented to charge the United States of America with having committed genocide against Africans in America.

Please note the terms "African," "African in America," "African-American," "Negro" and "Black" interchangeably throughout this work for articulation purposes and when I am directly quoting others.[1] I also capitalize the first letter of the racial group when addressing specific groupings of people like African, Indigene, and White. Lastly, the "N" word is directly quoted from those who call us that in their words and deeds.

Also, note that Ronald Weitzer discussed "settler states" as societies founded by migrant groups who assume a superordinate position vis-à-vis native inhabitant. These groups then build independent states that are *de jure* or *de facto* independent from the mother country and organized around the settlers' political domination over the indigenous population".[2]

---

[1] Please see the collection of speeches given at a 1960 lecture titled "The Name Negro: Its Origin, Purpose, and Evil Use" which were compiled and published as a collection of essays edited by Richard B. Moore in that same year. The lecture participants walked through the etymology of the word, the historical roots of how and why the word was used, and a call for Africans in America to ultimately discard their collective use of the word. The spirit of the lecture, which John Henrik Clarke was a participant in, was probably best captured by African Orthodox Church Archbishop Reginald Grant Barrow who stated that a magazine description of an African man from the Continent as a "Negro" and a "native" struck a chord with him and caused him to remark that "to him, meant someone inferior, somebody who had no right in the Africa of gold, the Africa of diamonds, the Africa of oil, and the Africa of great wealth"; please see Richard B. Moore <u>The Name Negro: It's Origin and Evil Use</u> (Baltimore: Black Classic Press, 1992); pp.30-1.

[2] Please see, Ronald Weitzer, <u>Transforming Settler States: Communal Conflict and Internal Security in Northern Ireland and Zimbabwe</u> (Berkeley: University of California Press, 1990) pp. 24

This describes the exact atmosphere that African lives, culture, and exploited labor were dumped into and had been trying to figure out a way to navigate or get out from under since the mid-sixteenth century. Therefore, I often refer to America, or the United States of America, as a settler state throughout this work.

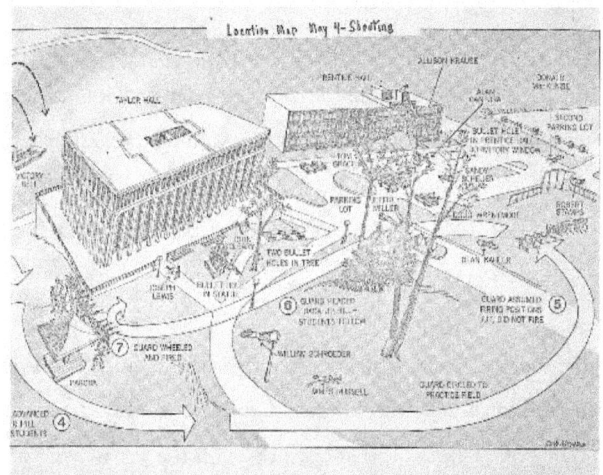

Printed map detailing the locations of structures, troop movement, bullet hole locations, and locations of casualties at the Kent State Lynching. May 4, 1970[3]
National Archives and Record Administration (NAID) No.596837

---

[3]Around 500 students began a protest of an expansion of the war in Vietnam on the campus of Kent State University in Kent, OH on May 1, 1970. On May 4, 1970, the crowds swelled to about 2,000 and the Ohio regiment of the National Guard were ordered to disperse the crowd after days of rioting. In a matter of thirteen seconds of crowd dispersal gunfire, nine protestors were wounded and four were killed.

Chapter Reviews

Chapter 1 offers an introduction of the work and frames the rest of the book by offering definitions of terms like Terrorism, lynching, trauma, and sets the legal framework for the rest of the work.

Chapter 2 looks at the ways and means Whites used lynching against African people in the Western Diaspora and the underlying rationale for it, including legal rationales.

Chapter 3 analyzes some of the colonial attitudes of African people as they were first brought here in chains.

Chapter 4 walks through the establishment of American jurisprudence and American law and how they are both used to allow, justify, and or curb the ebb and flow of the reality of American Terrorism on Africans in America through the Post-Civil War Reconstruction.

Chapter 5 examines some of the landmark Court cases and statutory laws of the period between the institution of Jim Crow Apartheid through the Civil Rights Movement of the 1960s that had significant impacts on American race relations with often bloody consequences.

Chapter 6 analyzes the modern lynching of African people in America through the end of the twentieth century.

Chapter 7 looks at lynching by law enforcement through its excessive use of force against Africans in America.

Chapter 8 offers suggestions on things that African people, and non-Africans, can do to change the course of this bloody history, especially the laws and American legal history that has set so many tragic events in motion. The footnotes should be thoroughly scrutinized as there are other lynching tales discussed within, some of which may not be known by the casual reader and may very well spark further study and analysis. These accounts further highlight the brutality of the lynching of Black folk in the twenty-first century, the callousness of the law, or both.

By George H. Farnum - Gelatin silver print. Real photo postcard. 5 1/2 x 3 1/2.Allen, James, and Lewis, Jon. Without Sanctuary: Lynching Photography in America. Twin Palms Publishers, 2000. See Allen's " Without Sanctuary website, image number 34, accessed August 25, 2010. For a discussion of the lynching, see James West Davidson. ' They say';: Ida B. Wells and the Reconstruction of Race. Oxford University Press, 2007, p. 6ff.Transferred from en.wikipedia to Commons by User: Russavia using CommonsHelper., (Public Domain), https://commons.wikimedia.org/w/index.php?curid=15057941

Lynching in Florida, Early twentieth century
Loewenthall Collection of African-American Photos
Cornell University Library, Rare Collections Department (Public Domain)

"Scourged from his home: hunted through the swamps, hung by midnight raiders, and openly murdered in the light of day, the African-American clung to his right of franchise with a heroism which would have wrung admiration from the hearts of savages"
Ida Bell Wells Barnett, 1895

Chapter 1
Introduction—American Terrorism as a Concept

The tales and reports of police brutality against African-Americans could fill volumes. One of the most glaring gaps seen throughout U.S. history, however, is the lack of precise analysis of the role that American jurisprudence (the philosophy of law) and the law itself plays in the perpetuation of the brutalization of Black folk in America.

From its earliest colonial stages and the passage of the *Black Codes* and *Fugitive Slave Laws*, just like *qualified immunity* and *stand your ground*, the various laws of this land have been both spears and shields raised against the sons and daughters of Africa. These generational struggles to survive this sojourn here since the early sixteenth century is as unending and unrelenting as the *American Terrorism* itself.

This historical record must be corrected if the people currently occupying this landmass ever hope to get out of these repeated loops. We see the killings (or attempted killings) of unarmed Blacks because they are Black. The angry explosions of justified outrage follow this. Next comes the image over-saturation, the Black *snuff films* splashed across corporate and social media platforms. The inevitable whitelash to the outrage and street action greeted by the rush to "blame the looters" surfaces at this point. The underlying Terrorism goes virtually ignored. Maybe the terrorists lose their jobs--depends. The Negro-spiritual fueled funerals, offers of forgiveness (sometimes), and lofty speeches then fill the churches and are almost always accompany a cooling of passions. If we are lucky, we might see a policy or two change in some city or some department but nothing systemic. Then the channel gets turned, and the loop goes on repeat until the next cold-blooded killing of the next unarmed Black person.

Developing a critical understanding of the historical underpinnings and legacy of this phenomena may eventually allow more folks to hop off this generational merry-go-round of predictability. Hopefully, leading to fundamental changes in how these tragic and traumatic events are addressed in the future.

Taking cues from Kenyan thinker, Ngugi wa Thiongo, who posits that "history is the result of struggle and tells of change that is perceived as a threat by all the ruling strata in all the oppressive, exploitative systems."[4] Thiongo goes on to state in summary that 1) history itself is subversive and 2) the leaders of tyrannical, oppressive regimes, and people that benefit from those regimes, not only fear the retelling of history, they seek to control it.[5]

Here in this "nation of laws," the role of the law in aiding (sometimes guiding) the repression of Black folk is hardly ever highlighted. This idea is real in every aspect of Black life and reflected in the fact that Black folks lead the states in poverty rates, incarceration rates, and childbirth mortality rates, for example.

This is also true when it comes to the most barbaric aspects of the existence of Black folk on these shores, American (domestic) terrorism, and its most favored tactic—lynching.

---

[4]Thiongo expresses these thoughts in the forward to the collection of letters Dedan Kimathi, leader of the Kenyan Land and Freedom Army (KLFA) drafted and exchanged with field generals during the Kenyan Struggle for Independence from the British between 1952 and 1960. The KLFA was also known as the Mau Mau and Kimathi was one of that movements moved famed leaders; see Kenya's Freedom Struggle: The Dedan Kimathi Papers (www.BookSurge.com, 2009) pp.xiii

[5]Ibid.

The concept of *American Terrorism* may unnerve some readers (of all stripes). Our history books, news sources, and traditions have taught us that Terrorism is something that "others" do, not Americans. Terrorism against African people is as profoundly "American" as any other symbolic tradition that defiantly continues even now. It follows that laws get passed, legal constructs are then executed, exemplified, and used to further the aims of *American Terrorism* unleashed upon African people in America.

According to the Federal Bureau of Investigation (FBI), domestic Terrorism involves violent, criminal acts committed by individuals and groups to further ideological goals stemming from domestic influences, such as those of a political, religious, social, racial, or environmental nature.[6] Important to note that the government of this land, otherwise known as the United States of America, has never declared the Knights of the Ku Klux Klan (KKK) a terrorist organization. The KKK is one of the oldest, and one-time boldest, White nationalist cell networks in America (discussed *below*) and is indeed a terrorist organization.[7]

---

[6]Please see the FBI website located here: https://www.fbi.gov/investigate/terrorism. Charles E. Cobb, Jr. offers a possible explanation when he notes that the head of FBI taskforce in McComb, MS had been in cahoots with the police chief and local sheriff in a conspiracy to jail a local Civil Rights leader named Willie Dillon, in the summer of 1964. Perhaps this shameful hesitancy is based in part on fear of embarrassment related to their past practices. See Cobb Jr., Charles E. This Nonviolent Stuff'll Get You Killed (Durham: Duke University Press, 2014) pp. 143. This amazing book will be revisited throughout this work.

[7]There is however a grassroots internet-based petition currently in circulation being pushed in the hopes of raising awareness about this gross miscarriage. Located here: https://www.change.org/p/department-of-counterterrorism-change-kkk-status-into-terrorist-organization. I repeatedly make the point that the Klu Klux Klan (KKK) is basically American "Al Qaeda". See the Anti-Defamation League (ADL) website for a report on Al-Qaeda where they note that Al-Qaeda is a "complex, international terrorist network made up of regional organizations and clandestine cells with various degrees of communication with (now deceased) Osama Bin Laden and Ayman Zawahiri; please see https://www.adl.org/resources/profiles/al-qaeda. The Knights of the Ku Klux Klan is a domestic terrorist network that has historically operated on a local, state, and regional level and as Morris Dees successfully argued in *Michael Donald v. United Klans of America (UKA)* discussed below will show that this network can be shown to operate with agency and authority between the various interdependent moving parts.

As we explore, these defenders of White nationalism and other settler state interests are indeed terrorists (along with other lynchers discussed below). They deserve that label and their rank among the wicked pantheon; they have most especially earned it through the sustained use of lynching.

Lynching, whether it's a physical lynching or a legal one, is one of the oldest and most painful weapons leveled against Africans in the U.S., by *American terrorists*, since we were first dragged off the continent of Africa and onto these shores. The practice is particularly brutal, consistently predictable in terms of reasoning and excuses, and appears to be a "go-to-move," so to speak.

The overall purpose of this work is to layout a condensed historical analysis of how the triangulated concepts of Whiteness, White supremacy, and anti-Blackness were cruelly hatched, dispatched, and then activated the brutal practice of lynching African people in America. Over the arc of our experience here, African people are collectively sent specific messages, reinforced concepts, and suffer the maintenance of the hegemony of this settler project.

We witness lynching expand, contrast, and adjust to (often bitterly slow) changes in the law and broader society.[8] These lynchings are and were notorious in the South, but they occur all across the territory. They occur in Northern states, Midwestern

---

[8]The idea that "Whiteness" and it's Janus-faced twin, "White supremacy", were created to not only "facilitate colonial administration, but to render racialization and subordination (of "others") more or less permanent" In other words, the hatching of those concepts set up the American social caste status as a pecking order and the bitter fights among "non-Whites" not to be at the bottom of that order. Please see Natsu Taylor Saito's Settler Colonialism, Race, and the Law (New York: New York University Press. 2020) pp.44. Gerald Horne adds that Whiteness was developed by the Dutch early on in Virginia in 1624, then as a concept used to convince those colonial settlers to engage in this project despite their lowly class status, setting the table for Whites to continue to vote against their economic interests to this very day. Horne talks about this particularly in several his works, but specifically in The Apocalypse of Settler Colonialism (New York: New York Monthly Review Press. 2018) pp.44.

states, and Western states. Folks like Henry Bibb and El hajj Malik el Shabazz (Malcolm X) taught us that when it comes to us, the U.S. Southern border starts in Canada.⁹

Historical Underpinnings

This exploration offered in remembrance of the journalistic and activist truth-telling, warrior wordsmithing spirit of the indefatigable Ida B. Wells-Barnett; she is legendary.

(Ida B. Wells Barnett and her children Charles, Herman, Ida, and Alfreda; 1909 (Public Domain)

The lion of the Abolitionist movement, Frederick Douglass, once remarked of her "Brave woman! You have done your people and mine a service which can neither be weighed nor measured. (Sic) If American moral sensibility were not hardened by insistent infliction of outrage

---

⁹Henry Bibb and El hajj Malik El Shabazz will both be discussed tangentially *below*. Henry Walton Bibb was born on May 15, 185 in Shelby County, KY into bondage but was a runner in every sense of the world, he escaped from enslavement and returned about a half a dozen times before finally settling in an area what is now called Ontario, Canada. Please see his public domain self-published biography, Narrative of the Life and Adventures of Henry Bibb, An American Slave, Written by Himself: Electronic Edition.

El hajj Malik el Shabazz (born Malcolm Little, changed his name to Malcolm X, and was given the name Omawale) was born on May 19, 1925 in Omaha, NB. He arose from the streets through various organizations to become a legendary leader of African people and staunch defender of Pan-Africanism; see Alex Haley's Autobiography of Malcolm X which was posthumously published in 1965.

and crime against colored people, a scream of horror, shame, and indignation would rise to Heaven, wherever your pamphlet shall be read".[10]

Her work, above most others, stands as a living testament to the exposure and erasure of the most blood-soaked weapon yielded against African people in the U.S. and still shines an eternal light on the nasty use, habit, and practice of physical racial lynching that continues today.[11]

According to the Tuskegee Normal and Industrial Institute (now Tuskegee University), and a conducted study (now archived), approximately three thousand

---

[10] Frederick Douglass wrote this letter to Ida B. Wells Barnett on October 28, 1892 and is published in a reprinted edition of Well's 1892 book which originally appeared in essay form in the *New York Age* earlier that same year. An easily accessible version can be found in the reprint of Ida B. Wells Barnett's Southern Horrors: Lynch Law in All Its Phases (New Delhi: Alpha Editions and VJJ Books. 2018).

[11] Ida Bell Wells Barnett was born on July 16, 1862 in Holly Springs, MS and had a distinguished career as an activist, journalist, organizer, business owner, educator, and platform amplifier at a time when dealing with hugely threatening and unpopular subjects including anti-lynching campaigns and getting international focus on those campaigns, suffrage, civil rights, etc. which was a dangerous endeavor for any African in America but most especially an African woman. Her seminal works include *The Red Record*, a masterful tabulation of the up-to-state statistics of racially motivated lynchings in 1895, the above mentioned *Southern Horrors* pamphlet, and the serialized pamphlet Mob Rule in New Orleans in 1900, Mob Rule in New Orleans with Southern *Horrors*: Lynch Laws in All Its Phases; Lynch law in Georgia, and The Red Record, etc.

Wells' work will be revisited throughout this book, and I argue that more focus needs to be placed on her work to highlight the effects of the lynching of African women who had been raped and sexually assaulted by White men, as African women were often afraid to report these incidents out fear of a) being lynched for lying themselves, b) not being believed or c) fearing that the men in their lives would seek vengeance and likely get lynched as a result.
The iconic post card photo of Laura Nelson hanging from a bridge in Okemah, OK in 1911 comes immediately to mind, as the brutality reigned down upon African women should be dealt with on its own terms and in its own light and just as in the way it was historically, as merely a means to pin pop the myths of African men raping White women as the justifiable excuse for lynching. The classic photo of Nelson, taken on May 25, 1911, is noted as Fig. 4 in Jonathan Markovitz's Legacies of Lynching: Racial Violence and Memory (Minneapolis: University of Minnesota Press, 2004) pp.21. See also Tucker, D. (1971). "Miss Ida B. Wells and Memphis Lynching". *Phylon (1960), 32*(2), 112-122. doi:10.2307/273997.

four hundred forty-six African people lynched in America between 1882 and 1968. This estimate is likely severely undercounted, Ibram X. Kendi notes, in his massive work, Stamped From the Beginning: The Definitive History of Racist Ideas in America, that the "White male redeemers" lynched someone every four days on average between 1889 and 1929.[12]

In many ways, the lynching of Black folk historically is as American as an afternoon game of baseball. (Incidentally, Emmett Till, teenage lynching victim discussed *below*, reportedly loved to play baseball), and just like baseball, lynching quite frankly was perfected here and served as a grand old excursion of sorts. Instead of clapping and cheering on hits and home runs, frenzied crowds would stand and cheer in adulation at the sight and sounds of black bodies crackling in an open smoky barbecue pit or tied to a tree, stripped of clothing, and left to exposure.[13]

---

[12]Tuskegee was founded by Booker Taliaferro Washington on July 4, 1881, and was the research center of luminaries like George Washington Carver, among others. Louis Harlan's biography on Washington covers the last few years of Washington's life and the dusk of his hey days as the pre-eminent Negro leader in the world until his death in his book Booker T. Washington: Wizard of Tuskegee from 1901-1915 (New York: Oxford University Press, 1983).

The digital imprint and breakdown of the overall numbers by state and race can be found on a link hosted by the University of Missouri-Kansas City Law School website at http://law2.umkc.edu/faculty/projects/ftrials/shipp/lynchingsstate.html; also see Kendi, Ibram X. Stamped From the Beginning: The Definitive History of Racist Ideas in America (New York: BoldType Books, 2017) pp. 259. And to put a finer point on the lynching numbers, there were 534 Africans lynched in Mississippi alone between 1882 and 1934 according to Akinyele Omawale Umoja in his excruciatingly detailed work We Will Shoot Back: Armed Resistance in the Mississippi Freedom Movement (New York: New York University Press, 2013) pp.16.

[13] This will be on full display in our discussion of the lynching of Sam Hose, *below*. And we will discuss Emmet Till in this essay as well. But the jovial, celebratory atmosphere that these lynchings attracted was vividly captured by Amy Louise Wood in Lynching and Spectacle: Witnessing Racial Violence in America, 1890-1940 (Chapel Hill: University of North Carolina Press, 2015) pp.30-3. Wood describes how the 3,000 people coming to Brandon, MS in 1908 to see the lynching of Will Mack, an African man accused of raping a White teenage girl, were "treated to vendors selling soda pop, ice cream, peanuts, and watermelon" and how the gallows were basically bum rushed and "raided" for souvenirs; one mother refused to stop

The Lorraine Motel Historical Preservation Site and National Civil Rights Monument, Memphis, TN.
A gunman lynched Dr. Martin Luther King, Jr. on April 4, 1968, at this location.
Photo Credit: FBI Images,
https://multimedia.fbi.gov/?q=civil%20rights&perpage=50&page=1&searchType=image

---

nursing an infant because she was so determined to watch the lynching "she had travelled such a long way to see".

See also Jonathan Markovitz's <u>Legacies of Lynching: Racial Violence and Lynching</u> (Minneapolis: University of Minnesota Press, 2004) where he notes that these lynchings were a peculiarly modern ritual that relied upon every form of communication and transportation of the day, up to the point, that railroad companies, starting as early as 1893, would designate special cars to brings folk to the "lynching" and even advertising those services if they had enough time to get the word out. pp.xxvi. One point Markovitz continually tries to make throughout his work is that lynching has largely faded away over the course of time and as we entered though the backend of the twentieth century and barreled into the next; my contention is that the lynchers have largely shifted back to law enforcement once again, acting under the "color of law"; and this is starting to be supported by the numbers of members of law enforcement who are finally starting to face some level of "justice" as a result of their extra judicial killings (lynchings) of African people. Not that these twenty first century "pattlerollers" are actually being punished, at least their being put through the ringers and rigors of criminal trials and facing judges and juries even if they ultimately get acquitted or no-billed from the grand jury.

Or perhaps it was Christmas Day for the mob, as the mob would turn deliriously giddy, at the mere thought of dead Africans strung up in a tree, like ornaments, often with their arms, legs, knuckles, genitals and, other parts butchered like a suckling pig with the horrible images of the devastation made into souvenirs and season's greetings cards.[14] Lynchings frequently became full-blown spectacles, an evil circus of vengeance, rage, and primal release.[15]

There were times when these macabre scenes would devolve into an orgy of blood lust of psychotic sport and debauchery as the participating audience, who would sometimes travel from miles around at the mere rumor of a lynching, might find themselves bidding and tussling over the dismembered body parts.[16] Pictures of

---

[14] One such incident occurred in 1891 in Texarkana, AR and was aptly described by Ida B. Wells Barnett. In this case a Black man named Ed Coy was burned to death after being charged with assaulting a White woman. Upon the unproven, hearsay claims, Coy was tied to a tree and tortured by the White men and White boys who were present and amused themselves by sticking him with knives and cutting off of pieces of his flesh. The males eventually covered Coy in coal oil and the women in the case set him on fire. Wells reported that over 15,000 stood by on that Sunday night and watched Coy burn up and die. This story is retold in <u>Mob Rule in New Orleans:</u> Op. Cit.pp.52.

Another incident, the lynching of Same Hose in 1899 about 40 miles outside of Atlanta, GA had a deeply profound effect on a young William Edward Burghardt DuBois which will be discussed at length *below*. There are countless books written on this subject, but I will only highlight a few of those stories and those works for the purposes of this brief essay. Also see, James Allen, <u>Without Sanctuary</u> (Sante Fe: Twin Palms Publishing 2000). This collection catalogues some of the most searing lynching photos publicly circulated and while it is often out of stock, it should definitely be a book that serious African people should get and share with others.

[15] Please see McTaggart, U. (2014). "The Empty Noose: The Trouble With Removing Spectacle From Lynching Iconography" *Journal of Black Studies, 45*(8), 792-811. Retrieved August 1, 2020, from www.jstor.org/stable/24573594. Mctaggert offers a biting critique of the symbolic, literary use and elevation of the "empty noose" by the Black Panther Party for Self Defense (BPP), playwright Ed Bullins, and novelist John Edgar Wideman, and how that fallacy lead to a false sense of power, reverse lynching, and mob violence.

[16] The White press served a key role and function in inciting the passions of the mob, wild tales of the ravaging of White women and the call to the defense of their "unblemished" chastity and was therefore faced with a torrent of acidic criticism from Ida B. Wells from the editorial pages of her publication *Free Speech* and fellow journalists of the day like Timothy

these events have survived. On August 7, 1930, in Marion, Indiana, one of the most iconic lynching photos was taken.[17]

On this date, three young Black men, J. Thomas Shipp, Abraham S. Smith, and James Cameron, had been accused of, and arrested for, robbing and raping a White woman named Mary Ball and the robbery and murder of her White boyfriend, Claude Deeter. In the middle of that fateful night, these young men were dragged from unlocked jail cells, severely beaten, and Shipp and Smith were strung up.[18]

The infamous Beitler photo of J. Thomas Shipp and Abraham Smith was reprinted on a postcard.
Marion, IN August 7, 1930
Loewenthall Collection Cornell University Library, Rare Collections Department

Thomas Fortune and the "Guardian of Boston" William Monroe Trotter. We will specifically see and further address this in the sections on the burning of Sam Hose and the Greenwood Massacre below, the incendiary role of the White press is key to understanding the full picture of those two lynching incidents and so many countless others.

[17] James Cameron's personal account of this incident can be found in his biographical recollection A Time for Terror: A Survivor's Story. (Wauwatosa: LifeWrightPress, 3rd Edition, 2016). Gripping and descriptive, Cameron's recall of the slightest details, from the knock on the door from the officer sent to collect him, a Black man ironically named Burden, to the moment he was surrounded by White men armed to the teeth who literally had to beat their way into the cell block and eventually drug him out to the roar of the crowd. pp.47-91.

The moment of mercy, where his life was spared is recounted on pp. 92-94. Katherine "Flossy" Bailey, the local head of the NAACP chapter, worked as ferociously behind the scenes to get the local sheriff to stop the lynching as she did in raising the successful campaign to get an Anti-Lynching law passed in Indiana a year later in 1931; her activist spirit should never be forgotten, (along with Walter White and the African attorneys Robert L. Bailey and Robert L. Brokenburr), this Is true the especially in the face of the buzz generated by the local papers and radio. pp.74-76. See also James H. Madison A Lynching in the Heartland: Race and Memory in America (New York: Palgrave McMillan, 2001) pp.96.

[18] Ibid. Op. Cit. Also see Madison, A Lynching in the Heartland, pp. 98.

That night the ancestors intervened on behalf of young Cameron, nicknamed "Apples," who was a mere 16 years old at the time of this carnage, as decent hearted Whites spared him. He went on to live a fruitful life, become a dedicated civil rights leader, and founder of America's Black Holocaust Museum and ultimately pardoned on February 3, 1993, at 62.[19]

Mr. Shipp and Mr. Smith, however, are the "strange fruit" dangling from that tree in front of that Grant County, Indiana courthouse, victims of American Terrorism, whose pictures still haunt viewers some 90 years later.[20] As Joy Degruy would likely agree, lynching is a traumatic experience.

---

[19]Cameron, A Time for Terror pp. 93. The pardon is mentioned in the beginning of the Epilogue as Mary Ball ultimately recanted her testimony and admitted that she was never raped. America's Black Holocaust Museum was founded in 1984 (originally named the National Black Holocaust Museum) in Milwaukee, WI and operated a storefront location until 2008. It currently serves as a virtual, online museum but is raising funds to purchase a new building for relocation of the archives with goals of serving as sacred, communal space for programming, organizing, and public commemoration. https://abhmuseum.org/.

[20] "Strange Fruit" is the anti-lynching clarion call belatedly belted out by Billie Holiday in 1939, this haunting and heart wrenching classic lays down markers and batons passed on to activist artists like Nina Simone and to a certain extent India Ire and Lauren Hill. That iconic picture was taken by Lawrence Beitler, who was able to sell thousands of copies (some as prints, others as souvenir postcards) at a hefty profit, in relatively short order after the fact In the end, Cameron was found guilty of an accessory to manslaughter charge and spent 2 years in prison. Cameron A Time for Terror, Op. Cit. pp. 157. Again Madison spends significant time addressing Beitler and his famous photo throughout the book and it was estimated that over 4,000 onlookers had gathered at the lynching site near the courthouse steps by 9:00 pm, please see Madison A Lynching In the Heartland, Op. Cit. pp. 7-11.

Meeropol, Abel and Milt Gabler (1939) Strange Fruit, Recorded by Eleanor Fagan (Billie Holiday) New York: Commodore

Lynching Definitions

"Oh my God, they hunted him like an animal. Oh, this is so horrific to watch".
Soledad O'Brien, tweet posted on May 5, 2020, in reaction to the posting of the video of the Lynching of Ahmaud Arbery.[21]

So, what exactly is a lynching? There are literal, physical lynchings and lynchings that occur during a legal process. The physical lynchings usually involve multiple individuals, and for some, the use of a rope must be present. For our purposes, the basic definition of a physical lynching formulated by researchers from Tuskegee Normal Institute, once heralded as "authorities on lynchings" by the late 1950s, provides a starting point. Those researchers posited that lynching had to have "legal evidence that a person was killed illegally, that a group of three or more must have been involved in the killing, the mob acted under the pretext of service to justice, race, or tradition."[22]

Another definition was offered by Geoffrey Abbott, which is "a form of violence in which a mob, under the pretext of administering justice without trial, executes a presumed offender. This execution often occurs after inflicting torture and corporal mutilation".[23] The term "lynch law," he posits, refers to a self-constituted court that

---

[21] https://twitter.com/soledadobrien/status/1257757613384744960

[22] Ginzburg, 100 Years of Lynchings, Op. Cit. pp. 245.

[23] https://www.britannica.com/topic/lynching. This is a useful definition, but as we will see this definition will have to be adjusted in the 21st century to account for "lone wolf" type activity and the popularization of problematic "Stand Your Ground" laws and "Castle Doctrines" which have been used to shield assorted murderers, including lynchers, from justice. Another useful definition can be found in Jonathan Markovitz's Legacies of Lynching: Racial Violence and Lynching, where he notes that a lynching has to have "legal evidence that a person has been killed and that he met his death illegally at the hands of a group acting under the pretext of service to justice, race, or tradition". Op.Cit. pp.xvii.

For our purposes, I will make the case that lynching victims don't actually have to be killed, like James Webster Smith, the first Black cadet at West Point in 1880 or Rodney King in 1992, Please see Ralph Ginzburg's book 100 Years of Lynchings (Baltimore: Black Classic Press, 1988 ed.), pp.9 for the report on Smith. Markovitz's brief analysis of the lynching of an African

imposes sentence on a person without due process of law. Both terms come from the name of Charles Lynch (1736–96), a Virginia enslaved owning justice of the peace who, during the American Revolution, headed an irregular court formed to punish loyalists.[24]

The operational definition of physical lynching is murder (or attempted murder) committed in the furtherance of a racial, ethnic, religious, national origin, or sexually-oriented goal, motive, or tradition or as a result of prejudice or animus based on race, gender, ethnicity, religion, nationality, sexual orientation. This definition is often modified and adjusted to adequately compensate for changes in the state of the law, societal reaction to those changes.

---

named Claude Neal, accused of killing a White woman named Nola Cannady, on October 26, 1934 outside of Greenwood, FL is highly instructive on this point, were in Neal's case, "all the Whites" from miles around (between eastern Alabama to northwest Florida) were invited to a "lynching party" (from radio station announcements as far away as Dothan, Alabama), saw Neal get killed by a smaller mob of about 100 White men, dragged to a spot in Marianna, FL and hung so that the larger mob between anywhere from 3-7,000 people could partake in the "festivities". Postcards memorializing the event were eventually sold for $.50 apiece. Subsequently, the Whites went on a rampage, attacking Africans, women, children, and men who didn't have anything to do with this, sending many to the infirmary, beating them, driving them away from their jobs, etc. Markovitz, 100 Years of Lynching; Op. Cit. pp.xxv-xxvi.

Amy Louise Wood makes note of the difference between a hanging, as official, formal capital punish sentenced by a judge or empaneled jury (or grand jury) versus a lynching is discussing the difference in the post mortem photography between the two, especially noting the lack of torture and brutalization of those that were "hung" and she also notes that the NAACP used this lynching in a report complete with pictures sent to over 144 newspapers across the globe, with at least one, El Nacional—Mexico City's leading paper publishing the report and it's scathing expose. Amy Louise Wood, Lynching and Spectacle: Witnessing Racial Violence in America, 1890-1940 (Chapel Hill: University of North Carolina Press, 2009) pp.36, 130.

[24]Ibid. And juxtapose this reality with Michelle Alexander's underlying theory that U.S. mass incarceration rates, supported by the "criminal clause" of the 13th Amendment, is yet another example of modern day chattel slavery in her work The New Jim Crow: Mass Incarceration in the Age of Colorblindness (New York: The New Press, 2010). Also see the documentary film Modern Day Slavery (2019) directed by Edwin Freeman.

The expanded definition accounts for the lawless, brutal actions of those that are convulsed by the changing racial demographics of this settler project and die-hard adherents to the withering concept of White supremacy. This definition includes the trigger happy cops who "assume Blacks fit some description and are guilty of something," "lone wolf" types, and other miscreants who feel like taking the law in their own hands and have learned to leave their ropes in the shed figuring they could just shoot someone in the back instead.[25] This expanded definition of physical lynching provides a more explicit context to examine the full range and scope of American Terrorism unleased upon Black folk in the United States and sharper lenses to see it through.

Physical lynchings occur with ropes, chains, guns, vehicles, firebombs, burnings, trees, posts, fences, and other assorted weapons and props, and usually result in death, usually gruesome death. Not all lynchings are the same.

While bodily mutilation does not occur during a legal lynching, those legally lynched usually end up discarded, nonetheless. Some of the characteristics of a legal lynching include predetermined outcomes, failure to bring charges against assailants, all White juries, and implicates jury nullification [26]. Disparate criminal sentences handed out to non-Whites is another hallmark of legal lynching. This book engages these issues and places them in a historical context as well.

---

[25]An analysis of the vigilante mob of White settlers and White nationalists will be repeatedly examined throughout this work. And support for the concept of including law enforcement in the lynch mob comes from the historical fact that so many members of law enforcement were members of the Klan (as we will highlight in the Freedom Summer lynchings, or whole towns were essentially controlled by the Klan (as in Tulsa, OK in 1921), or modern law enforcement lynch mob are starting to get charged for lynching Africans under theories of felony murder, for example (as in the lynching of George Floyd); all of these incidents will be discussed *above*.

[26]Nullification occurs when the jury issues a Not Guilty verdict even though it believes the State has proven it's beyond a reasonable doubt in a criminal case, or rules in favor of a party despite the required legal burden not being met in a civil matter.

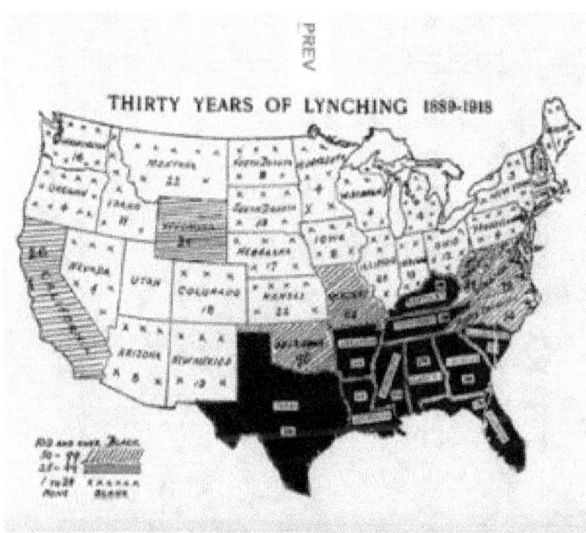

National Association for the Advancement of Colored People, Lynchings of Last Ten Years 1909–1918 from Thirty Years of Lynching in the United States, 1889–1918, *1919, New York:* NAACP, NAACP Collection, Manuscript Division, Library of Congress, Courtesy of the NAACP (Public Domain)

Portrait of Mary "Molly" Church Terrell circa 1919.
Terrell was an activist, educator, and staunch anti-lynching crusader in her own right.
Scurlock, Addison N., 1883-1964, photographer / (Public domain)

Santo Domingo Revolution-African Liberation 1791-1804
Artwork Credit: Yan'D, 1813 (Public Domain)

Santo Domingo Revolution-African Liberation 1791-1804
Unknown Artist (Public Domain)

February 28, 1741, African Rebellion, New York City By Unknown author - http://www.suppressedhistories.net/secrethistory/stakenorth.html, (Public Domain)

https://commons.wikimedia.org/w/index.php?curid=15209450

"Untitled Image (Revolt on a Slave Ship)," *Slavery Images: A Visual Record of the African Slave Trade and Slave Life in the Early African Diaspora*, accessed September 15, 2020, http://slaveryimages.org/s/slaveryimages/item/2548 (Public Domain)

Laurens County, GA Race Riot 1919 (Public Domain)

The lynching of Lige Daniels inn Center, Shelby County, TX August 3, 1920; he was 18 (Public Domain)

The lynching of Leo Frank, Marietta, GA August 17, 1915
Loewenthall Collection of African-American Photos
Cornell University Library, Rare Collections Department (Public Domain)

Lynching of Non-Africans

"Ed Pratt was again ordered to turn over the keys to the jail and again told the crowd the keys were not in his possession. Refusing to believe the county sheriff did not possess the keys, the mob fell upon Pratt"
Jim Conover, 1992 describing the mob storming the jail to lynch a White man accused of criminal activity in 1868

While lynching wasn't always strictly racialized throughout American history, as Whites, Asians, Latinx, and Indigenes were lynched as well, and there was always an aura of "vigilante justice" associated with American Terrorism and Africans did receive the brunt of the "justice" meted out. Nevertheless, it is useful to offer a bit of context for extra-judicial killing, lynchings of non-African people on these shores. A colorful book published in 1992 on the non-racialized practice of lynching is titled Lynch Law by Jim Conover and James Brecher. It follows the lethal mob activity against a family of White brothers, the notorious Berry Gang, emanating from a deadly barroom brawl over a woman which occurred on September 1, 1868.[27]

In the end, chaos ensued, and after Deputy sheriffs were killed, mobs were assembled and disassembled. There were jail breakouts, break-ins took place, a suicide, manhunts, and the mob lynched an innocent White man. This book gives an excellent overview of the non-racialized use of lynching on the frontier. This incident went down in the small town of Pekin, Tazewell County, Illinois, and all the main characters were non-African.[28]

Also, there was the 1915 lynching of Leo Frank in Atlanta, GA, where a Jewish businessman got strung up for the alleged murder of a teenage employee. As it turns

---

[27] Conover, Jim and James Brecher Lynch Law (Pekin: Lynch Law, 1992)

[28] Ibid. pp.120-31; also note the brutal lynching of twenty-one year old Matthew Shepard on October 6, 1998, where he was jumped, beaten, and left to die tied to a fence ostensibly for being gay. Jennifer Petersen analyzes this lynching in connection with the lynching of James Byrd, Jr discussed below in Murder, the Media, and the Politics of Public Feelings: Remembering Matthew Shepard and James Byrd, Jr. (Bloomington: University of Indiana Press, 2011).

out, Oscar Micheaux, a legendary pioneer of film making in general but especially Black film making, used this story as a basis for his 1921 film *The Gaunsualus Mystery*. Jonathan Markovitz's book <u>Legacies of Lynching: Racial Violence and Memory</u> highlighted the Frank lynching.[29]

Whether a lynching took place in the small towns that dotted the ever-expanding American landscape in the genocidal wake of "manifest destiny." Or the glorified "wild, wild west," the sense of "frontier justice" had been used to mask the evil underbelly of the fascination with death through authorized state action. That same guttural energy is still observed and felt today when the masses show up to protest or celebrate the governmental murders of convicted serial killers turned celebrities, as they did with Ted Bundy.[30]

This work attempts to take a broad look at lynching over the scope of the African "New World" experiences with American Terrorism since the mid-sixteenth century. It is mainly focused on Africans in America up through the very next time a member of law enforcement guns down an unarmed Black person as they see fit or mercilessly chokes their life right out of them.

---

[29] Markovitz, Jonathan <u>Legacies of Lynching: Racial Violence and Memory</u>; Op.Cit pp.38.

[30] One simply needs to revisit the video of the scene outside of Raiford, Florida state prison on January 24, 1989 in the hours leading up to Bundy's execution. It looked and felt like a spring break block party, including on lookers dressed up in various cosplay and holding signs and placards meant to mock and ridicule the condemned. Laura Barcella offers an insightful reminiscence in a post uploaded to the Disney owned Arts and Entertainment Network ("A & E" Network) *Real Crime* blog on January 24, 2019. https://www.aetv.com/real-crime/ted-bundy-execution

Overview

"When the next conflagration happens, the next uprising....So what's going to happen? You know what Jeff Sessions is going to be saying: he's going to be talking about "law and order." And they want the police officers to have all the military equipment. And God knows what President Trump will be tweeting. All of this is going to fan the fires. So, it's deeply problematic".[31]
Sherilyn Ifill, President, and Director-Counsel of the NAACP Legal Defense Fund, February 27, 2017

Using an abbreviated chronology of Colonial and U.S. law as a backdrop, I chose to highlight a handful of the thousands of lynchings of Black folk in the U.S. This book shows the interplay between the movement of African people in America and the various forces that have continually weaponized the law to be used against non-Whites. Individuals (like the aforementioned former U.S. Senator (R-AL) and Attorney General Jefferson Beauregard Sessions III) have been historically aligned to stop that progressive movement (both literally and figuratively) of Black folk in particular and make frequent appearances in every chapter[32].

I offer a brief examination of the lynchings as a result of the Stono Rebellion, the lynching of Marie-Joseph Angelique, the Denmark Vesey, Gabriel Prosser, and Nat

---

[31] Ifill, Sherrilyn, et. al. <u>A Perilous Path: Talking Race, Inequality, and the Law</u> (New York: Center on Race, Inequality, and the Law , New York University School of Law (2018) pp.42; this commentary was made during a ceremony commemorating the launching of the Center (in the spirit of legendary Civil Rights attorney and law school professor Derrick Bell.) Ifill was joined on the panel by former U.S. Attorney General Loretta Lynch, Executive Director of the Peace and Justice Initiative Bryan Stevenson, and Center faculty director Anthony C. Thompson.

[32] Saito, <u>Settler Colonialism</u> Op.Cit p.2. Returning to Saito, she offers a clear critique of the current manifestation of the "settler state" using Trump (45) and his appeals to that sense of cloistered and subdued White nationalism, what main stream corporate media often referred to as "populism" and his use of age-old, even Klu Klux Klan inspired slogans of "America First" and "Make America Great Again".

Saito points out that "Trump is not being merely "divisive" when he blasts these dog whistles so much as he is actually exposing some of the deepest schisms to permeate (and percolate) in this society". Therefore she finishes the point by asserting that the untethered "vision of America as a White supremacist, patriarchal settler society is as alive and well as ever today. And that most importantly, ignoring that option is no longer a reality".

Turner Rebellion lynchings, the Sam Hose lynching, the attempted lynching of Dick Rowland, and the ensuing Greenwood Massacre, the legal lynching of Clyde Dennard, the Emmett Till lynching, the 16th Street Bombing, the Freedom Summer lynchings, the Michael Donald lynching, the Trayvon Martin lynching, and the lynching of Ahmaud Arbery, Breonna Taylor, and George Floyd respectively along with dozens of others. Each of these tragedies highlights the status of American jurisprudence at the time, as it directly impacted and interacted with the lives of African people.[33]

I hope to show that three of the main through lines presented throughout the African experience with lynching, from the days of American streets filled with settler-colonists, troops, and politicos from their home countries to the days of American streets filled with *Black Lives Matter* protests and protestors are a) our trauma, b) White fear, and c) our resistance.[34] Lynching was meant to never, ever be forgotten and conducted to leave lasting, permanent, and painful marks on the "collective memory" of African people on these shores with deeply traumatic outcomes.[35]

---

[33] Again these incidents have been chosen to highlight a specific point but not to elevate them over other atrocities, in fact, these cases are used to show how African bodies have been handled as various changes in the law shaped society at different points and shows some of the different purposes lynchings served. Again, Wells, <u>A Red Record</u> and Ralph Ginzburg's <u>100 Years of Lynchings</u> are two of the most gripping compilations of accounts of multiple lynchings that are fairly easy to get a hold of.

[34] Here I follow a similar construction that Ronald Walters employed in <u>Pan-Africanism in the African Diaspora: An Analysis of Modern Afrocentric Political Movements</u> (Detroit: Wayne State University Press. 1998) p. 12. One of the main questions and tapestries Walters weaves is that Africans in the Americas never really stopped being African and that this is true politically, culturally, phenotypically etc. but most importantly we never stopped being African in our minds and imaginations. This should be taken in close conjunction with Gerald Horne's overriding thesis that Africans have never ever stopped resisting oppression as discussed at length *below*.

[35] See generally Markovitz, Jonathan <u>Legacies of Lynching: Racial Violence and Memory</u> (Minneapolis: University of Minnesota Press, 2004) and Jennifer Petersen <u>Murder, the Media, and the Politics of Public Feelings: Remembering Matthew Shepard and James Byrd, Jr.</u> (Bloomington: University of Indiana Press, 2011)

Joy DeGruy, then defines trauma for us as "an injury, caused by an outside, usually violent force, event, or experience."[36] The lynching phenomena fits this definition of a trauma causing event to a tee and has been a vitally important part of the legacy of using this weapon against Africans in America. The flip side of this coin is our equally important resistance to these practices and events.[37]

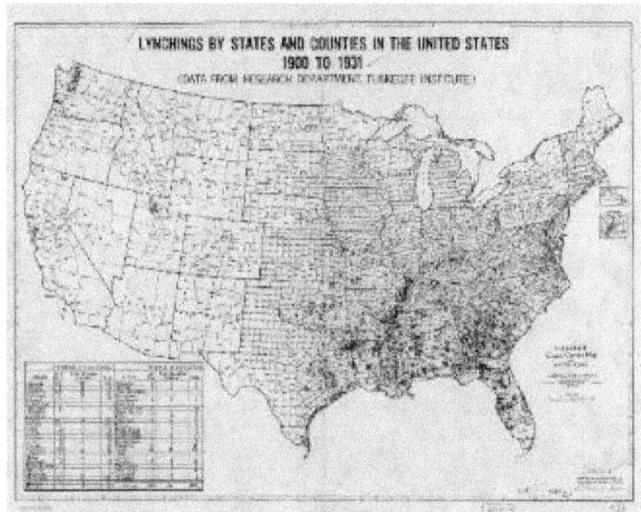

Lynching Tracking Map, Tuskegee Institute Library of Congress Online Catalog (1,149,050) 1931 (Public Domain)

---

[36] DeGruy, Joyce, Post Traumatic Slave Syndrome (Portland: DeGruy Publications, 2005) p.5. According to her bio page on Speakoutnow.org, Dr. Degruy is a nationally and internationally renowned researcher, educator, author and presenter.

[37] Horne, Gerald, The Counter-Revolution of 1776, (New York: New York University Press, 2014). Horne gives a rigorous analysis of the various communities that Africans formed as they confronted their chattel slavers and the systems of oppression that they were confronting. Beginning on pp. 30. These free Africans, from Canada to Brazil, waged absolute war against their oppressors; unrelenting, no-hold barred war.

Illustration of the lynching of Robert Lewis in Port Jervis, NY. And appeared in the *Evening World*. Lewis was accused of attacking a White woman named Lena McMahon and was set up by a man named P.J. Foley. 1892 (Public Domain)

"This is a White man's government" "We regard the Reconstruction Acts (so-called) of Congress as usurpations, and unconstitutional, revolutionary, and void" - Democratic Platform / / Nast, Thomas, 1840-1902, artist, 1868; Library of Congress (Public Domain)

Postcard of the lynching of Laura Nelson. She was lynched along with her son Lawrence. Okemah, OK May 25, 1911 (Public Domain)

In fact, in a number of his works, Gerald Horne has not only documented and highlighted hundreds of cases of individual and collective organized rebellion against the onslaught of systemic White settler oppression during the early nineteenth century, he argued that the American Revolution itself was waged in part because

Diasporic Africans fought so hard and so long against England it forced that nation to end the practice of chattel slavery. This forced American "founding father" slave owners to break away from England in a "Counter-Revolution" in large part to protect its ability to enslave African people perpetually.[38]

Our immediate ancestors then ensured the colonial settlers never had a moment's sleep, so much so that some of them who were double agents for the Crown hatched a plot to abduct and assassinate George Washington, slaveholding first president of the United States.[39] Black people over here have always resisted. But they have always had reason to, whether they found themselves on these shores or in other parts of the Diaspora.

One of the things that Africans in America always strived for was the inclusion in that maxim that sits above the entrance of the Court. We have wanted to see the day when "equal justice under the law" applies to us fully. It took the passage of the fourteenth Amendment to the Constitution, in 1868, to extend this idea that every individual is supposed protected from discriminatory, overbearing, or burdensome state action. These are the very issues that African people in this grouping of people—this settler state, are still grappling with today.

---

[38] Ibid. pp. 234-52. Horne dedicates the seminal chapter of this work to fleshing out this concept.

[39] Ibid. pp. 246-47. A free African named Benjamin Whitcuff, from Long island, NY, and an unnamed African conspirator were involved in the plot. This occurred towards the beginning of the War, but the Africans had very good reasons to attempt this as over a decade later Washington (1) was absolutely giddy at the prospects for American success in helping Paris squash the Africans who started the Haitian Revolution, in fact he was quoted as saying "I am happy about how well disposed the United States are to render every aid in their power to our good friends and allies (the French) to quell the alarming insurrection of Negroes in Hispaniola" as he was thinking about his own Africans he held in bondage; please see Horne's Confronting Black Jacobins: The United States, the Haitian Revolution, And the Origins of the Dominican Republic (New York: Monthly Review Press, 2015) pp. 30.

October 16, 1995-Protestors on the National Mall, facing the Washington Monument. Addressing police brutality was one of the calls for the Million Man March.
By The Library of Congress - A glimpse of the 1995 Million Man March - from the recently cataloged Roll Call Photograph Collection, No restrictions, https://commons.wikimedia.org/w/index.php?curid=52019808

Chapter 2

Historical Uses of Lynching Against African People in the Western Diaspora—American Terrorism in Practice

"For your own safety, there must be needful guard over your slaves and put not too much confidence in the women or the children least they happen to be instrumental to you being surprised which may be fatal"
Sound advice from a Massachusetts ship captain, 1731[40]

The abolition of the slave trade or the inhumanity of dealers in human flesh exemplified in Captn. Kimbers treatment of a young Negro girl of 15 for her "virjen" (sic) modesty.
S.W. Fores, London, April 10, 1792 (Public Domain)

Lynching was weaponized against Black folks across the settler state and became the sword and shield of *American Terrorism*. I look at just a sampling of the reasons in this brief history, including but not limited to a) outright fear of Rebellion and Insurrection, b) a direct punitive or psy-op response to the various Maroon communities and freedom fighters, c) Post-Reconstruction Racial Terror, d) Perpetuation of Jim Crow laws, e) Modern "Alt-Right" reaction to changing societal demographics and perceptions of forced Multi-Culturalism," and f) Law Enforcement use of excessive force.

---

[40] Horne, The Counter-Revolution; pp.81, later in this work Horne spends some time discussing Captain Cudjoe and the maroon society that struck fear in the hearts of the settlers he encountered and the countries he maneuvered with his power plays, Op.Cit.pp. 100-01.

Some of the other reasons like protection of myths of the purity of the White woman, the White man's desire to assault women, especially Black women, with impunity, class, jealousy, religious purity, for example, are rolled into and analyzed along with these listed sub-categories. For example, among the litany of excuses for the burning of Sam Hose (discussed below) were to cow Black criminals, threaten educated Blacks, and teach Blacks their civic duties.[41]

---

[41] Matthews, Donald, At the Altar of Lynching: Burning Sam Hose in the American South (New York: Cambridge University Press, 2018). Some of the other cited works helping me to discuss these points are definitive history of the liberation of Haiti in 1791, The Black Jacobins originally published by Cyril Lionel Roberts James in 1938 and the previously referenced works by Gerald Horne especially discussing the Buck breaking and corporal punishment along with the response to the African world family Maroons and insurrections. Chapter 1 of the Black Jacobins, titled "the Property" offers some of the most gripping recounts of the brutalization of the "slave" making and breaking process from the Island of Santa Domingo. C.L.R. James The Black Jacobins (New York: The Vintage Books ed. 1998) beginning on p.6.

The Reconstruction Racial Terrorism is clearly highlighted by Ida B. Wells Barnett, but another true historian of our ancestors during this time period, Rayford Logan refers to this dismal period as the "nadir" or the darkest hour our people faced and squarely lays the blame for this on the shoulders of US president Rutherford B. Hayes (19) and absolute abandonment of the masses of African people in the South at the end of Reconstruction. Hayes surmised that this act led to an almost generational acceptance of presidential neglect that helped to feed the ever-growing monsters of disenfranchisement, terror, bloodshed exemplified by the unrelenting lynchings and burnings. Rayford Logan, Betrayal of the Negro (New York: McMillan 1965.) pp. 23, 62.

And during this time Carter G. Woodson and Charles Wesley, in their massive compilation work originally published in 1922, The Negro in Our History (Washington, D.C.: The Associate Publishers, 1972) p.547 estimated that 2, 522 of the 3, 224 9 (or 78.2%) individuals who were lynched were Africans. The section on the perpetuation of Jim Crow laws will be highlighted in Tim Madigan's book on the Burning of Greenwood, The Burning: Massacre, Destruction, and the Tulsa Race Riots of 1921 (New York: St. Martin's Press, 2001), by James Cameron's book Time for Terror: A Survivor's Tale (Baltimore: Black Classic Press. 1994) and the accompanying history of his event by James H. Madison, A Lynching in the Heartland: Race and Memory in America (New York: Palgrave McMillan, 2001), the Magnum Opus of charging the US with the international crime of genocide in the wake of this aspect of brutality, William Patterson's 1951 petition to the United Nation's Genocide Convention, Patterson, William, We Charge Genocide: The Crime of Government Against The Negro People (New York: International Publisher's Co. 4th Edition, 2017).

And the so-called "Alt-Right" reactions and over-reactions to their perceptions of forced diversity and Multi-Culturalism will be highlighted by the Michael Donald lynching and the crippling lawsuits levied against the United Klans of America (UKA) in Alabama documented

Legal Framework

"Negroes had for more than a century before been regarded as beings of an inferior order, and altogether unfit to associate with the White race, either in social or political relations; and so far inferior, that they had no rights which the White man was bound to respect"
Supreme Court Chief Justice Roger B. Taney, majority opinion *Scott v. Sanford* 60 U.S. 383 (1857)

It may be necessary to pause here to make a brief comment on how the state and federal laws are made. There are primarily five ways that I analyze and juxtapose throughout the bulk of the remainder of this work as they come up.

The most popular way to make a law is through the democratic representative process through elected legislatures (i.e., House of Representatives, U.S. Senate, state assemblies). The other ways are a) Colonial/Papal announcement, b) Judicial rulings through established case law, c) Executive order and action, and d) Executive Agency Rules Regulation. I also take a snapshot of some of the ways our ancestors tried to bring pressure through raising issues and critiques via International law and governing bodies.[42]

Some of the broader legal questions to be examined are does "equal protection of the law" really extend to African people on these shores? Can the families and estates of lynching victims present viable claims and pursue damages? Against citizens or law enforcement operating under the "color of law"?[43] These issues become central themes of the work.

---

by Laurence Leamer in his book <u>The Lynching: The Epic Courtroom Battle that Brought Down the Klan</u> (New York: Harper Collins, 2016).

[42] A handy guide that first year law students across the country may have used or are familiar with called <u>Finding The Law</u> ed. Robert C. Berring and an Elizabeth A. Edinger (St. Paul: West Group, Am. Casebook Series, 11th ed. 1999) is a great single resource which lays out the interplay between all the ways the laws are made here and how to locate them. I will address the work of William Patterson and El hajj Malik El Shabazz tangentially *below*.

Just a side note, when I use the capitalized term "Court," I am usually referring to the United States Supreme Court or specific court that issued a particular ruling.

Baseline Legal Concepts, Fictions, and Fallacies

"This is a Gentile organization, and as such has as its mission the interpretation of the highest ideals of the White Gentile peoples...our forefathers founded this as a Protestant country and our purpose is to reestablish and maintain it as such. This Republic was established by White Men. It was established for White Men. Every effort to wrest from White Men the management of its affairs in order to transfer it to the control of blacks or any other color, or to permit them to share in its control, is an invasion of our sacred constitutional prerogatives and a violation of divinely established laws ".
From Ideals of the Ku Klux Klan, reprinted in Atlanta, GA June 7, 1948[44]

This settler state has manifest into what has come to be known as the United States of America. It has always been conceptually held together by faulty baseline legal concepts and myths, and it was these legal fictions and lies that allowed the practice of lynching to persist for so long.

We examine a few of those projections briefly discussed *below* in no particular chronological order; they are 1) the idea that Indigenous nations needed to get wiped out so that their ancestral lands could be fully utilized; otherwise, they would go to waste; 2) the United States is a "nation of laws" and that the law then is paramount, but we see that a lot of the most aggressive actions taken against African people here have been under the protection of and "color of law"; 3) that the settlers have the God-given right to defend themselves and their property; and 4) the concepts of Whiteness, White supremacy, and anti-Blackness had to be created and activated to

---

[43] Again according to Black's Legal Dictionary, "Color of Law" refers to the appearance or semblance, without the substance, of legal right. *McCain v. Des Moines*, 174 U. S. 108, 19 Sup. Ct. (H4, 43 L. Ed. 936) (1899).

[44] Patterson, William L. (ed.) We Charge Genocide pp. 211. This recount is taken from Appendix A of the 1951 petition to U.N. to charge the U.S. government with genocide on behalf of Africans in America. This petition will be analyzed in more details *below*.

get the landless Whites, one step out from under indentured servitude themselves, to buy into the establishment of the project based on the hopes of opportunity and the fact that at least they aren't savage "darkies" or dreaded "redskins".

A group of African-Americans marching near the Capitol building in Washington, D.C., protesting the lynching of four African-Americans in Georgia 1946.
Library of Congress Online Catalog (1,149,050)

Stone Mountain Monument
Stone Mountain Monument of Jefferson Davis, Robert E. Lee, and Thomas "Stonewall" Jackson
Stone Mountain, GA Public Domain/CC0

Genocide of Indigenes

"The legitimacy of acquiring Indigenous lands in violation of treaties, by aggressive warfare or through agreements with other colonial powers is never seriously questioned, for the narrative begins from the premise that the United States was divinely ordained to exist in its current form"
Natsu Taylor Saito, 2020[45]

Exhibit in the Oakland Museum of California, USA. Extracted From Bonds for Expeditions Against the Indians; State of California, 1854. (Public Domain)

Among one of the baseline legal concepts that used to help set the stage for the eventual brutalization of Africans across the New World was this wholesale destruction and genocide of Indigenous populations for easier plunder, as handed down initially by the Catholic Church through the Spanish conquistadors and colonial governors.[46]

---

[45] This quote from Chief Justice Taney will be discussed in a bit more detail below in the section on the Dred and Harriet Scott case.

[46] Here Saito lays out the premise that, what she refers to as "emerging bodies of international law addressing racial discrimination and Indigenous rights" explicitly prohibit forced assimilation and articulate the rights of people to maintain their distinct identities, traditions, cultures, social, political, and economic structures. Saito further notes that the first treaty of the UN's Convention on the Prevention and Punishment on the Crime of Genocide (Genocide Convention) defined genocide as: any of the of the following acts committed with the intent to destroy, in whole or in part, a national, racial, ethnic, or religious group, involving a) Killing members of the group, b) Causing serious bodily or mental harm to members of the group, c) Deliberately inflicting harm on the group conditions of life calculated to bring about its physical destruction in whole or in part, d) Imposing measures intended to prevent births

Bartolome De Las Casas retells one of the most detailed accounts of the devastation of Indigenous civilization. De las Casas, as an eighteen-year-old Spaniard in 1502, arrived on the island of Hispaniola (modern-day Haiti and the Dominican Republic) and witnessed first-hand the destruction of indigene civilization between that island and the island of Cuba.[47]

De Las Casas returned to Spain, and his calls to end the slaughter and plundering fell on deaf ears. He returned to Hispaniola, became a Dominican friar, and began his writing career. He eventually became a Bishop in 1543, finished his opus The History of the Indies in 1561, and his A Short Account of the Destruction of the Indies in 1552. De Las Casas became one of the loudest and most vigorous critics of the West's wholesale destruction of Indigenous culture in Central America, South America, and the Caribbean.[48]

But like with most things in history, when it comes to us and our dealings with others, we typically do not find angels only angles. Before we go too far down the road congratulating De las Casas on his enlightened stances, Gerald Horne reminds us that De las Casas was present in Seville, Spain, when Columbus was busy parading kidnapped Indigenes through the streets. De las Casas' father joined Columbus' second voyage across the Atlantic. Horne goes on to State that De las Casas had owned enslaved people at multiple points in his life, while he was a college student,

---

within the group, and/or e) Forcibly transferring children of the group to another group. Saito, Settler Colonialism Op.Cit. pp. 174.

[47] De Las Casas, A Short Account of the Destruction of the Indies in 1552 (London: Penguin Publishing Group, 1992).

[48] Ibid. Please see the imbedded chronology section in the Introduction listed on pp. xlii, xliii. The History of the Indies was published posthumously at De Las Casas' request.

during his trips to the settler project in 1502, and during his involvement with the conquest of Hispaniola.[49]

And fast forward a hundred fifty years or so. The Virginia Company in 1607, for example, thoroughly established the Jamestown Colony and, through its provincial Governor Thomas de La Warr (apropos name), went to full-blown war with the Alonquin people and their leader Powhatan. This genocide, marked by indiscriminate attacks, where members of that nation were killed, villages were raised and burned to the ground, and crops were outright destroyed.[50]

The only real question at the time was, should the "Indians be killed or enslaved?".[51] Given this historical backdrop, that National Football club located 160 miles or so north of Jamestown, VA in Washington, D.C. should have dropped its genocidal moniker and iconography decades ago and quite frankly never should have adopted it in the first place.[52]

---

[49] Horne, Gerald The Dawning of the Apocalypse (New York: Monthly Press Review 2020) pp.81

[50] See Saito, Settler Colonialism Op. Cit pp. 60-61

[51] Ibid. In another section of this work, Saito lays part of the blame of the appropriation of Indigenous lands on seventeenth-century English philosopher John Locke's "productive use" theory and the idea that land should not go to waste. Saito points out however, that local Indigenous populations had extensive methods of agricultural cultivation throughout the settlers' experience with them but those systems were summarily ignored by the Whites. P.31.

[52] In the wake of the #BLM protests in the response to the lynchings of Ahmaud Arbrey, Breonna Taylor, and George Floyd respectively and the seeming unending street actions, a sea change occurred where numerous corporations and media saw themselves with numerous aspects of a burgeoning racial reckoning. The once vaunted National Football League (NFL) and their football clubs were no exception, with the most obvious being the formerly named "Redskins" franchise. The club announced an official name change on July 3, 2020. No new name has been announced (at the time of drafting), but there were calls to rename the team the "Red Tails" in honor of the famed Tuskegee Airmen who reached acclaimed fighting during WWII. At the time of this writing, the Washington Football's Team press release is still available on the team's official website, https://www.washingtonfootball.com/news/redskins-announce-franchise-will-be-called-washington-football-team-pending-adop.

The lynching of Indigenes continued through the late nineteenth century as well, as Ida B. Wells cited the example of Lewis McGeesy and Hond Martin on January 7, 1898.[53] These two poor souls, accused by the Whites of murdering a White woman, and based on that hearsay evidence alone, they were summarily tied to a post at the Post Office in Maud, OK (Indian Territory) and burned alive. Curiously though, as the men were "Indians," Wells notes that the Indian Commissioner at the time was able to eventually get "reparations" from the town of Maud payable to the Commission.[54]

A cartoon threatening to lynch carpetbaggers, Tuscaloosa, AL *Alabama Independent Monitor*, 1868 (Public Domain)

---

[53] Wells, Ida B. Mob <u>Rule in New Orleans</u>; Op.Cit. pp.53.

[54] Ibid. Also see The Bureau of Indian Affairs website, The Board of Indian Commissioners was established on April 10, 1869 as authorized advisors and consultants to the federal government on Indigene affairs; the Bureau of Indian Affairs offers a brief history of the organization of the Commission and its metamorphosis over the centuries; located on this link here: <u>https://www.bia.gov/bia</u>

Color of Law, Vigilante Justice

"Get a gun, get a nigger"
Unnamed police officer handing out loaded guns and ammo in the streets of Tulsa, OK in the midst of the Greenwood Massacre, 1921[55]

According to Black's Legal Dictionary, "Color of Law" refers to the appearance or semblance, without the substance, of a legal right.[56] In real life, this manifests in multiple ways. During the Red Summer of 1919 (discussed later), Ida B. Wells Barnett, who recently moved to Chicago and offered a first-hand account of the skirmishes and noted that Cook County state's attorney, Maclay Hoyne, said that, "there is no doubt that a great many police officers were grossly unfair in making arrests. They shut their eyes to offenses committed by White men while they were very vigorous in getting all the colored men they could get".[57]

Another shockingly clear example of this lethal legal construct on full display resulted in the lynching by gunshot of civil rights activist Jimmie Lee Jackson. Jackson was organizing with the Southern Christian Leadership Conference (SCLC) for the right to vote and for the integration of local restaurants in Marion, Alabama, about 60 miles northeast of Montgomery.[58]

---

[55]Madigan, The Burning Op.Cit. pp.108. The Burning of the Greenwood section of Tulsa, "Black Wall Street" will be discussed *below*.

[56]*McCain v. Des Moines*, 174 U. S. 108

[57]Harris John and Ida B. Wells Barnett (Narrated by Acie Cargill) Red Summer Race Riot Chicago 1919 (2019) Op.Cit. pp 11-12. Ginzburg's 100 Years of Lynchings is chock full of various governors, sheriffs, senators, congressman, and retired judges making similar statements.

[58]Leamer, Laurence, The Lynching: The Epic Courtroom Battle that Brought Down the Klan (New York: Harper Collins Publishers, 2016). pp.169. Leamer discusses the Jackson lynching in this work where he gives an excellent account of the lynching of nineteen year old Michael Donald and the successful lawsuits Morris Dees, fabled Mobile civil rights attorney, levelled against the UKA which will be addressed *below*.

On February 18, 1965 (just three days before the assassination of El hajj Malik el Shabazz up in Harlem, NYC), the group had a regular meeting. Still, that night decided to march to the courthouse in support of a jailed leader. On that dark road, they met the Alabama Public Safety Director Al Lingo along with twenty-one state police cars, Marion police officers, county deputy sheriffs, and civilians wielding clubs and ax handles. And as if on cue, the police rushed the non-violent protestors dealing blows left and right, and in the melee, a State Trooper got wounded and shot Mr. Jackson in retaliation accusing him of assault.[59] So many of the events touched upon and fleshed out involve members of law enforcement masquerading as law-

---

This SCLC office was headed up by field secretary James Orange who had just been arrested. Also see superstar organizer Louise Thompson, spouse of William L. Patterson, and her 1934 article published in *The Crisis Magazine*, the journal of the NAACP which at one time was edited by W.E.B. DuBois. In "Southern Terror", Thompson aptly describes a time when she was arrested in Birmingham, AL while trying to visit a friend and received especially harsh treatment from courts and law enforcement alike, primarily for being African, a woman, an organizer, a communist, and from outside of the South; her stinging critique of the use of the "N-word" from law enforcement and the bench, the weaponization of statutes and ordinances against Africans and communists alike, and the sham criminal disposition process is well worth the read and can be found in Herbert Aptheker's edited compilation A Documentary History Of the Negro People in The United States, Vol. IV: From The New Deal to The End of World War II (New York: Carol Publishing Group, 1992) pp.120-25.

The Southern Christian Leadership Conference (SCLC) was established on January 10-11, 1957 (originally as the Southern Leadership Conference) in response to ultimate success of the Montgomery Bus Boycott which ended a few weeks prior on December 20, 1956. The sixty-six civil rights leaders met in Atlanta, GA and selected Rev. Dr. Martin Luther King, Jr. to lead the organization and take up the break of American Apartheid across the South. While the SCLC (which added the "Christian" moniker to its name in order to ward off accusations of being run by communists to no avail) preached the need for a commitment to nonviolence, King stayed strapped, especially in his home—a frequent target for threats and an eventual firebomb on January 30, 1956, please see Cobb's That Nonviolent Stuff'll Get You Killed (Durham: Duke University Press, 2014) pp. 7 For a discussion of the usual presence of multiple weapons at the King family home. Cobb recounts a tale of one visitor to the King family home, a journalist named William "Bill" Worthy, being quickly warned about sitting in a particular armchair by legendary organizer Bayard Rustin from out of fear of shooting himself in the buttocks, King, as Cobb noted, would have weapons secreted throughout his home.

[59]Ibid. State Trooper James Bonard Fowler, at the age of 77 years old, finally pled guilty to a charge of manslaughter and served 6 months in prison.

abiding citizens while secretly being leading members of the Klan, Citizen's Councils, sympathizers, or supporters.[60]

Numbers of officers are found not only letting the killers off the hook but virtually handing out the rags they used to wipe their bloody hands.[61] And for every jailer we find willing to risk their standing, and that of their overwhelmed staff, to protect their prisoners, we find far too many who somehow or another manage to leave the front, back, and side doors unlocked, and unsecured cellblocks wind up wide open just in time for the mob to swoop right in.[62] This shameful behavior occurred far too frequently.

In the appendix to their 1951 petition to the United Nations, William Patterson and Paul Robeson offer a stunning indictment on Klan activity just in the State of

---

[60] Rosser, L. (1921). The Illegal Enforcement of Criminal Law. *The Virginia Law Register, 7*(8), 569-586. doi:10.2307/1107032

[61] Essentially the story Ida B. Wells recounts in my hometown back in the fall of 1900 in her harrowing account of the race riots that rocked that city found in Wells Mob Rule in New Orleans offers a dynamic and riveting report of the event. Wells paints a picture of mobs and hordes, led by law enforcement and elected officials, attacking random Africans in the hunt for a Robert Charles, who along with Leonard Pierce, killed a couple of NOPD officers in self-defense. In fact, the mayor of western suburb Kenner, LA (the city where Louis Armstrong International Airport sits today) was quoted as yelling to the mob that "I am from Kenner, gentlemen, and I have come down to New Orleans tonight to assist you in teaching the blacks a lesson. I have killed a Negro before, and in revenge of the wrong wrought about you and yours, I am willing to kill again. The only way you can teach these Niggers a lesson and put them in their place is to go out and *lynch* a few as an object lesson. String up a few of them, and all the others will trouble you no more. That is the only thing to do—kill them, string them up, lynch them! I will lead you, if you will but follow. On to the Parish Prison and lynch Pierce!" Wells, Mob Rule in New Orleans Op.Cit. pp. 14-15.

[62] We saw this in the James Cameron case, in fact the State of Indiana had a law on the books at the time, according to Cameron, that local sheriffs could actually be prosecuted for letting the mob drag a prisoner out of the jail. Cameron A Time for Terror Op.Cit. pp.152. We will also see this during the Greenwood Massacre in Tulsa, OK, where that sheriffs' refusal to turn over Dick Rowland to the White mob coupled with the audacity of the heavily armed "Defenders of Greenwood", like O.B. Mann and Andrew Smitherman, provided the White nationalists with the perfect cover to burn the prosperous African community to ashes and plunder what was left.

Georgia alone and that American terrorist group's intimate relationship to numerous members of that state's power elite and their shared ideology between 1940 and 1950. This evil détente resulted in the systemic disenfranchisement of Africans longing to participate in the electoral process fully. That marriage played out in every form of American Terrorism, including "threats, cross burnings, masked parades, floggings, lynchings, voter purges, and other acts of discrimination" meant to deter Africans from voting, organizing, running for office, or otherwise participating in the political process.[63]

One of the most glaring examples of this monstrous mix Patterson highlights was on April 15, 1946. On that date, Ex-GA Governor Eugene Talmadge's *Statesman* titled published a poem titled "White Georgia Thanks God for the Klan" in Augusta. This poem was designed to drum up support for Roy Harris, GA Speaker of the Legislature, his "Cracker Party," and the joint call to keep Africans from participating in any of the pending primary elections in any capacity, whether they wanted to be poll workers, candidates or voters.[64]

Another example of this wicked marriage is the creation of the Mississippi Sovereignty Commission after the inauguration of "moderate" James Plemon "J.P." Coleman as Governor of the State in 1956. This Commission, which was called for by Mississippi House Bill 880, according to Rick Bowers, would eventually "be granted extraordinary powers, including the power to investigate private citizens and

---

[63] Patterson, William L. (ed.) <u>We Charge Genocide: The Crime of Government against Negro People</u> (New York: International Publishers Co., 4th Ed. 2017) pp.201-16; this shocking compilation is found in Exhibit A of the petition, which will be discussed in a more detailed fashion *below*.

[64] Ibid. pp. 205.

organizations, to maintain secret files, to force witnesses to testify, and even to make arrests."[65]

Section 5 of the bill stated that:

> "It shall be the duty of the Commission to do and perform any, and all acts and things deemed necessary and proper to protect the sovereignty of the State of Mississippi, and her sister states, from encroachment thereon by the Federal Government…and to resist the usurpation of the rights and powers reserved to this state and our sister states by the Federal Government or any branch, department, or agency thereof."[66]

On March 29, 1956, the Commission styled as "Mississippi's segregation watchdog agency" with State Rep. Ney Gore and Hal C. DeCell at the helm. The Commission,

---

[65] Bowers, Rick <u>Spies of Mississippi</u> (Washington, D.C.: The National Geographic Society, 2010) pp. 4, this is the companion book to the 2014 film of the same name directed by Dawn Porter. Governor-elect Coleman was a snarling White nationalist and prior to inauguration he put a marker down meant to serve notice that White supremacy would be defended in high office, take his seven point program he presented to the Legal Education Assistance Committee (LEAC) which was set up by the MS legislature in order to slow-down the integration of public schools post *Brown and Brown II*. His plan was 1) To prohibit common law marriages by statute, 2) to repeal the compulsory school attendance law (as plans were being made to close public schools in a hope of circumventing integration), 3) To provide penalties for "illegal bargains" made by an outsider with a party to a suit and to punish "agitation court suits" to end segregation, 4) To provide penalties for abusive and obscene telephone calls and strengthen the law on criminal libel, 5) To provide penalties for persons interfering with state law under the color of federal authority, 6) To create a permanent authority for maintenance of segregation with a full staff and funds for its operation to come out of tax money , and 7) a requirement that all teachers paid from public funds to make affidavits as to all organizations they hold membership in. These proposals were supported by LEAC and submitted to the full legislature in 1956; Please see Yashihiro Katagiri's book <u>The Mississippi State Sovereignty Commission: Civil Rights and States Rights</u> (Jackson: University Press of Mississippi, 2001) pp. xxxiv.

[66] Katagiri, <u>The Mississippi State Sovereignty Commission</u>; pp. 6

through its development of private investigators and recruited spies, would wreak havoc, sometimes terror, on the African people in Mississippi and their burgeoning movement for Civil Rights, especially voting rights.[67]

This spy network included folks from all walks of life and from all over the state. To their eternal shame, there were numbers of Africans that joined the ranks like high-profile individuals, including the editor of the largest Black facing newspaper in the state at the time, the *Jackson Advocate*, Percy Greene, and renowned preacher Henry Harrison Humes, leader of the New Hope Baptist Church in Greenville, MS.[68] These two, and the countless, nameless others at the time like the anonymous turncoats dubbed "Agent X" were in the rooms where plans were made, decisions were made, and the news was shared and then would make beelines for their Commission handlers to "run, go tell."

They provided information on Medgar Evers, James Meredith, the Freedom Riders, and an Agent X were actually at the seminal organizing training session in Oxford, OH, where James Earl Chaney, Michael Henry Schwerner, and Andrew Goodman decided to make that fateful trek to Neshoba County, MS in 1964. He told, and those three organizers got lynched as a result. We discuss in more detail *below*.[69]

---

[67] Ibid. Bowers notes that this despicable snitching turned into a lucrative side hustle for some, especially Humes and Greene; in fact, Greene earned $3,200 in 1958 which is the equivalent of $29,794 in 2020. Spies of Mississippi;Op.Cit.pp.17; also see Katagiri The Mississippi State Sovereignty Commission; Op.Cit.pp.8-9.

[68] An Associated Press story published in July 1957 boldly stated that Humes and Green were paid $400 each for conducting investigations on behalf of the State, this disclosure signaled the beginning of the end for Humes, Green was able to slither around a bit longer however; Katagiri; The Mississippi State Sovereignty Commission; Op.Cit. pp. 42.

[69] Bowers, Spies of Mississippi. pp. 83-95. This shameful record reflects that the treasonous Africans were often inspired by a mix of greed, lure of access to powerful elites, good old fashioned classism, and a serious doubt in the ability of the Civil Rights movement to defeat White Supremacy in bloody Mississippi. It made sense then that the Commission would want to keep up-to-the-minute tabs on Medgar Evers though, he was reportedly incredibly inspired

According to Rick Bowers, in his Book Spies of Mississippi, based on evidence gathered from the Mississippi Sovereignty Committee documents, a man named R.L. Bolden, who later worked as the Vice President of the Mississippi statewide chapter of the NAACP, admitted to working for the Day Detective agency and providing information in exchange for cash payments; but according to Bolden he only passed on publicly available information. He was "not the only one."[70] The Commission was able to survive, despite redirecting funds and responsibilities, until July 1, 1974.[71]

The law is a tool used to blunt the positive movement of African people in this country; sometimes, used to control our bodies, other times used to protect those that desecrated us. Even the few and fleeting moments where it offered some alleviation from generational oppression, defenders of White nationalism and the settler state used it as an excuse to wage their terror campaigns against us.

---

by the Kenya Land and Freedom Army (KLFA) and Jomo Kenyatta, first president of independent Kenya; please see Umoja, We Will Shoot Back; pp.42.

It was reported that at one point, Evers was hoping (planning?) for an organic development of "Mau Mau" style African guerilla insurgents roaming the Mississippi countryside liberating their people left and right. Katagiri also does a deep dive into the African turncoats that chose to spy and snitch on their community's efforts to participate in the electoral process in Chapter 2 of his book The Mississippi State Sovereignty Commission; pp. 36-63; it is important to note the role the Black press and Black preachers played in assisting the Commission.

[70] Bowers, Spies of Mississippi, Op.Cit pp.104; questions still swirl about this as upon Bolden's passing as even Charles Evers, Medgar's brother and president of the Mississippi NAACP, vouched for Bolden in a statement to the Jackson, MS ABC affiliate WAPT on June 19, 2012 located on its website here: https://www.wapt.com/article/civil-rights-activist-r-l-bolden-dies/2079420. Katagiri notes that it was a confidential informant known as T-I who supplied damaging information on Evers, along with the various Agent X's, among others. See The Mississippi State Sovereignty Commission; Op.Cit. pp. 56.

[71] Katagari, The Mississippi State Sovereignty Commission; Op.Cit pp.224-25.

The law and its duly sworn officers have played a seminal role in shaping our experiences on these shores along with those terrorizing us under the "color of law" or vigilantes taking the law into their own hands like discussed immediately below.[72]

---

[72] Ibid. pp. 88, here Bowers mentions that the White Knights of the Ku Klux Klan, one of the most lethal klaverns in Mississippi in the 60's were entering dozens of recruits into newly formed auxiliary police units (like they pattleroller forbears, or we can look at cops just handing out guns to the lynch mob in the streets of Tulsa during the Greenwood Massacre, or the Sheriff and Deputy Sheriff involved with the Freedom Summer lynchings, etc.

Castle Doctrine/Stand Your Ground Laws

"A man's house is his castle and where shall a man be safe if not in his own home."
Sir Edward Coke, 1628

The legal tenets of the Castle Doctrine and the Duty to Retreat are traced back to English common law, with the rationale credited to seventeenth-century jurist Edward Coke.[73] Coke lays out his thesis in his work, which ultimately served as the first volume of a posthumously published set, <u>Institutes of the Laws of England</u>.[74] The basic idea of the Castle Doctrine is that an individual can defend himself in his own home, which was logically extended to being able to defend herself within her person.[75]

Aspects of the doctrine, including the concept of "defending oneself to the wall," have been examined and re-examined over the centuries as American jurisprudence matured, with the State of Florida being no exception. Jason C. King notes that the Supreme Court of Florida "allowed for a jury instruction to state that (the defendant) used all other reasonable means in his power (defending himself "to the wall"), which is consistent with his safety, to avert the danger—which encompassed the common law of duty to retreat" in a 1905 criminal case.[76]

---

[73] Please see Jason King's book the <u>Duty to Retreat: A Review of the Evolution of the Duty to Retreat, the Castle Doctrine, Florida Stand Your Ground Law and Relevant Court Cases</u> (Coppell: 2015) pp.1-2; here King offers a quick review of the development of the legal concepts that made the judicial basis for the passage of the Florida Stand Your Ground statutes which were at least implicated in the George Zimmerman trial discussed *below*.

[74] Ibid. It was noted that this text was transported on the Mayflower and served as a basis for early Colonial law in the beginning of the settler project.

[75] Ibid. pp.2-3.

[76] Ibid. pp. 29, see also *Snelling v. State*, 49 Fla. 34 (1905), this case had to do with the murder of an intruder in a home by the homeowner.

For the course of the twentieth century, Florida's reliance on the common law principles of self-defense, amount of requisite force, and duty to retreat had been affected by shifts in public policy concerning domestic violence and mental health awareness.[77] And in 2005, the Florida State Legislature passed the Stand Your Ground Law (SYG) drafted by the National Rifle Association (NRA). This law formally melded the common law Castle Doctrine and Duty to Retreat to the Wall and, in effect, stated that a man carries his castle on his back.[78]

Florida Statutes 776.012, 776.031, and 776.032 make up the corpus of the laws around the use or threatened use of force in defense of a person, defense of property, and immunity from criminal prosecution civil action for justifiable use or threat of force.[79]

King notes that whenever a criminal defendant asserts the SYG defense and seeks immunity, the Court must hold an evidentiary hearing based on the subjective "reasonable person" standard instead of the "objective" standard. In this case, the defendant had the burden of proof to show that he had justifiable reasons to use

---

[77]Ibid. pp.64: see also *Weiand v. State*, 732 So.2d 1044 (1999), this case had to deal with a murder in a domestic violence situation.

[78]Ibid. pp.83, also see the U.S. Commission on Civil Rights Report "Examining The Race Effects of Stand Your Ground Law" pp.7; Commissioner Michael Yaki noted, in his report, that the NRA actually wanted the Florida SYG law to grant total immunity, both civil and criminal, to anyone asserting SYG law and found to be "justified" in the use of deadly force. This extreme vision was not ultimately carried out, but the overall thrust remained in place when the actual law was passed.

While Yaki recognizes that the law has been used by individuals across racial groups and acknowledges the lack of implicit racial bias in the use and applications in the law itself, he does make the point that the individuals themselves carry their own implicit racial biases with them in their use of force decision making process and the implicit racial bias in the criminal justice system, re over policing, inconsistent criminal sentencing, voir dire, etc. still have a deleterious effect.

[79] Fla. Stat. 776.012 (2005), Fla. Stat. 776.031 (2005), Fla. Stat. 776.032 (2005), also see Jason King, The Duty to Retreat; pp. 84-5.

deadly force or the threat of such force.[80] In a plot twist, however, former Governor Rick Scott signed a bill in 2017, which shifted the burden from the asserting defendants to the state.

In other words, Florida prosecutors now have to prove that a "reasonable person" would have, for example, escaped, called for help, done nothing, or made different choices other than using force in a given situation.[81] If the state fails to meet its burden, the defendant can assert SYG as ana affirmative defense.

This rule may become more apparent if applied to the Trayvon Martin lynching discussed below, even though it's a hypothetical example. The defendant George Zimmerman refrained from ultimately asserting the immunity defense.

If SYG, as understood at the time of the lynching, applied to the Zimmerman defense, then all a jury would have to believe is that a "reasonable person" in Zimmerman's shoes would have done the same thing and used force as well. This is a far different question than was it necessary for Zimmerman to use deadly force to defend himself. We explore the facts of the lynching of Trayvon Martin below.

---

[80] Ibid. pp.86, the rub is that, according to King, the evidentiary hearing is determined by a preponderance of the evidence (more likely than not standard) which is the standard for the burden of proof in most civil cases and far less than the beyond reasonable doubt and clear and convincing evidence standards often used in other civil and criminal litigation.

[81] Please see Brandon Farrington, Florida Law Shifts 'stand your grand' Burden of Proof, June 11, 2017 *Associated Press* located on its website here: https://www.news-press.com/story/news/local/2017/06/10/stand-ground-law-shifts-burden-proof-prosecutors/102721106/

1920 UNIA March, Harlem, NY (Public Domain)

Cyril Briggs and Richard B. Moore founded the self-defense oriented African Blood Brotherhood for African Liberation (ABB) in New York City in 1919. (Public Domain)[82]

---

[82] This organization, a one-time ally of Garvey's UNIA, eventually grew disillusioned over Garvey's brand of Pan-African nationalism, the handling of the Black Star Lines, and the AAB's move towards Communism. The beef between Garvey and Briggs was epic, even leading to a legal beef between the UNIA's *Negro World* and the ABB's *Crusader* magazine after Garvey accused Briggs, a light skinned African, of actually being a White man trying to pass for Black within the pages of the *Negro World* (confronting racial and cultural appropriation is nothing new for us, even when it's misguided). Please see Edmund David Cronin's biography on Garvey entitled Black Moses: The Story of Marcus Garvey and the Universal Negro Improvement Association (Madison: The University of Wisconsin Press, 1966) pp.75

Map of Free and Enslaved States Credit: by William C. Reynolds (Public Domain)

Tallahatchie River, Emmett Till was fished out of this river in Sumner County, MS
On August 31, 1955. (Public Domain)

Neshoba County Sheriff Lawrence Rainey, flanked by FBI agents, is brought to court in October 1964 in connection with the Mississippi Burning murders. A.P. Photo. FBI Website: https://www.fbi.gov/history/famous-cases/mississippi-burning (Public Domain)

School Segregation rally, Little Rock, AR 1959
John T. Bledsoe / Library of Congress (Public Domain)

Random White Man in Black Face
Loewenthall Collection of African-American Photos
Cornell University Library, Rare Collections Department
(Public Domain)

David Shankbone / CC BY (https://creativecommons.org/licenses/by/3.0) 2012
Clip Art Credits https://www.uihere.com/free-cliparts/trayvon-martin-racism-black-clip-art-service-clipart-2325920 (Public Domain)

Trayvon Martin

"You kill a dog, you go to jail, you kill a little black boy, and nothing happens".
Civil Rights attorney Benjamin Crump, after the killers of fourteen-year-old Martin Lee Anderson, was acquitted by an all-White jury in 2006.

The heart-breaking lynching of seventeen-year-old high school junior Trayvon Martin on February 26, 2012, was a shock to the system of African people in America. Partly because the story took so long to come out, partly because law enforcement had to be shamed into making an arrest, partly because this young

African was walking home from the neighborhood store and died with nothing more in his possession than a bottle of iced tea and a bag of candy.[83]

Around 6:30 pm, after watching the NBA All-Stare game action, Trayvon left his father's girlfriend's townhouse, whom he was visiting, in Sanford, FL. Sanford, FL, was a town that once denied Jack Robinson a motel room during his minor league baseball days. At any rate, Trayvon decided to walk to the 7-Eleven convenience store he had visited earlier that day.[84] His first visit to the store was with his older cousin, "Boobie" the second visit was to get something to drink for himself and a bag of Skittles candy for his brother Chad.[85] It was on Trayvon's return that things took a terrible turn for him because he was stalked by a lone wolf—out for who knows what.

The stalker, the resident watch captain named George Zimmerman, a twenty-eight-year-old, wannabe cop, was armed with a nine-millimeter handgun and on the phone with 9-1-1 while tailing Martin. A review of the 9-1-1 transcripts is revealing on several fronts and show that a) Zimmerman recognized Martin as a teenager, b) recognized Martin as Black, and c) he was told by the 9-1-1 dispatcher not to pursue Martin, whom he claims at one point was "running away."[86] The critical factor here

---

[83] The story of Trayvon Martin co-authored by his parents, Sybrina Fulton and Tracy Martin tells the tale of his lynching and subsequent aftermath of the fate of the lone-wolf lyncher, George Zimmerman, and his acquittal based on Florida's Stand Your Ground Law as an affirmative defense, but it also tells the story of Trayvon's life, in vivid and detailed recollection from those who knew and loved him. Please see Rest in Power: The Enduring Life of Trayvon Martin (New York: Spiegel and Grau, 2017); also see the 2018 documentary *Rest in Power: The Trayvon Martin Story* directed by Jennifer Furst and Julia Wlloughby Nason and with Shawn "Jay Z" Carter on the Executive Producer team.

[84] Ibid. pp.29, the Jack Robinson event occurred in 1946 and he was also escorted right of the dugout during the Spring Training game he tried to play in, please see pp. 77.

[85] Ibid. pp.29. Trayvon and Chad were not blood relations, but their parents were dating and apparently loved and respected each other just like blood siblings.

[86] Ibid. pp.30. The transcripts were archived by the University of Missouri Kansas City School of law and can be located here: http://law2.umkc.edu/faculty/projects/ftrials/zimmerman1/zimcalls.html; those transcripts

is that to Zimmerman, young Martin "fit the description," and it didn't matter what that "description" was and what the description was for. Black men, by and large, have always fit the description, a painful truth we revisited through this book.

Zimmerman's 9-1-1 call began around 7:09 and ended at approximately 7:15 pm; a short time after that call ended, Zimmerman and Martin got into an altercation. Martin, apparently at that point filled with the spirit of Emmett Till, Michael Donald, and countless other Africans facing death at the hands of the White nationalists aiming to kill him, began to get the better of Zimmerman who then, realizing he picked the wrong fight and instead of just taking his whipping, shot Martin one-time in the heart, killing him on the spot.[87] This lynching was both brutal and efficient.

Zimmerman was questioned and released that same night since he was the only eye-witness to the lynching. He raised a self-defense argument, and the local cops citing Florida Stand Your ground law (discussed *above*) stood by their decision.[88] Once Attorney Benjamin Crump became involved and began an aggressive media campaign did the story of this lynching leave the cozy and controlled confines of

---

read as if they came straight out of a nineteenth century pattleroller's employee handbook; compare those transcripts to Edward Cantell's 1860 judicial hornbook "The Practice of Law in North Carolina" where he asserts that "the patrol shall visit the negro houses in their respective districts as often as may be necessary, and may inflict a punishment, not exceeding fifteen lashes on all slaves they may find off their owner's plantations, without permit or pass, designating the place or places to which the slave has leave to go; also please see Hadden <u>Slave Patrols</u>; pp.105. Hadden goes on to note that neighborhood watches, like the one Zimmerman captained, can be traced to communities that needed to keep an eye on the Africans inspired by Lord Dunmore's Promise of Manumission and their attempts to leave the work farms and the settler project and seek liberation with the Brits. pp.159.

[87] Ibid. 60-6,

[88] Ibid. 55-6, it was the press conference held by Sanford Chief of Police Bill Lee announcing that "there were no immediate plans to arrest the killer" which helped to seal the deal for Attorney Crump to get involved.

Sanford, FL and became a global saga. That tragedy inspired thousands of Africans to mobilize and would, later, help to galvanize them.[89]

The media onslaught forced action, the FBI opened a civil rights investigation, and the Florida State Attorney's office became involved in the case, filed charges. Zimmerman was finally arrested on April 11, 2012, and charged with second-degree murder.[90] The *Justice for Trayvon* campaign led the calls for this case to go to trial and challenge the Florida Stand Your Ground Laws. A goal of the campaign was to keep publicizing their narrative that Zimmerman initially Martin based on "racial profiling" and ultimately lynched Martin because he couldn't take a butt whipping.[91]

The trial, in this case, was set to begin with voir dire (jury selection) on Monday, June 10, 2013, but was delayed due to the successful removal of the original Judge. While the Stand Your Ground law was never formally raised as an affirmative defense at trial, the self-defense story still played out. The final hearing began on July 11, 2013, and within two days of testimony, the mixed-race jury returned with a non-guilty verdict.[92]

The world saw, in the middle of the second term of the first leader of the settler state who just so happened to be Black, that young African men on these shores could be lynched, armed with nothing more than a bottle of iced tea and a bag of candy. And

---

[89] The month of March began the movement for gaining *Justice for Trayvon*, there were countless rallies, speeches, lobbying efforts on the local, state, and federal level including lobbying visits to the Congressional Black Caucus. The pressure was beginning to mount on the Florida State's Attorney office and after almost six weeks charges were eventually filed against Zimmerman.

[90] Ibid.

[91] Ibid. pp.174-75.

[92] Ibid. 315-6.

that Black man was lynched because he (again like so many of his ancestors as far back as Crispus Attucks) "fit some description," and he was confronted by some White man who refused to mind his own business.[93]

The *Justice for Trayvon* campaign and Zimmerman's acquittal in the lynching, as an outgrowth of the fiery passion and savvy of the two devastated parents and a talented team of attorneys, support staff, and teammates, helped drive and inspired a larger movement spearheaded by Black Lives Matter (#BLM). This organization was founded by three Black organizers, Alicia Garza, Patrice Cullors, and Opal Tommel, in that long-standing tradition of legends like Ella Jo Baker, Fannie Lou Hamer, Ruby Doris Smith, among countless others.[94]

Zimmerman lynched Trayvon Martin for the classic reason White supremacy has ingrained in Whites, that age-old premise that Whites get to control Black bodies. An American "truth" is that there is still a bedrock belief that Africans are to be

---

[93] Ibid. pp. 320-1. Almost a week after the verdict came down Obama (44) finally got around to saying something to appease his most loyal and faithful disciples, Africans-American voters, and while he couldn't muster the words to condemn global White Supremacy or even anti-Blackness in any forceful or full throated way, he did say "that when Travon got shot, I thought he could have been my son...or he could have been me thirty-five years ago". Obama ended his remarks by calling on the U.S. Department of Justice to help train local law enforcement to address "mistrust in the system" (not curbing behavior or stopping the wave of law enforcement lynchings that were becoming prevalent during the latter stages of his watch) and offered a critique of local laws, like the Stand Your Ground law at issue in this case.

[94] #BLM is a youthful, dynamic organization, that while appears to be decentralized, serves as a "brand" that organizers, activists, and participants can mobilize around; in that sense the galvanizing effect has been positive and far more effective in turning young African people out than any other organization since the heyday of the 60's. Information on Black Lives Matter can be found on its website located here: https://blacklivesmatter.com/; Ruby Doris Smith-Robinson was a stalwart SNCC organizer and activist from the very beginning until her untimely death in 1967, her niece Kiesha Lance Bottoms is the current Mayor of Atlanta, GA (at the time of drafting). SNCC was founded at a conference held between April 16-18, 1960 and was convened by Ella Jo Baker on the campus of Shaw University. See, Clayborne Carson's In Struggle, (Cambridge: Harvard University Press, 1995) pp. 19.

stopped, questioned, made to show papers (passes, birth certificates, licenses), made to prove we "belong" or have a right to be where we are found out in public.

This is a bedrock principle of the settler state put into practice and maintained by White supremacy. It has been acted upon by American Terrorists for centuries now. White supremacy and anti-Blackness are two of the deadliest
concepts ever conceived and unleashed on Black populations across the globe, especially in the United States.

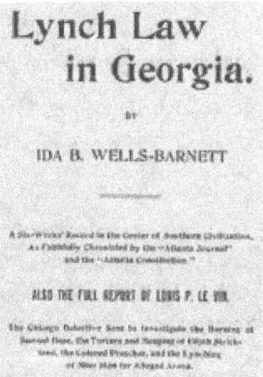

Ida B. Wells Barnett Lynch Law in Georgia (1899)
(Public Domain)

Smoldering homes in the wake of the burning of Greenwood, Tulsa, OK June 1921
Alvin C. Krupnick Co. / Public Domain

Mother Emmanuel AME Church, scene of the June 2015 gunshot lynching known as the Charleston Massacre
Cal Sr from Newport, NC, US / CC BY (https://creativecommons.org/licenses/by/2.0)

Denmark Vesey Memorial, Hampton Park, Charleston, S.C.
March 25, 2018
Photo Credits: ProfReader / CC BY-SA (https://creativecommons.org/licenses/by-sa/4.0)
(Public Domain)

Hanging Black Man, Anonymous Late Nineteenth Century
Loewenthall Collection Cornell University Library, Rare Collections Department
(Public Domain)

The Duluth (M.N.) Herald June 16, 1920 (Public Domain)

Duluth, MN June 1920 (Public Domain)

The lynching of Redmond, Robertson, Addison May 17, 1892
Somewhere in Georgia (Public Domain)

The lynching of an unnamed African man sometime between 1880 and 1890.
Loewenthall Collection of African-American Photographs
Cornell University Library, Rare Collections Department (Public Domain)

August 16,
1904-
Statesboro,
G.A.

https://digitalcollections.nypl.org/items/510d47df-a034-a3d9-e040-e00a18064a99, Public Domain, https://commons.wikimedia.org/w/index.php?curid=86570469

Whiteness, White supremacy, and anti-Blackness

"A White woman's honor was more important than a Black man's life"
Sentiment from a Southern newspaper around the time of the Scottsboro Boys" case[95]

The "wonder twins" of Whiteness and White supremacy had to be created and activated for the colonial settler project to hold up all these years. Gerald Horne argues that part of the underlying thrusts for this development in Colonial times had to do specifically with a) England's army depleted due to involvement in constant wars with European neighbors (namely France and Spain) b) the need to invite the recently defeated Irish and Scots to join the settler project on England's behalf, and c) to help offset any complications from the increased "dragooning of Africans."[96]

This toxic stew resulted in the ultimate creation of a new type of aristocracy called "Whiteness," whereby newly arrived Europeans of all stripes could be united against the interests of dispossessed Indigenes and enslaved Africans. And no matter how bad things were for them, economically, socially, or historically, they weren't the "god awful" redskins or blackies.[97] To further drive home this point, Horne states that by 1587, the birth of Virginia Dare marked the advent of the first "White" born child on these shores and had practically become a holiday celebrated by White supremacists, "the vanguard of the settler state," for centuries on end.[98]

---

[95] Klarman, From Jim Crow to Civil Rights; Op.Cit. pp. 118.

[96] Gerald Horne, The Apocalypse of Settler Colonialism Op.Cit p. 13.

[97] Ibid. See also p. 151

[98] Gerald Horne, The Dawning of the Apocalypse Op.Cit p. 147.

And while Horne gives us the practical explanations for the need to implement a concept of Whiteness and a notion of White supremacy, Jacob Carruthers traces the underpinnings of those ideas directly to eighteenth-century European thinkers David Hume and Charles Montesquieu, respectively.[99]

According to Carruthers, Hume noted in 1777 in his posthumously published work that "Negroes are naturally inferior to the Whites, any evidence of accomplishments attributed to them are exaggerations (like in the ancient Nile Valley Civilizations, for example), that Negroes are comparable to talking parrots." Negroes are unsophisticated to the point that "you may obtain anything from them by offering them strong drink, and may easily prevail with them to sell not only their children but their wives and mistresses for a cask of brandy."[100]

Carruthers also notes that Montesquieu, an early proponent of the concept of "social evolution," attempted to separate humanity into "three stages of social development," ranging from civilized, barbaric, and savage; it shouldn't be any mystery to which camp he summarily subscribed Africans to.[101] Montesquieu declared that "since it is natural to look upon color as the criterion of human nature, it is impossible then for us to suppose these creatures to be men, because allowing

---

[99] Carruthers, Jacob H. "Intellectual Warfare: The Battle for Kemet" in his collection of essays entitled Intellectual Warfare (Chicago: Third World Press, 1999) pp.6-7. This collection represents the texts of essays and published speeches which were produced in various places and spaces over a number of years; this particular speech was delivered at the Eighth Annual National Association for the Study of Classical African Civilization (ASCAC) Conference in 1991. Here, Carruthers is drawing on Hume's Essays: Moral, Political, and Literary and Montesquieu's The Spirit of the Laws, respectively. Please note, that several Africana scholars have posited definitions of White supremacy over the years, I found Carruthers' intellectual genealogy to be most useful and timely (chronologically speaking) for my purposes here.

[100] Ibid. pp.6.

[101] Ibid. pp. 6-7

them to be men, a suspicion would follow that we ourselves are not Christians."[102] This sentiment gets to the core of the White nationalist mindset that Whiteness is divinely ordained to be superior to all other races.

Armed with the intellectual rationale to undergird the creation and implementation of the concept that had been on the ground for almost two hundred years by then, the colonial settlers were set to turn up the pressure on African people across the Diaspora; our focus is on those Africans on this side of the North Atlantic for now.

A concise definition then is provided by Elizabeth "Bertita" Martinez, who asserts that "White supremacy is a historically based institutionally perpetuated system and exploitation and oppression of continents, nations, and people of color, by White people and the nations of the European continent to maintain and defend a system of wealth, power, and privilege.[103] This definition eloquently sums up the menace of White supremacy. Still, I would add the United States of America as a leading driver of the concept. These systems seek to defend and advance White wealth, power, privilege, cultural hegemony, and its particular brand of *Terrorism*.

So with these four cornerstones in place, 1) genocide of the Indigenes, 2) color of law and vigilante justice, 3) castle doctrine, and 4) Whiteness-White supremacy-anti-Blackness, we can now turn our attention to some of the legal approaches to combat the plague of lynching, starting with the push for federal law as a means to get some relief from American Terrorism.

---

[102] Ibid.
[103] Martinez, Elizabeth B. "What is White Supremacy?" This essay can be found on the Philadelphia Yearly Meeting of the Religious Society of Friends (Quakers) annual meeting website posted here: http://www.pym.org/annual-sessions/wp-content/uploads/sites/7/2017/06/What_Is_White_Supremacy_Martinez.pdf

Condensed Summary of Federal US Anti-Lynching Legislation

"Black lives have not been taken seriously as being fully human and deserving of dignity, and it should not require a maiming or torture in order for us to recognize a lynching when we see it."
Senator and Democratic Vice-Presidential nominee Kamala Harris (D-CA), June 4, 2020[104]

The U.S. federal government has an utterly dismal track record when it comes to passing legislation geared towards putting an end to the practice of lynching. Obviously, with the freeze on the Emmett Till Anti-Lynching Act of 2020, it has yet to pass a single anti-lynching bill in its two hundred forty four-year history.[105] One of the earliest formal attempts was the Dyer Anti-Lynching Bill in 1918.

The National Association for the Advancement of Colored People (NAACP) was instrumental in supporting that passage effort and the effort to pass the Costigan-

---

[104] Sen. Harris delivered these remarks during her floor speech during the Senate votes on the *Emmett Till Anti-Lynching Act of 2020*. The bill was eventually held up by yet another Southern politician (following the long line of his ideological and geographical forbears), Rand Paul (R-KY), and incidentally on a day of one of the home going celebrations of George Floyd, one of the recent ancestors whose lynching kicked off of weeks of massive protests all over the world.

And Senator Harris herself made settler state history by becoming the first Black woman to be selected to as a VP candidate when presidential Democratic nominee, Joe Biden, selected her as his running mate on August 11, 2020, please see the Biden Harris 2020 website located here: https://joebiden.com/

[105] Smith, David (June 11, 2020) :Rand Paul stalls bill that would make lynching a federal hate crime" *The Guardian*; also note that Michael Klarman states that during the Great African Migration, heating up after WWI, that this movement of Black bodies may have "tempered" some of the hostilities of members of the "planter classes" as there were actually some local anti-lynching legislation and ordinances to keep prisoners "safe" (from the White mob) passed in an effort to keep Africans from packing up and leaving town in droves. Klarman, Michael, *From Jim Crow to Civil Rights*; Op.Cit. pp.102

Wagner Anti-Lynching Bill in 1934.[106] The NAACP brilliantly lays out the history on its website:

> "Congressman Leonidas Dyer of Missouri first introduced his Anti-Lynching Bill–known as the Dyer Bill–into Congress in 1918. The NAACP supported the passage of this bill from 1919 onward; they had not done so initially, arguing that the bill was unconstitutional based on the recommendations of Moorfield Storey, a lawyer and the first president of the NAACP. Storey revised his position in 1918, and from 1919 onward, the NAACP supported Dyer's anti-lynching legislation. The House of Representatives passed the Dyer Bill on January 26, 1922. He was given a favorable report by the Senate Committee assigned to report on it in July 1922, but a filibuster halted its passage in the Senate. Efforts to pass similar legislation were not taken up again until the 1930s with the Costigan-Wagner Bill. The Dyer Bill influenced the text of anti-lynching legislation promoted by the NAACP into the 1950s, including the Costigan-Wagner Bill".[107]

---

[106] The NAACP was founded on February 12, 1909 in direct response to a violent race riot in Springfield, IL by White folks like Henry Moskovitz, Mary White Ovington, and Moorfield Storey and Africans like W.E.B. Dubois (who would eventually serve as research director), Ida B. Wells-Barnett, Mary "Molly" Church Terrell, and Archibald Grimke; see generally Charles Flint Kellogg's History of the National Association of the Advancement of Colored People 1909-1920 (vol.1) (Baltimore: The Johns Hopkins Press, 1967). White nationalists and defenders of the settler project had a particular disdain for the NAACP however, in fact MS Governor, Paul Johnson, during his election sneeringly referred to the organization as the National Association of "Apes, Coons, Niggers, and Possums". He belatedly ate those words, but the damage was still done; however, please Rick Bowers Spies of Mississippi (Washington, D.C.: The National Geographic Society, 2010) pp.96.

[107] https://www.naacp.org/naacp-history-dyer-anti-lynching-bill/ See also, Hixson, W. (1969). "Moorfield Storey and the Defense of the Dyer Anti-Lynching Bill" *The New England Quarterly, 42*(1), 65-81. doi:10.2307/363500. Hixson penned this article based on the available history and perusal of Storey's private correspondence. The Dyer bill carried a penalty of up to 5 years imprisonment and a $5,000 fine, these proposals had been put on the table as early as 1917 but were coalesced and presented by Congressman Dyer after he was deeply impacted

While the two proceeding legislative efforts typify the types and styles of U.S. laws that were being debated, discussed, and bandied about by Whites occupying the highest elected offices in the land, Africans in America were never content with the pre-ordained results or the behavior of our well-known enemies, nor should we have been.[108]

The lynching of Henry Smith, Paris, TX 1893 (Public Domain)

For example, in his work, <u>Legacies of Lynching: Racial Violence and Memory</u>, Jonathan Markovitz notes in the opening lines of his introduction that fierce debates around this act were reflected in the sentiments of individuals like Congressman Thomas Upton Sisson (D-MS) when he stated "he would rather the whole Black race of this world were lynched than for one of the fair daughters of the South to be ravished or torn by these Black brutes"; and Sisson received a co-sign from House

---

by a race riot that went down in East St. Louis, Illinois in July of 1918 where over 40 African women, children, and men were murdered. On page 67, Hixson notes that Dyer's bill also allowed the U.S. Attorneys to target both the complicit and negligent local law enforcement members as well as members of the mob. Also See Zangrando, R. (1965) "The NAACP and a Federal Ant lynching Bill, 1934-1940" *The Journal of Negro History, 50*(2), 106-117. doi:10.2307/2715996 for an analysis of the Costigan-Wagner Anti-Lynching Bill. The Costigan-Wagner bill died in committee but in addition to the penalties defendants faced, $5000 fine and 5 years in jail, this bill made provisions for the imprisonment of negligent or complicit members of law enforcement similar to the Dyer Bill. The Southern Democrats were successful in blocking both bills. Text of Dyer's speech on the House floor in support of his bill and a snippet of the Floor debate can be found in <u>The Negro American: A Documentary History</u> (ed. Leslie Fisher and Benjamin Quarles) Op.Cit. pp.427-32.

[108]Markovitz, Jonathan, <u>Legacies of Lynching: Racial Violence and Memory</u> (Minneapolis: University of Minnesota Press, 2004) pp. xv-xvi. Markozitz's book is focused on how lynching, as a metaphor for the "most vivid symbol of racial oppression" has changed and been remixed over time.

Minority Leader Finis Garrett, one time Chief Justice of the U.S. Court of Customs and Patent Appeals, (D-TN) when he loudly and proudly proclaimed that this bill should be renamed "a bill to encourage rape."[109]

---

[109]Ibid. Markovitz does attempt to cut Sisson and Garrett the benefit of the doubt on the question of lynching used as a tactic to concertize Whiteness, White supremacy, and Anti-blackness however, which in my mind is utterly inexcusable.

THE SHAME OF AMERICA

Do you know that the United States is the Only Land on Earth where human beings are BURNED AT THE STAKE?

In Four Years, 1918-1921, Twenty-Eight People Were Publicly BURNED BY AMERICAN MOBS

3436 People Lynched 1889 to 1922

For What Crimes Have Mobs Nullified Government and Inflicted the Death Penalty?

Is Rape the "Cause" of Lynching?

83 WOMEN HAVE BEEN LYNCHED IN THE UNITED STATES

AND THE LYNCHERS GO UNPUNISHED

THE REMEDY

The Dyer Anti-Lynching Bill Is Now Before the United States Senate

THE DYER ANTI-LYNCHING BILL IS NOW BEFORE THE SENATE TELEGRAPH YOUR SENATORS TODAY YOU WANT IT ENACTED

NATIONAL ASSOCIATION FOR THE ADVANCEMENT OF COLORED PEOPLE

NAACP Flyer in support of the Dyer Anti-Lynching Bill in 1922 (Public Domain)

Given the slow-motion nature of the federal law making process, International law has served as a club folks have used to beat the settler state over the head with.

Formal Charge of US Genocide to the UN

"Although we believe that the evidence tabulated below proves our case, we appeal to the General Assembly not as a court of law, which it is not, but as the conscience of mankind which it should be. We appeal not to the legal sense of mankind but its common sense. When a crime manifestly and overwhelmingly true, known to history and notorious to the world, that fact itself becomes part of the evidence before the General Assembly."
William Patterson, 1951

Africans, especially Africans in this part of the Diaspora, have always turned to the International community to fight White supremacy and the brutality of the settler state. An outgrowth of the tenth-anniversary meeting of the National Negro Congress (NNC) was a decision to deliver the first *"Petition to the United Nations on Behalf of the Thirteen Million Oppressed Negro Citizens of the United States of America"* to seek the elimination of political, economic, and social discrimination against Negroes in the United States of America.[110] This petition was delivered to U.N. Secretary-

---

[110] The text of this petition can be found in the appendix of Herbert Aptheker's book <u>Afro-American History The Modern Era: A Pioneering Chronicle of the Black People in Twentieth-Century America</u> (New York: Carol Publishing Group, 1971). This was a ground breaking move for Africans at that time, and was typical of the type of involvement Africans engaged in during this round of their "Double V" campaigns post World War II. The National Negro Congress (NNC) was formed in Chicago, IL in February 1936 and the keynote address was delivered by Asa Phillip Randolph. Randolph's speech and the NNC platform can be found in Herbert Aptheker's <u>A Documentary History of the Negro People in the United States Vol. IV</u>, Op.Cit. pp.211-20.

And it wasn't just activists who used their opportunities to marshal international support for the African-American liberation movement, some celebrities and other "known quantities" of their day would also use their respective platforms to deliver the message, like Langston Hughes did during his presentation at the Second International Writers Conference , in Paris, France in July of 1937; the text of the speech was reprinted in the September, 1937 edition of The *Crisis Magazine* found in the same Aptheker compilation, pp.279-82. Hughes explicitly calls out the U.S. as a "king hypocrite" in the wake of its attacks on other fascist world leaders without ending the American terrorism Africans faced on these shores daily.

General Trygvie Lie on June 6, 1946, but severe opposition raised from delegates from the settler project effectively blunted any serious movement.[111]

Five years later, in his role as President of the Communist Party, USA, William Patterson, and consummate activist celebrity Paul Robeson presented official documents at the fifth assembly of the United Nations in 1951, held in Paris, France, the United States with Genocide.[112] The argument itself was logical, immaculately organized, and bone-crushingly effective over nine separate articles and the "Evidence." The Petitioners were able to show that the wholesale killing of Africans in America was brutal, efficient, and again often dispatched under the "color of law."[113]

Throughout near 80 pages, they were able to layout the extrajudicial killings (some of which were lynchings under the "operational definition") of Black men, women, and children between 1945 and 1951. The descriptions are as biting as they were in Ida Wells' *Red Record* and tragically could be ripped straight from the headlines of any twenty-first-century social media posting.[114] While the larger U.N. body rejected the

---

[111] Ibid.
[112] Patterson, William <u>We Charge Genocide: The Crime of Government Against The Negro People</u> (New York: International Publisher's Co. 4th Edition, 2017). This was a revolutionary move as well, especially considering the tragic and staggering evidence presented to support the case. El hajj Malik El Shabazz called for similar UN action in 1964, See *generally* George Breitman, <u>The Last Year of Malcolm X: The Evolution of a Revolutionary</u> (Atlanta: Pathfinder Press, 21st. Edition 2011) and specifically the speech he handed out at the former Organization of African Unity (now African Union), at its second meeting in 1964 in Cairo, Egypt, where he called for the African nations in attendance to petition the United Nations on behalf of the oppression faced by Africans across the Diaspora, especially those in this settler state; please see the link posted by the Organization of Pan-African Unity located here: http://www.oopau.org/2.html.

[113] Ibid.

[114] Ibid. pp.58-134. See Also Martin, C. (1997). Internationalizing "The American Dilemma": The Civil Rights Congress and the 1951 Genocide Petition to the United Nations. *Journal of American Ethnic History, 16*(4), 35-61. Retrieved July 28, 2020, from www.jstor.org/stable/27502217

charges, similar to the presented petition in 1946, the message sent by our ancestors was delivered directly to the settler state, loud and clear.

Emmett Till Anti-Lynching Bill 2020

And lastly, here we are just a few short weeks out from the settler state's latest attempt to bring a level of critical seriousness to lynching, that ever-present scourge and scornful face of American terrorism. Congressman Bobby Rush, a former member of the Black Panther Party for Self Defense, turned federal legislator, introduced the bill in 2019[115].

The text of the bill contains a factual error and gross oversight on its face; it does note that Congress had introduced over 200 anti-lynching bills over the first half of the twentieth century and that seven separate presidents personally petitioned Congress to pass the legislation. The bill also calls for a formal apology from the whole of the federal government apparatus (not just the U.S. Senate), reconciliation, and a reckoning with U.S. history. The calls for reparations do not appear in this legislation, even though planters would frequently get paid reparations from the government for enslaved Africans slain by pattlerollers and reparations were finally paid to Japanese-American descendants of citizens interned during WWII.[116]

---

[115]H.R. 35 Emmet Till Anti-Lynching Act, 116th Congress H. Rept. 116-267 (2019-2020). Volumes have been written on the Panthers along with numerous documentaries and feature length films. Their sharp style of dress and 10-point program captivated Africans on this soil towards the tail end of the 1960's, younger and older alike.

[116]Ibid. The actual text of the bill is located here: https://www.congress.gov/bill/116th-congress/house-bill/35/text. The bill mistakenly claims that the Peace and Justice Museum and Memorial (P&J) in Montgomery, AL, spearheaded by attorney Bryan Stevenson is the first ever memorial dedicated to the lynching of Black folks across the settler state, but as previously noted the American Black Holocaust Museum (ABHM) addressed all of the issues credited to the P & J and was founded decades ago by lynching survivor James Cameron discussed *above* and again at one time operated an actual physical location.

This bill seeks to codify the shameful practice of lynching as a federal crime that carries an increased sentence of "not more than 10 years".[117] Yet, like the other efforts discussed above, yet another Southern politician stood proudly, defiant in the way of passing this critical legislation. *American Terrorism* has sanctioned yet again, this time through benign neglect. It was Kentucky Senator Rand Paul (R) carrying the torch of his Southern ancestors this time.[118]

The record reflects that while the law (and the various makers of the law) have awarded seeming victories to Black folks, on the one hand, they have always delivered generational punches to the gut with the other. With this firmly in mind, we begin examining the historical roots of this seemingly unending set of contradictions.

Also this bill should have definitely honored and credited the work of Ida B. Wells-Barnet in some way no matter how small and not even mentioning her in the recitation of the facts is downright disrespectful. My argument for the inclusion of Ida B. Wells Barnett and her tireless work on exposing lynching is not meant in any way to denigrate the equally legendary work of Walter White and the NAACP however, who is credited in the bills findings, in fact White should be heralded as Kendi reminds us that "Walter White passed for White and conducted lynching investigations throughout the South in the 1920's and also astutely linked the oppressive conditions Africans in America faced to oppressive conditions we faced in Europe and South Africa as well"; please see Kendi, <u>Stamped from the Very Beginning</u>. Op.Cit. pp. 330. And the quick note on reparations for bondagemen can be found in Hadden's <u>Slave Patrols</u>; Op.Cit. pp.123. and the payment of Japanese-American descendants was codified under *The Civil Liberties Act of 1988* Pub.L. 100–383, Statutes at Large: 102 Stat. 904.

[117] Ibid.

[118] Sweet, Lynn "How Rand Paul Blocked the Emmett Till Anti-Lynching Bill while nation mourned George Floyd" Chicago Sun-Times June 5, 2020

1917 NAACP Silent Lynching Protest, New York, NY
Underwood & Underwood / CC BY-SA (https://creativecommons.org/licenses/by-sa/4.0)

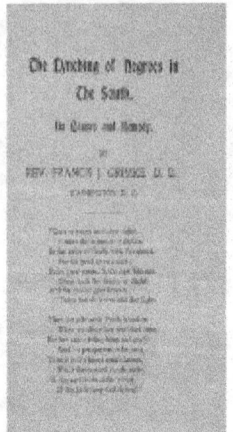

1899 Book of Sermons by Rev. Francis James Grimke, 1899, LOC (Public Domain)

William Jones lynched on Clarkson Street, New York, NY
July 13, 1863 -NY Draft Riot
By Harper's Weekly - Modified from a secondary source at http://www.sonofthesouth.net/leefoundation/civil-war/1863/august/draft-riots.htm, (Public Domain) https://commons.wikimedia.org/w/index.php?curid=1067142

Postcard of the lynching of Lawrence Nelson
Okemah, OK May 25, 1911 (Public Domain)

Martin Luther King and El Hajj Malik el Shabazz before a press conference, March 26, 1964 (Public Domain)

Unidentified farmer and unidentified COFO organizer keeping "fire watch" at a Holmes County, MS Library Freedom School location, 1964. Photo Credits: 1976 Matt Herron / Take Stock / TopFoto (licensed use)

Paul Robeson, Library of Congress Prints and Photographs Division, Farm Security Administration-Office of War Information Photograph Collection, June 1942 (Public Domain)

Chapter 3

Early Colonial Attitudes Towards Enslaved Africans-American Terrorism before America

"The nightmare scenario for settlers was avoiding precisely what eventually befell them in Hispaniola in 1791, that is, an uprising where they were liquidated or forced to migrate and the Africans seized power. The problem was that settlers were so drunk on the incomparable riches delivered by the African Slave that they found it hard not to deliver more gravediggers determined to prepare their indecent burial."
Gerald Horne, 2018

Early attitudes about enslaved Africans were a mix of condescension, wonderment, and fear. These are the base ingredients of *American Terrorism*. Whether they were the Spanish conquerors and French traders in the Caribbean or the English who emerged, later on, the maroons wreaked havoc on the plans for smooth sailing and coasting towards domination and struck a deep sense of fear and wariness in the hearts of the settlers who tried to subjugate them.[119]

The constant trick bag that settlers across the landscape kept falling into was that the more chained Africans they accumulated meant more profit they could maximize.
+
The more chained Africans that accumulated also meant more incensed Africans would soon multiply and outnumber the settlers in many places.[120] Those incensed Africans needed to be broken for this settler project to survive through the night, let alone through the centuries.

---

[119] Horne, The Apocalypse of Settler Colonialism pp.90, here Horne notes that those Africans who escaped to the hills and hinterlands of Santo Domingo, Hispaniola, Jamaica, Cuba, etc. almost single-handedly drove the colonizers off those islands.

[120] Ibid. pp.135.

The brutal enslaved breaking process showed the very depths of the European settlers' depravity and dehumanization of the Africans as Cyril L.R. James lays out in the first chapter of The Black Jacobins.[121] And Horne reminds us that it was a British ship captain in the sixteenth century, George Best, who "extended the Curse of Ham—a purported Biblical injunction mandating degradation of Africans to all of Ham's descendants, which served to rationalize enslavement and brutalization of African people.[122]

And when physical brutality was not enough, the settlers established laws and codes to propel the enslaved breaking agenda further.

What came to be known as the state of Florida was likely ground zero for the establishment of Black Codes, and the record indicates that it should be. For example, in his work, The Dawning of the Apocalypse, Gerald Horne notes that both free and enslaved Africans were present in that state as early as 1526, and later on that year, they were on the warpath along with their indigenous counterparts in South Carolina and on Sapelo Island, Georgia.

Horne argues that 1526 is a more seminal year for marking the nascent African presence on these shores where the date of 1619 is merely notional at best and seeks to "understand the man without understanding the child." Not to belabor the point but using 1526 as the seminal date effectively restores almost a century of armed, active rebellion and maroon society history to the story of African response to American Terrorism. That later date would unintentionally ignore; generations of Africans who came here kicking, screaming and scrapping.[123]

---

[121] James, C.L.R. The Black Jacobins Op.Cit. P.6

[122] Horne, The Dawning of the Apocalypse, Op.Cit. pp. 99.

[123] Horne, Gerald The Dawning of the Apocalypse (New York: Monthly Review Press, 2020); pp. 12-5; also see Benjamin Brawley, another earlier giant of the African in America experience

In Virginia in July 1640, an escaped African named John Punch felt the lash of *colonial law* when he and his "White" counterparts that he absconded with all got recaptured and faced the justice of the peace. Victor, the Dutchman, and James, the Scotchman, each received thirty lashes and an extra year of indentured servitude on top of whatever they had left on the books. But John Punch, oh, he got the thirty lashes as well, but the Court held that "being a *Negro*, (he) shall serve his said master or assigns for the time of his natural Life or elsewhere."[124] As we see, the stark reality of racial disparity in criminal sentencing goes back to the very beginning of the colonial settler project. On that score, nothing changed all these centuries later.

In Virginia in 1661, the provincial government enacted a *"fugitive slave law"* of sorts; when it declared that any English indentured servant who ran away "in company with negroes" and got caught would get years added to the servitude. The custom was that the indentured would receive a life sentence if the Negro also received a life sentence. This law set the stage for subsequent laws for escaped Africans discussed *below* and concretized chattel enslavement as a "life sentence."[125]

In 1664 Maryland passed a law stipulating that any White woman that married an African in bondage would have to join her husband in bondage until he gained his freedom. Virginia was soon to follow and added that all her children from this marriage would join in bondage with her husband.[126]

---

who agrees with Horne's assessment, by highlighting that groups of those Africans arriving in 1526 were so troublesome that they were almost immediately shipped back to the island Hispaniola after burning down their encampments and trying to escape. Brawley notes this in A Social History of the American Negro (London: Collier Books Limited, 1970) pp.5.

[124] The Negro American: A Documentary History (ed. Leslie Fisher and Benjamin Quarles) (Glenview: Scott, Foresman, and Company 1967) Op.Cit. pp. 19.

[125] The Negro American: A Documentary History Op.Cit. pp. 20

[126] The Negro American: A Documentary History pp. 20-1, citing William H. Henning, ed. The Statutes at Large: being a Collection of All the Laws of Virginia, 1619-1792 (13 vols., Richmond, published by the State of Virginia, 1809-1823).

And in keeping with the times, the settlers in South Carolina passed *"An Act for The Better Ordering and Governing of Negroes and Slaves"* in 1712.[127] This remarkably prescient Code in summary established that: 1) Africans, Mulattos, Indigenes, and Mestizos who are in bondage are in fact in bondage along with their children, 2) that the enslaved are meant to labor without leave (ever), 3) the dwellings of the enslaved are meant to be searched diligently once every fourteen days for fugitives, guns, weapons, or for anything that was not given to them by their "master", etc., 4) banned any settlers from trading with any enslaved person under penalty of losing their property subject to the ruling of the justice of the peace, 5) weapons bans outside of the plantation for enslaved African people, 6) mandatory gun safes for settlers with enslaved Africans on their property, 7) authorization of the slave patrols and paddle rollers (police), 8) fines for settlers who give enslaved Africans "travel papers" to conduct business outside of the plantation on Sundays except in case of unavoidable emergency, 9) authorization for the death penalty (lynching) for any enslaved person proven to have committed a common felony in the view of the justice of the peace (we have been catching death sentences since we've been here), 10) authorization for 40 lashes for any enslaved person having been found to have committed a misdemeanor, except for children as their punishment will be left up to the justice of the peace, 11) authorization of full value restitution (reparations) between one settler to the other if an African in bondage kills another African in bondage, and lastly 12) authorization of the death penalty (lynching) for any Africans engaging in any acts of resistance or insurrection, same sentence for any settlers that assist any of Africans engaging in insurrection or resistance.[128]

---

[127] Ibid. Op.Cit. pp. 21-6. This edition only posts the first twelve of the twenty-three sections of the Code. This Code had been based on earlier codes passed in 1696 and based solely on Codes that had been passed in Barbados. See Hadden, *below*.

[128] Ibid. Op.Cit. pp.21-6

South Carolina was also the earliest colony to establish standing, standard, compensated patrol forces meant to keep Africans in line, the "patterollers." These forces assembled out of fear of Indigene attack or African Rebellion. Before relevant U.S. laws were written, the old English concept of "hue and cry" was more than enough to snatch some random African from right up off the streets, but those old common laws metastasized amid the settler project. Sally Hadden offers a detailed history of how, when, and why this system was created and developed over the centuries in her book <u>Slave Patrols: Law and Violence in Virginia and the Carolinas</u>.[129]

Hedden notes that counties mainly used patrols to monitor and control African bodies when settlers would not do so independently, and in most cases, could not do the job individually. Early on, conscripted groups of men (planters and workers alike) joined in breaking up nighttime gatherings or haul in suspicious characters. The groups also prevented mischief before it happened and capture the alleged lawbreakers after the fact. The big difference was that in the South, the Africans were always the most "suspicious group."[130] She goes on to make the explicit point that while slightly different, these early "patterollers seemed most like constables because both had duties that were police like in nature. Slave patrols and constables

---

[129]Hadden, Sally <u>Slave Patrols: Law and Violence in Virginia And The Carolinas</u> (Cambridge: First Harvard University Press, Paperback ed., 2003) pp. 4. While Hadden makes the point within the very first few pages of her work that Southern enslaved patrols continued to engage in police functions she failed to clearly see the connections between modern policing and their attitudes towards Africans today and their colonial predecessors. The discussion on the "hue and cry" system is covered on pp,25-6.

[130]Ibid. Op.Cit. pp.16-40 Hadden lays out the various codes that were passed across the Mid-Atlantic in support and development of the slave patrols and confirms that at different times patrols consisted of settlers, indentured servants, militiamen, landed gentry, even manumitted Africans looking for a few less lashes or their "freedom". Another dynamic that was consistently at play was the ever present threat of invasion from the Spanish forces to the South, the greedy Whites were scared that at one point a law was passed that for every four settlers that were trained and armed, one African had to be trained and armed as well, African rebellions quickly got laws like that tossed out. These laws were all heavily influenced by "Bondage Codes" used in Barbados.

eventually gave way to paid police forces, and in cities like Richmond, Raleigh, and Charleston, the police force's main function was controlling enslaved Africans.[131]

The Colonial South Carolina Black Codes, modeled after the Codes of Barbados, differed mightily from the 1724 Code Noir in Louisiana, which primarily modeled the Codes in place on the island of Santo Domingo. In fact, Gerald Horne, in his book Confronting Black Jacobins, remarks that this code almost mirrored the 1685 Santo Domingo "Slave Codes" and was almost "liberal" concerning the breaking up of families, for example.[132]

Horne suggests that the Africans already here, including mulattoes and "octaroons," and growing numbers Africans arriving every day deeply worried provincial Governor William Charles Cole Claiborne. Claiborne was concerned about the prospects of Rebellion against the vastly outnumbered the Whites and figured a "softer approach" would serve Paris' interests best.[133] Regardless of this "egalitarian" and refined Apartheid employed in Louisiana at the time, pattlerollers were ever-present.

---

[131]Ibid. pp.84, here Hadden notes that the overlap wasn't a secret as she quoted John Tompkins saying that "with a well-regulated police in the way of patrols we can proclaim to the world that slavery is an inestimable blessing; See the quote from enslaved African S.S. Taylor where he summed it all much more eloquently, "police were for White folks, patterollers were for niggers".

[132] Horne, Gerald Confronting Black Jacobins: The United States, the Haitian Revolution, And the Origins of the Dominican Republic (New York: Monthly Review Press, 2015) pp. 32-3; the 1724 law forbade slavers from selling spouses or prepubescent children to different slavers; this concept was still in place for British slavers for another forty years.
[133] Ibid., pp.114-15.

The Rise of the Pattlerollers-Foot Soldiers of American Terrorism

"Historians have often described patrollers as men of very low social rank, but slave patrols between 1704 and 1721 frequently included men of superior social status, not just poor slave less Whites. Wealthy South Carolina men angled for appointments as slave patrollers to avoid having to serve in the militia when it was called away from home"
Sally Hadden, 2003[134]

Sally Hedden effectively closes the point by commentating that it did not matter what region enslaved persons were in. What set the pattlerollers apart from private citizens, militia, overseers, catchers, and constables was the "official appointment that authorized slave patrollers to act on the community's behalf." Pattlerollers also had "the indemnification and protection from the courts to brutalize enslaved Africans if they wanted to with the full blessing of the communities they were assigned to "protect and serve."[135]

The same energy was carried over as pattlerollers transformed into paid police officers and firefighters across the South. These are the same forces that showed up on the streets of New Orleans and exacted revenge on the African community they had grown accustomed to brutalizing. They sent the shameful Black pattlerollers packing during the race riot of 1900.[136]

---

[134] Hedden, Sally <u>Slave Patrols</u>; Op.Cit. pp.21

[135] Ibid. pp.102-3. It's useful to keep in mind however that not all of the Whites felt so compelled and duty bound to serve as pattlerollers, in fact as the Confederate Congress began to flail and falter, land-owning Whites began to appeal for patrol service waivers and finally got the "Twenty Nigger Law" passed which made concessions for any White man who ran a solo operation with at least twenty enslaved Africans on his roll to be able to skip pattleroller service; this was amended but originally passed to "secure proper police of the country", see pp.176; reminds me of the reports of how Trump (45)'s pa was able to weasel him out of serving in Vietnam; shirking "duty" is sometimes a calling card of the loudest progenitors of both the need for and protection of the settler state, other White nationalists apparently flock to the U.S. military or join American Terrorist groups after getting out of service.

[136] Barnett, Ida B. Wells<u>, Mob Rule in New Orleans</u>; please see generally

The police force in Seattle, WA 1918, pandemic ready (Public Domain)

It should never be forgotten that the law duly authorized these brutal defenders of White nationalism and the settler state, the codes of the day, to perpetuate *American Terrorism* against African people and their children. That was part of the Code. And that South Carolina Code was indeed wicked, dehumanizing, and oppressive, but it was prescient. And the whole world would soon find out just how prudent it was for these settlers to worry so much about "their" African-Americans, nods to Trump (45), in a little over twenty years or so, as we explore in our examination of the Stono Rebellion *below*.

The Lynching of Angelique (1734)

"You are killing me"
Marie-Joseph Angelique while sitting in a jail cell being tortured by judicial decree during a forced confession at a cell block trial in Old Montreal, Quebec, Canada, June 21, 1734

The spirit of "New World" African resistance was literally on fire in the mid-eighteenth century across the various settler projects. Like so many times in our history, African women were blazing the way. Take the story of Angelique, "the enslaved woman" who burned down Montreal.[137]

On April 10, 1734, Marie-Joseph Angelique, a twenty-nine-year-old enslaved African woman from Portugal, who previously tried to escape, rebelled and set fire to the Frenchville farmhouse. That work farm is the spot where she was held in bondage, and the fire itself ultimately consumed forty-six buildings, including "homes, shops, warehouses, and a convent."[138] Afua Cooper offers a brilliant and heartbreaking analysis of this event and the aftermath in her fantastic work, <u>The Hanging of Angelique: The Untold Story of Canadian Slavery and The Burning of Old Montreal</u>.[139]

---

[137] Cooper, Afua <u>The Hanging of Angelique: The Untold Story of Canadian Slavery and the Burning of Old Montreal</u> (Athens: University of Georgia Press, 2006) offers an excellently written and utterly harrowing account of this story that had not really been well known or highlighted by the masses. Op.Cit. pp. 14-23.

[138] Ibid. pp. 20, 201.

[139] Cooper's book is amazing and a shock to the conscious of anyone who engages it fully and critically and hopefully it will help kick start much needed exploration, again, into the brutal realities that African women face existing in a world that lynches so many of them, their children, and their loved ones; like the 1920 case of Rachel Moore. Moore was lynched after her son-in-law shot a White man in a dispute over work that the son-in-law completed; Moore was completely innocent and didn't have anything to do with the killing of the White man, but the mob strung her up anyway; please see Umoja's <u>We Will Shoot Back</u>; pp. 19.

Angelique was eventually caught and arrested, and after being excruciatingly tortured by use of the "boots," she confessed but refused to name any accomplices. It was the final defiance that enraged authorities, led by Judge Pierre Raimbault and notary Charles-Rene Gaudron de Chevremont.[140]

The Boots was a torture practice geared towards drawing confessions from the accused and was based on a medieval technique which would put you in the mindset of the "hobbling scene" from the 1990 movie "Misery."[141] The story revolves around Angelique's role as a reluctant "breeder," and her liaison with a French soldier turned Frenchville worker, named Henry Thibault.[142]

Judge Raimbault tortured Angelique during her "cell block trial" because he was convinced that a) as a good "slave" and wouldn't just rebel on her own. Raimbault believed this despite the years of forced sexual abuse she suffered and the ultimate relinquishment of her babies on demand. And b) Raimbault was convinced that Angelique's White lover Thibault, had to be the mastermind of the operation.[143]

This tale highlights the need for modern, critical analysis of the brutality African women faced throughout the history of lynching and the unique role sexual assault played in general, especially the sexual assaults against African women. Ida B. Wells

---

[140] Ibid. pp.14

[141] Ibid. pp. 17-9, the "laced boots" involved the use of four wooden boards about two feet high and placed on the inside and outside of the legs of the tortured. They were bound together leaving enough space for wedges to be placed in between the board and the leg. The judge would ask a question and for every incorrect answer (truth be damned) would result in an iron wedge being placed between the leg and the board and hammer striking the wedge and driven it into the leg; one past torture victim, Urbain Grandier, reportedly had bone marrow oozing out of his legs after his time in the "boots".

[142] Ibid. 171

[143] Ibid. pp. 17-9.

Barnett's baton needs to be picked up and ran with as these stories need to be told and reexamined.[144]

Finally, after the torture, humiliation, and begging for death, Angelique confessed to the burning down the Frenchville farmhouse. In an ultimate move to humiliate her, she was paraded through the town, taken to a church to confess to the crime publicly, and marched through the streets, labeled an arsonist, and lynched on a shoddy gallows set up in the ashes of the devastation she leveled. Sadly, a fellow African man was her hangman.[145]

After letting Angelique's lifeless body dangle like tinsel on the Christmas tree, she finally got cut down and thrown into a bonfire that had been ready and waiting on

---

[144] Barnett, Ida B. Wells The Red Record Revisited (ed.) pp. 105-7, here Wells-Barnett planted some seeds on the subject when she made the brilliant point that White men, often old pedophiles, typically escaped justice when they were accused of assaulting African women, often children but obviously African men would often get lynched off the mere allegation that they even looked at a White woman funny. Well's Southern Horrors: Lynch Law and All It is Phases briefly touches upon this as well.

In that same vein, Sally Hadden discusses in heart breaking detail some of the exhaustive brutality enslaved African women faced at the hands of the pattlerollers who would burst into homes and quarters during their inspections, sometimes dragging the men out and whipping them then raping the women. Hadden addresses this on pp.116-7 in her book Slave Patrols; Op.Cit.

[145] Ibid. pp. 20-23. There is a long standing history of African treachery against other Africans especially in this context, in fact in the early to mid-nineteenth century New Orleans' "free-Blacks", in putting an ante-bellum spin on that classic Lawrence "Kris" Parker cut "Black Cop", were not only used but relied heavily upon to supplement their pattleroller forces according to Sally Hadden, Slave Patrols; Op.Cit.pp.103, the enslaved rebellions and insurrections are replete with traitors and turncoats including the ones we will address *below*, and the various Civil Rights organizations that formed and sought to help lead the liberation struggle from the UNIA, to the Black Muslims, to SCLC, to SNCC, to the BPP, on down the line have long traditions of being infiltrated by State agents, whether they were working for local cops or State and Federal agencies. The race traitor is nothing new to African people in America and their work often led to bloodshed; we will discuss the crushing role spies and traitors played in the Freedom Summer lynchings *below*.

Parker, Lawrence "Kris" (1993) track 3

her; at the end, her ashes were scooped up and set to the four winds.[146] That courageous ancestor Angelique was made an example of because her rebellious act, likely meant to destroy her little slice of hell and not that whole hellacious town, hit that one nerve that would always set the settlers off, regardless of where they slept—fear.

White fear is palpable; fear of attack from other colonials, fear of attack from the Indigenes, and fear of African rebellion. Angelique got lynched, at the behest of and under the ever-watchful eye of the law, out of fear. Period.

Stono Rebellion (1739)

"The Stono Uprising was led by Angolans; it was concluded with disconsolation"
Gerald Horne, 2014.[147]

And like the tale of Angelique, the settler fear of African resistance was also summed up beautifully by Gerald Horne in the subtitle to his chapter on the Stono Rebellion in The Counter Revolution of 1776, "will the Africans become masters and the Europeans slaves?"[148]

Five years after the burning of Old Montreal in South Carolina, the settlers had every right to fear for their lives. The Stono Rebellion was a massive uprising engaged by Africans, initially sparked by a group of Angolans posted near the Stono River. These Africans may have been inspired in part by the Spanish colonists posted up at St. Augustine, Florida, and their overtures of freedom for escapees. Twenty-nine Whites

---

[146] Ibid.

[147] Horne, The Counter Revolution of 1776; Op.Cit. pp.111

[148] Horne, The Counter revolution of 1776; Op.Cit. pp.110-30.

were killed, and the threat of another event struck fear throughout the Southern territories.[149]

Ultimately, the settlers and their provincial governors would careen from arming and attempting to disarm groups of Africans (some in chattel bondage, some not). Then they pitted those Africans against fellow colonizers, indigenous nations, and sometimes each other. The Africans would get offers of manumission and promises of freedom from enslavement and property ownership along the way. But those Africans were brave and bold, even as they were summarily lynched as punishment for the White blood they shed and their audacity to revolt.[150] The chaotic game of bumper cars that the Europeans had fashioned in their colonies was headed for the home stretch.[151]

The Stono Rebellion shook the entire colonial settler project from across every false provincial border, to every outpost, every fort, and the various thrones, Crowns, and churches pulling strings and collecting the profits across the Atlantic. For example, just a couple years later, on February 28, 1741, paranoid White settlers in New York City were so petrified of an African insurrection (and desertion to Spanish forces) that when a series of fires started breaking out across the City; panicked settlers figured "it was on," a massive race riot ensued, and in the aftermath twenty-five Whites were arrested for their roles.[152]

One hundred and thirty-four Africans brought to trial resulted in thirteen lynchings being burned alive, eighteen lynched by hanging, seventy shipped off to the

---

[149] Ibid.

[150] Ibid. pp. 111.

[151] Ibid.

[152] The Negro American: A Documentary History; Op.Cit pp.26-7

Caribbean, and thirty-three sent back into bondage. And at the time, New York had the largest number of Africans in bondage above what would come to be known as the "Mason-Dixon" line a century or so later.[153]

Progenitors of the settler project, and the creators of Whiteness, White supremacy, and anti-Blackness felt like chattel bondage was their divinely ordered birthright. It is little wonder then that the Crown's move to abolish the system, as a result of *Somerset (discussed below)*, sent tidal waves crashing upon the shores of its western colonies.

Somerset v. Stewart 98 ER 499 (1772)[154]

"The question is not whether slavery is lawful in the Colonies (where a concurrence of unhappy circumstances has caused it to be established as necessary) but whether in England? Not whether it ever existed in England; but whether it not now be abolished?"
William Murray, 1st Lord of Mansfield; opinion of the Court

This case, decided in June 1772, had a direct and definitive effect on African people surviving the settler state; it abolished chattel slavery in England and sent a tsunami-like shockwave across the Atlantic.[155] The backstory is riveting, as the case namesake African born James Somerset (ancestral precursor of Henry Bibb, and other African runners), was so prone to escaping bondage his "owners" frequently had to capture him, recapture him, and finally ship him all over the English colonies until he ended up in the bowels of a ship moored in the Thames River in London.[156]

---

[153] Ibid. For a partial list of the names of the arrested Africans and their fates, please see The Negro American: A Documentary History pp.27, citing Daniel Horsmanden, "A Journal of the Proceedings in the Detection of the Conspiracy For the Burning of the City of New York in America, and Murdering the Inhabitants" (New York, 1744); Op.Cit. pp.11-15.

[154] (1772) 98 ER 499

[155] Horne The Counter Revolution of 1776; Op.Cit.pp.210

[156] Ibid.

While in England, he was discovered, taken into custody, and eventually brought before the Court. The question arose as to whether he could stay in bondage on English shores, and the Court profoundly said, "No." The dander that was kicked up by American settlers once this decision came down, and the Africans who found out about it helped set the stage for the "patriot" led Counter-Revolution of 1776.[157]

The April 13, 1937 lynching of Roosevelt Towns and Robert McDaniels in Duck Hill, MS.
Photo Credits: Anonymous-AP Photo-Public Domain

---

[157] Ibid. Again, Horne argues that African resistance across all the Crown's "New World" possessions so enraged the so-called "patriot" colonists that when England abolished slavery, they revolted just so that they could maintain their divine rights to hold our ancestors in bondage.

A poster highlighting the Duck Hill, MS Lynchings in 1937 (Public Domain)

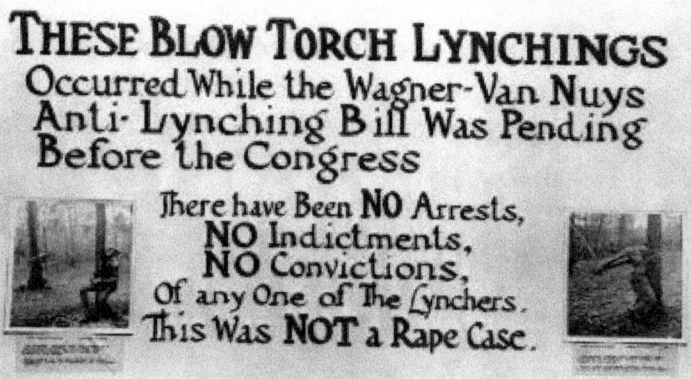

Postcard of Lynching of Bennie Simmons, who was soaked in coal before being set on fire. June 13, 1913, Anadarko, OK. (Public Domain)

Chapter 4

American Law and American Terrorism through Reconstruction

"It was part of my business to arrest all slaves and free persons of color, who were collected in crowds at night, and lock them up. It was also part of my business to take them before the Mayor. I did this without any warrant, and at my own discretion. Next day they are examined and punished. The punishment is flogging. I am one of the men who flog them. They get not exceeding thirty-nine lashes. I am paid fifty-cents for every for every Negro I flog. The price used to be sixty-two and half cents. I am paid fifty-cents for every Negro I arrest and fifty-cents more if I flog him. I have flogged hundreds. I am often employed by private persons to pursue fugitive slaves. I have been thus employed since 1838. I never refuse a good job of that kind"
Constable John Capeheart Norfolk, VA, was listed on that City's rolls from the 1830s through the 1850s.[158]

The African flight, either to the King's army or away from the work camps during the Revolutionary War in the eighteenth century, set the stage for the nineteenth century. The nineteenth century was a pivotal time for Africans in America regarding their collective interaction with American wartime society, the passage of major American law directly affecting Africans on these shores, and their reactions to both chattel enslavement and the continual, unchecked state of American Terrorism.

In every stage and every phase of the nineteenth century, as African people began to find their collective voices, their main focus was to get out from under the yoke of bondage and find some relief from the pattlerollers, the enslaved catchers, and militias. If that meant fleeing to Canada or fleeing to Santo Domingo, they were open. At times, it meant siding with the British against the settler state.

On the eve of the Revolution, London took pride in its ability to rouse Africans against the settlers who worked, raped, beat, and otherwise set upon them. This sentiment was highlighted in the treatment and impact of Lord Dunmore's Proclamation.

---

[158]Hadden, <u>Slave Patrols</u>; Op.Cit. pp.83.

Lord Dunmore's Proclamation

"And I do hereby further declare all indented servants, Negroes or others (appertaining to Rebels) free that are able and willing to bear arms They joining his Majesty's Troops for the more speedily reducing the Colony to a more proper sense of their duty, to His Majesty's Crown and Dignity"
John Murray, 4th Earl of Dunmore, November 1, 1775

As the settlers waged war against the Brits, the provincial Governor of Virginia did all that he could to stir the pot effectively and, at the same time, had to bolster his forces. In the fall of 1775, aboard a British warship the William, Dunmore issued a proclamation that sought to turn the tables on the settlers.[159]

Dunmore declared martial, ruled the disloyal settlers as traitors, and extended the most sweeping offer of emancipation to the bondage Africans in the Western Diaspora. The settlers were freaked out, especially Founding Father enslaved owners like James Madison (2), Patrick "Give me liberty or give me death" Henry, William Bradford, and others.[160]

Despite their very best efforts to conceal the Proclamation, once Africans started getting the word and getting the word out, they would leave "America" in droves three-hundred risked all the threats of punishment within the first week; all told, upwards of two-thousand Africans moved to join the British army; not out of patriotism, loyalty, or love; this was about (and has always been about) liberation because upwards of fifty-five thousand merely absconded.[161]

---

[159]Quarles, B. (1958). "Lord Dunmore as Liberator". *The William and Mary Quarterly, 15*(4), 494-507. doi:10.2307/2936904; also see Hadden, Slave Patrols; pp. 158-62.

[160]Hadden spends some time revealing the worrying correspondence dispatched by Henry and Madison (2), but surprisingly they seemed to be more concerned with enslaved Africans running away than they were with them taking up arms. Hadden Slave Patrols; Op.Cit. pp. 158-9. Also see Quarles, "Lord Dunmore as Liberator" pp. 501-02, where he gives the numbers of Africans who left their settlers high and dry.

[161]Ibid. see also Hadden, Slave Patrols; pp. 160-62.

Dunmore's Ethiopian Regiment Uniform (Public Domain)

History turned out that the settlers won their Independence from London. Still, it would be another eighty-seven years before Africans in America would see the end of chattel slavery and a four hundred ninety-four year fight to liberate ourselves from White Supremacy and anti-Blackness on these shores.

One of the recurring themes throughout this work is that American law is always concerned about what happens to African bodies, where we can go, where we can't go, what we can do, what we can't do, and as the reigns eased up just a little bit White nationalists and defenders of the settler state would react, constrict, and reassert themselves; often with incredibly traumatic consequences for African people. This has been true from the earliest days that this settler project ejected its colonial masters and unleashed American Terrorism on Black folk.

Eric Arnesen, "The fugitive slave acts of 1793 and 1850" *Cobblestone* 1 Feb. 2003: n. pag. Print. (Public Domain)

Three-Fifths Compromise (1789)[162]

Representatives and direct Taxes shall be apportioned among the several States which may be included within this Union, according to their respective Numbers, which shall be determined by

---

[162] U.S. Const. art I §2.

adding to the whole Number of free Persons, including those bound to Service for a Term of Years, and excluding Indians not taxed, three fifths of all other Persons. The actual Enumeration shall be made within three Years after the first Meeting of the Congress of the United States, and within every subsequent Term of ten Years, in such Manner as they shall by Law direct. The Number of Representatives shall not exceed one for every thirty Thousand, but each State shall have at Least one Representative; and until such enumeration shall be made, the State of New Hampshire shall be entitled to three, Massachusetts eight, Rhode-Island and Providence Plantations one, Connecticut five, New-York six, New Jersey four, Pennsylvania eight, Delaware one, Maryland six, Virginia ten, North Carolina five, South Carolina five, and Georgia three.[163]

The actual text of the compromise in the italicized section was overturned with the passage of the thirteenth amendment in 1864. Federalist 54, the essay penned by James Madison under the joint pseudonym "Publius," where Madison engages in oratorical jiu-jitsu as he argues for the duality of Africans being human property should be compared to the August 21-22 1789 Constitutional Convention debates dominated by the Anti-Federalists. It becomes clear that, at best, we were always viewed as the little black ping pong balls meant to color the games played as the settler project was being conceived.[164]

Fugitive Slave Act (1793)[165]

"Now, in a slave-holding state, color always raises a presumption of slavery, which is directly contrary to the presumption in a free or non-slave-holding state; for in the latter, prima facie, every man is a freeman. If, then, under this most monstrous assumption of power, a freeman may be seized, where is our boasted freedom? What says the fourth article of the amendments to the constitution of the United States? 'The right of the people to

---

[163]What the Framers of the Federal Constitution Thought of the Negro. (1918). *The Journal of Negro History, 3*(4), 381-434. doi:10.2307/2713818
[164]Hamilton, Alexander et al The Federalist Papers (New York: Penguin Group and Signet Classic Printing, 2003) pp. 333-38; also see Ketcham, Ralph (ed.) The Anti-Federalist Papers (New York: Penguin Books Signet Classic Printing, 2003) Op.Cit. pp. 153-58. There is a handy copy of the U.S. Constitution in this edition of the Federalist Papers.
[165]1 Stat. 302

be secure in their persons, houses, papers and effects, against unreasonable searches and seizures, shall not be violated.' Art. 5 'No person shall be deprived of life, liberty, or property, without due process of law"
Supreme Court Chief Justice Roger B. Taney, majority opinion, *Prigg v. Pennsylvania*[166]

This Act of Congress sought to fashion an enforcement mechanism supporting the old Fugitive Slave Clause in Article 4 of the Constitution (which was later abolished by the enactment of the thirteenth Amendment). The dispute arose down the road a bit between the States as more and more Northern states would move to abolish chattel slavery, and the Southern states dug in their defiant heels.

This friction is precisely captured in *Prigg v. Pennsylvania* 41 US 539, published in 1842.[167] This Court case stemmed from the assault of an African woman named Margaret Morgan of York County, Pennsylvania, by a handful of enslaved catchers, led by Edward Prigg. He kidnapped her and tried to drag her into bondage down in Maryland. Pennsylvania had passed a law in 1780, abolishing the enslavement of citizens born in the state, and this case was a challenge to that state law.[168]

While the somewhat brokered majority decision ruled against Ms. Morgan, as the Court ruled to overturn Prigg's conviction in Pennsylvania, it did leave the door open for states to individually refuse to allow its citizens to be dragooned from their borders and disappeared to lands south of the Mason-Dixon line.[169]

---

[166] *Prigg v. Pennsylvania* 41 US 539 at 577

[167] Ibid. See also David, C. (1924). The Fugitive Slave Law of 1793 and its Antecedents. *The Journal of Negro History, 9*(1), 18-25. doi:10.2307/2713433. David provides a critical analysis of early Colonial fugitive slave laws, beginning as early as the 1629 proclamations of "freedoms" and "exemptions" to those willing to settle in the Netherlands in exchange for returning enslaved and indentureds to bondage and servitude and he also notes a 1750 circular in the *Boston Gazette* looking for the kidnapping and return to bondage of Crispus Attucks, I will revisit this in the body of the text *below* but see pp 18 for this cite.

[168] Ibid.

[169] Ibid.

C.J. Taney, while raising the pertinent questions, still ruled with the majority primarily because Congress has the exclusive right to legislate in matters concerning interstate recapture and return of Africans who escaped bondage; it should be noted that this decision came down just fifteen years before C.J. Taney wrote the infamous majority opinion in *Scott v. Sandford*, the Dred, and Harriet Scott case.[170]

Marbury v. Madison 5 U.S. 137 1803

"It is emphatically the province and duty of the judicial department to say what the law is. Those who apply the rule to particular cases, must of necessity expound and interpret that rule. If two laws conflict with each other, the courts must decide on the operation of each. So if a law be in opposition to the constitution; if both the law and the constitution apply to a particular case, so that the court must either decide that case conformably to the law, disregarding the constitution; or conformably to the constitution, disregarding the law; the court must determine which of these conflicting rules governs the case. This is of the very essence of judicial duty".[171]

While the main thrust of this decision would only touch upon Africans tangentially, the underlying issue stemmed from a philosophical beef between two Founding Father enslaved "owners" (namely John Adams (2) and Thomas Jefferson (3), respectively). *Marbury* stands as the landmark decision from the Supreme Court. This case stands for the proposition that Congress cannot pass laws that violate the Constitution and that the role of the Court is to say what the law "is."[172]

Insurrection Act (10 USC §§ 251-54) 1807

"If a city or state refuses to take the actions that are necessary to defend the life and property of their residents, then I will deploy the United States military and quickly solve the problem for them."
Donald J. Trump (45), 2020

---

[170] The 1857 *Plessy v. Ferguson* decision will be discussed *below*.

[171] *Marbury v. Madison*, 5 U.S. 137, 2 L. Ed. 60, 1 Cranch 137, 178 (1803)

[172] *Ibid.* See also Corwin, E. (1914). *Marbury v. Madison* and the Doctrine of Judicial Review. *Michigan Law Review, 12*(7), 538-572. doi:10.2307/1274986

Trump (45) was rocked by the images of the millions of people in the streets across the world protesting in the name of #BlackLivesMatter and against the law enforcement lynching of George Floyd in the early summer of 2020. Understanding his authoritarian tendencies, some advisor somewhere must have dusted this relic of a statute off and explained it to him in a way he could understand.[173] Armed and ready with this dangerous weapon in the wrong hands, Trump (45) began his media blitz, including propaganda, empty threats, and angry tweets.[174]

There has been evidence of the federal government grossly overstepping its boundaries and violating the whole notion of federalism, one of the ideological glues—like White nationalism and hyper-capitalism, which hold the settler state

---

[173] Trump requested his Presidential briefs to have bullet points and pictures and it took a while for aides to figure out how to "dumb down" the critical information needed to serve as the executive of the U.S. Please see Veronka Bodarenko, "Trump wants his daily intelligence briefings short and full of killer graphics" May 30, 2017 Business Insider Daily located on the link here: https://www.businessinsider.com/trump-daily-intelligence-briefings-short-and-full-of-killer-graphics-2017-5.

Trump, by most accounts lack any real knowledge base, desire to gain one, or even curiosity about some of the most basic things you would expect from the "commander-in-chief" of the most powerful military forces in the world, and this became painfully obvious during a trip headed to Asia in early November 2017. As recorded in their blistering book, A Very Stable Genius, Phillip Rucker and Carol Leonnig, the presidential entourage stopped over in Honolulu, HI for a fill up of Air Force One and it was decided that a smaller group including the Trumps and then Chief of Staff of Staff and retried U.S. Marine Corps General John Francis Kelly. On the way to one of the most hallowed sites in the entire settler state, where the Japanese sneak attack cost the lives of two-thousand, three hundred soldiers, and forced the U.S. off of its hands, into WWII, and eventually leading to the nuclear bombing of Japan; a "date of infamy" most sixth-graders would be able to tell us, simply did not register with this head of the U.S. federal government and highest office holder in the land, as he was quoted as asking Kelly "Hey John, what's this all about? What is this a tour of? This question was again asked to a former U.S. Marine Corps General by the sitting president of the United States on their way to a solemn tour of the *USS Arizona*; let that sink in. Please Rucker and Leonnig's Very Stable Genius; pp. 167-69.

[174] Montanaro, Domenico "What is the Insurrection Act that Trump is Threatening to Invoke" *NPR* June 1, 2020 located here: https://www.npr.org/2020/06/01/867467714/what-is-the-insurrection-act-that-trump-is-threatening-to-invoke

American myth together. It allowed unnamed and unmarked federal agents to show up in the streets of Portland, OR, and started throwing protestors into the backs of equally unmarked "kidnap" vans and SUVs.[175]

§ 251. Federal aid for State governments

Whenever there is an insurrection in any State against its government, the President may, upon the request of its legislature or of its governor if the legislature cannot be convened, call into Federal service such of the militia of the other States, in the number requested by that State, and use such of the armed forces, as he considers necessary to suppress the insurrection.

§ 252. Use of militia and armed forces to enforce Federal authority

Whenever the President considers that unlawful obstructions, combinations, or assemblages, or rebellion against the authority of the United States, make it impracticable to enforce the laws of the United States in any State by the ordinary course of judicial proceedings, he may call into Federal service such of the militia of any State, and use such of the armed forces, as he considers necessary to enforce those laws or to suppress the rebellion.

§ 253. Interference with State and Federal law

The President, by using the militia or the armed forces, or both, or by any other means, shall take such measures as he considers necessary to suppress, in a State, any insurrection, domestic violence, unlawful combination, or conspiracy, if it—

(1)

so hinders the execution of the laws of that State, and of the United States within the State, that any part or class of its people is deprived of a right, privilege, immunity,

---

[175] Booker, Brakkton "Oregon Governor Says Federal Officers Will Begin Phased Withdrawal From Portland" NPR July 29, 2020 located here: https://www.npr.org/2020/896840086/oregon-governor-on-federal-agents-leaving-portland07/29/

or protection named in the Constitution and secured by law, and the constituted authorities of that State are unable, fail, or refuse to protect that right, privilege, or immunity, or to give that protection; or

(2)

opposes or obstructs the execution of the laws of the United States or impedes the course of justice under those laws.

In any situation covered by clause (1), the State shall have denied the equal protection of the laws secured by the Constitution.

§ 254. Whenever the President considers it necessary to use the militia or the armed forces under this chapter, he shall, by proclamation, immediately order the insurgents to disperse and retire peaceably to their abodes within a limited time.

This codified law has been used from the earliest days of the settler state. It has been to activated to assist African people in integrating public spaces, protecting civil rights protestors, and to attack the KKK. On the other hand, this law was used to quell the Nat Turner Rebellion (discussed next), to commit genocide against Indigenous nations, to break up the LA Rebellion after the verdict came out on the attempted lynching of Rodney King, and after Hurricane Katrina.[176]

The "Presidential Proclamation" clause of the Act is significant to pay attention to, especially given what had been going on in Portland, OR in the summer of 2020 and

---

[176] Cokely, Robert <u>The Role of Federal Military Forces in Domestic Disorders: 1789-1878</u> (Washington: Center of Military History, U.S. Army) pp. 93-4. Cokely discusses the various military detachments, active duty and national guardsmen, that were used to shut down the Nat Turner Rebellion, we will address this again *below*. On a personal note about Katrina, I was born in New Orleans, LA and just happened to find myself back home working as the LA District Manager for the food, hospitality, and textile manufacturing union UNITE HERE! in New Orleans at the time of the storm and actually got stuck for four days in the 7th ward with 18 members of my family, including my wife and seven year old son, as the flood waters so desperately tried to drown my beloved city.

the threats to send more federal forces to occupy the streets of Chicago, Detroit, and other blue-state cities caught in the run-up to the upcoming fall elections.[177]

March 3, 1991 video footage of pattlerollers from the California Highway Patrol attempting to lynch Rodney Glen King during a traffic stop on the I-210 in Los Angeles, CA. The acquittal of these patrollers, on April 29, 1992, despite the horrific video evidence, set off a six-day Rebellion which caused Gov. Pete Wilson (R) to ask for federal assistance thereby causing President George Bush (410 to invoke the *Insurrection Act of 1908*. Photo Credits: (Public Domain)

---

[177]Jalonick, Mary Clarke, Michael Balsamo, Eric Tucker William *Barr Vigorously Defends Federal Law Enforcement Response to Protest During House Testimony*, Time July 28, 2020

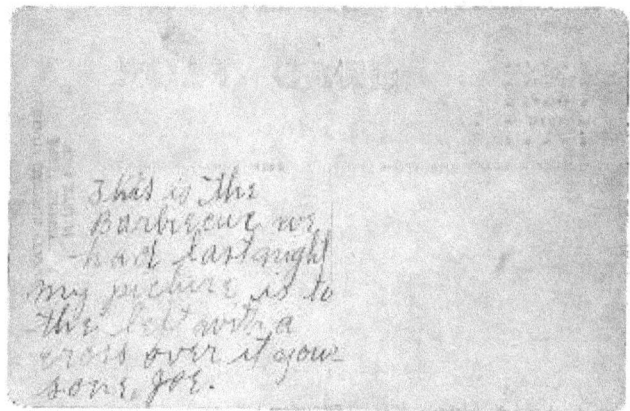

Postmark and Note on the Jessie Washington Lynching Postcard
May 15, 1916, Waco, TX (Public Domain)

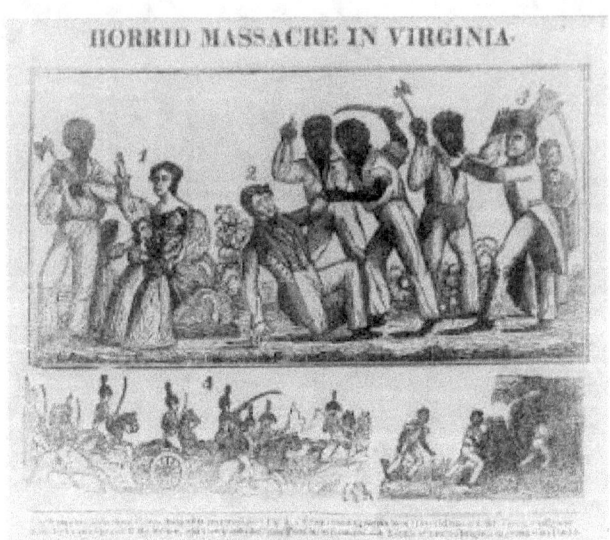

Nat Turner Rebellion, Southampton County, VA 1831 (Public Domain)

Vesey, Prosser, Turner Lynchings (1800-31)

"Do not open your lips, die as I do"
Peter Poyas, before getting lynched, 1822

The following short summaries aren't meant to walk through the history, chapter and verse, but to highlight how the formal law on a local and state level in the case of Vesey and Prosser and federal law in the case of Turner had been used in the process of the lynching of our ancestors, setting the predicate for what we see today. And also to show how the "color of law" plays into the reactionary violence of the settler state.

Gabriel Prosser's Insurrection was planned over the summer months of 1800 and was set to spark off in Richmond, VA, on September 1st.[178] The plan was for the

---

[178]Brawley, <u>A Social History of the American Negro</u> Op.Cit. pp. 115-7. Prosser, and his chief lieutenant Jack Bowler, were both on the run with bounties, Governor Monroe put $300 on

forces, over 1,100 enslaved Africans, to meet up by the river and march on the armory building. Unfortunately, a terrible mix of bad luck, bad weather, and treachery thwarted the plan, and Prosser was finally captured a few weeks later.

Prosser was lynched vis-a-vis state-backed execution both as a form of retribution for daring to plot an insurrection and send a message to others. By itself, the Prosser incident was enough to send shockwaves of terror and tension through the souls of the settlers, but couple that with Santa Domingo (Haitian) Revolution about nine years prior and you can quickly see the powder keg being set up.[179]

In 1822 in Charleston, SC, another significant African Rebellion was led by Denmark Vesey.[180] The size, scope, organizational thrust of the Vesey Rebellion was undeniable. Vesey gained his "freedom," he was multi-lingual and working as a carpenter. Vesey began reading and thinking about the condition of his people, and like so many others (and the settlers feared), he became electrified by the Santa Domingo Revolution. The plot began in secrecy and marked with signs, codes, and signals, and the word spread far and wide outside of the circumference of Charleston, where even slaves of the sitting Governor Thomas Bennett had joined the crew.[181]

Prosser head and more on Browler's head. They caught Prosser in the bowels of a ship getting ready to set sail.

[179] Ibid. As far as the plot went, a huge thunderstorm rose on the night the Rebellion was supposed to jump off and the river flooded. The other thunderstorm that ripped through the Rebellion came from a "scared slave" who wanted to save his "master" and snitched on the Africans that were joining the Insurrection, high treachery indeed.

[180] Ibid. 171-78.

[181] Ibid. 172-73. Some of the ancestors involved were named Ned and Rolla Bennett, Peter Poyas, Jack Purcell, Gullah Jack, and Monday Gell. As a rule, Prosser did not seek to involve any African women as they had to be the primary caretakers of the children. The quote from Peter Poyas can be found on pp.172.

Weapons caches had been stored all over the city. The overall plan was to take over the armory, commandeer a ship (as Vesey came of age on a ship in his youth and recruited sailors and stevedores in the plot) and set sail for Santa Domingo.[182] And yet again, the Rebellion was thwarted by fearful Africans who reported to the authorities. Eventually, the Rebellion and its organizers were either convicted, killed, or banished. Vesey, the Bennett's, Peter Poyas, and Gullah Jack were among those that were lynched in retaliation; all told, thirty-five rebels were killed, and another forty-three were banished.[183]

And then, in 1831 in Southampton County, VA, the devout leader of the most famous the three coastal Rebellions, Nat Turner was organizing his plot.[184] As directed by the signs and signals, Turner began to communicate and organize with his closest allies. Their plot was simple, kill as many settlers and enslaved "owners" as they could with Turner dispatching of his "owner" Joseph Travis and his family first.[185]

This liberatory crew grew in size and fervor throughout the night, taking their justice and revenge on their way to the county settlers but were met by the local Whites who had called for reinforcements. The Rebellion eventually dispersed, and like the others, Turner went into hiding. He holed up for several weeks close enough to the

---

[182] Ibid. 175.

[183] Ibid. 177. One of the traitors to the Rebellion was a slave named William Paul. And on another note, Colonel R. Y. Hayne organized the detachment that was dispatched to put the Rebellion down and was able to parlay his role in the incident into a governorship and eventual U.S. Senate seat.

[184] Ibid. 179.

[185] Ibid.

Travis place to snatch rations only coming out at night. There was a $500 bounty put out on Turner, and he was eventually captured.[186]

While incarcerated, Turner reportedly relayed his "Confessions" to his defense counsel Thomas C. Gray and was subsequently lynched on November 11, 1831, less than two weeks after being caught.[187] They had to lynch Nat Turner. White blood was shed repeatedly. Roughly sixty Whites were killed, and the settlers were so freaked out that the Governor called Washington D.C. and asked for federal assistance resulting in Andrew Jackson using the *Insurrection Act of 1807* (and the full force of the settler state government apparatus) to federalize the state militia to put down the Rebellion, mostly for show.[188]

Emboldened by the show of force, the settlers sought their revenge. They kicked off one of the bloodiest sanctioned lynching sprees on record, in comes cases with full knowledge and support of various members of law enforcement, military, or public officials, with one party that went from Richmond (likely with memories Gabriel Prosser from a generation before) with the "intention to kill every Negro in Southampton County.[189]

---

[186] Ibid. 184

[187] Ibid. 184

[188] Cokely, The Role of Federal Military Forces in Domestic Disorders: 1789-1878; Op.Cit pp.93-4.

[189] Brawley, A Social History of the American Negro; Op.Cit. pp.183-5. The stories coming in the aftermath of the Nat Turner Rebellion are brutal. The indiscriminate murders, torture, maiming, and the activation of those brutal pattlerollers are forerunners to the lawless cops we keep reading about today; brutally lynching Black folks as if all the parties involved in a sick, repetitive loop the 80's cult smash television show *Quantum Leap*.

James Hamlet, the First enslaved African, returned to captivity under the Fugitive Slave Law of 1850, New York City Hall; October 17, 1850
Reprinted from the Atlas and appearing in the National Anti-Slavery Standard
(Public Domain)

Fugitive Slave Act (1850)[190]

"As I was going across the field a Black snake bit me on my heel; Run nigger run, de Patrol catch you, Run nigger run tis almost day"
African warning song that the patrols were nearby, circa 1850

This rather pernicious law passed by Congress and signed by President Millard Fillmore (13) on September 18, 1850, absolutely wreaked havoc among African people across the entire settler state.[191]

Mid- Eighteenth Century Pattleroller Poster, Boston MA (Public Domain)

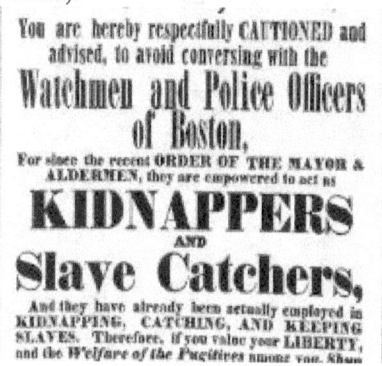

---

[190]Pub.L. 31–60, see also Johnson, A. (1921). "The Constitutionality of the Fugitive Slave Acts" *The Yale Law Journal, 31*(2), 161-182. doi:10.2307/789306.

See also Landon, F. (1920) and "The Negro Migration to Canada after the Passing of the Fugitive Slave Act". *The Journal of Negro History, 5*(1), 22-36. doi:10.2307/2713499. Landon article cites quotes directly from Henry Bibb's paper *The Voice of the Fugitive* and offers a birds eye view from an African who escaped Southern bondage via Midwest underground railroad hotbeds of Michigan, Ohio, and Wisconsin multiple times and notes that almost every issue in 1852 offers statistics on the number of arriving Africans in flight from chattel enslavement, including three of his own brothers. Landon, The Negro Migration to Canada after Passing the Fugitive Slave Act pp.23-4.

The song and sheet music from 1867 are found in Hadden's <u>Slave Patrols</u>, Op.Cit. pp.119.

[191]Ibid.

Where the *Fugitive Slave Act* of 1793 left a door halfway cracked open for Abolitionist-led states of the North to prevent the kidnappers from plying their wicked trade, the *Fugitive Slave Act* of 1850 slammed that rickety door shut, reinforced it with steel plates, and set up barbed wire fencing around the perimeter.[192]

In the years bracketing this law, Africans were caught in a generational flight or fight struggle, and even in flight, they often had to fight. A great example of this is the tale recounted by Ohio Congressman Joshua R. Giddings, who noted the Houston, TX *Telegraph* reported in 1850 there were over fifteen hundred escaped Africans aiding the Comanche Nation in Mexico. With roughly five hundred or so on the run from Texas, who enslaved catchers were desperate to round up. Giddings was writing that the catchers were still unsuccessful as late as 1858, and maroon communities in south Florida were getting their dander up as well.[193]

---

[192]Ibid. See also Landon, F. (1922). The Anderson Fugitive Case. *The Journal of Negro History,* 7(3), 233-242. doi:10.2307/2713418; The text from this Act can be found at the following posted by www.govtrack.us: https://govtrackus.s3.amazonaws.com/legislink/pdf/stat/9/STATUTE-9-Pg462.pdf
[193]Aptheker, Herbert To Be Free: Pioneering Studies in Afro-American History, (New York: Carol Publishing Group ed. 1991) to Maroon counter-insurgency. Op.Cit. pp. 11-31.

Scott v. Sandford 60 US 393 (1857)

"They had for more than a century before been regarded as beings of an inferior order, and altogether unfit to associate with the White race, either in social or political relations; and so far inferior, that they had no rights which the White man was bound to respect; and that the negro might justly and lawfully be reduced to slavery for his benefit. He was bought and sold, and treated as an ordinary article of merchandise and traffic, whenever a profit could be made by it. This opinion was at that time fixed and universal in the civilized portion of the White race. It was regarded as an axiom in morals as well as in politics, which no one thought of disputing, or supposed to be open to dispute; and men in every grade and position in society daily and habitually acted upon it in their private pursuits, as well as in matters of public concern, without doubting for a moment the correctness of this opinion".
U.S. Supreme Court Chief Justice Roger B. Taney, majority opinion [194]

The *Dred Scott* decision, and the infamous pronouncement concerning African rights in the settler state from Chief Justice Roger B. Taney, was one of the seminal moments from the Supreme Court which legally reinforced the concepts of Whiteness and White supremacy. [195]

This 7-2 decision stood for the prepositions that a) Africans located here were never intended to become full "citizens" under the U.S. Constitution and that Dred and Harriet Scott (and any other Africans by extension) did not have "standing" to file any suits for damages or otherwise, b) the Property Clause restricted federal reach to lands owned at the time of the ratification of the Constitution in 1787, and c) that the Due Process Clause of the 5th Amendment forbade the government from banning the abolition of slavery into federal territories. [196]

---

[194] *Dred Scott v. Sandford* 60 US 393, 407 (1857),

[195] Ibid. also see Mallison, A. (1920). "Political Theories of Roger B. Taney" *The Southwestern Political Science Quarterly*, *1*(3), 219-240. Retrieved July 28, 2020, from www.jstor.org/stable/42882963 See also Woodson, C. (1916). "The Negroes of Cincinnati Prior to the Civil War". *The Journal of Negro History*, *1*(1), 1-22. doi:10.2307/2713512 Here Woodson offers a vivid description of the daily lives of Africans living in the literal shadows of bondage, as Kentucky is literally a stone's throw from that other river town I grew up in. Woodson credits the City with being progressive for Africans and touts the per capita earnings they were able to achieve due mainly to a) the rise of the steamboat and b) the proliferation of African mechanics. pp.10. Ironically, these are precisely the types of ingredients that when mixed with jealousy, fear, and White supremacy lead directly to Africans getting lynched.

[196] Ibid.

Dred Scott, to quickly summarize, was enslaved but taken by the Whites who "owned" him from Missouri to locations in Illinois and Wisconsin, where chattel slavery had been abolished. Scott was then taken back to Missouri and filed suit against John F. A. Sandford, for his immediate release as he had spent so much time in the "free" territories, he was deemed "free." Chief Justice Taney disagreed, stating that the Africans "had for more than a century before been regarded as beings of an inferior order, and altogether unfit to associate with the White race, either in social or political relations; and so far inferior, that they had no rights which the White man was bound to respect."[197]

This sentiment marked the law of the land for the next 8 years until the enactment of the thirteenth, fourteenth, and 15th amendments, the "war amendments."

Emancipation Proclamation (1863)[198]

"That on the first day of January, in the year of our Lord one thousand eight hundred and sixty-three, all persons held as slaves within any State or designated part of a State, the people whereof shall then be in rebellion against the United States, shall be then, thenceforward, and forever free; and the Executive Government of the United States, including the military and naval authority thereof, will recognize and maintain the freedom of such persons, and will do no act or acts to repress such persons, or any of them, in any efforts they may make for their actual freedom"
Abraham Lincoln (16), January 1, 1863

President Abraham Lincoln (16) read off the Emancipation Proclamation (or Proclamation 95) while Civil War battles still raged on. This historic, yet limited document only actually applied to enslaved Africans living within the borders of the

---

[197] Ibid. at 407
[198] The historical document is currently held in the National Archives and was actually issued on September 22, 1862 but William H. Seward, Lincoln's Secretary of State, thought the idea was too radical and that the Union army needed a victory prior to publication; the Battle of Anteitam delivered that much needed victory. The link to the National Archives section on the Emancipation Proclamation is located here: https://www.archives.gov/exhibits/featured-documents/emancipation-proclamation

District of Columbia. The express wording was directed at the Southern states in active Rebellion of the settler state at the time but as the Civil War dragged on to its conclusion in 1865 and Union detachments, often led by African soldiers, began liberating fellow Africans still in bondage, culminating with the "freedom pronouncements" of General Gordon Granger read off in Galveston, TX on June nineteenth, 1865 which effectively ended the de facto practice of the chattel enslavement of Africans based solely on race[199]

The legal question of chattel enslavement was finally answered by the "War" amendments enumerated below. At war's end, the "Negro Question" was raised. And the Lake Mohonk Conferences of 1890 and 1891, was called to address it. As the settler-state moved on, Africans were forced to survive independently and under severe pressure from White oppression.[200]

---

[199] The National Archives has a handy summary of the history and impact of the Emancipation Proclamation, see also https://www.archives.gov/exhibits/featured-documents/emancipation-proclamation#:~:text=President%20Abraham%20Lincoln%20issued%20the,and%20henceforward%20shall%20be%20free.%22; see also Welling, J. (1880)" The Emancipation Proclamation" *The North American Review, 130*(279), 163-185. Retrieved July 29, 2020, from www.jstor.org/stable/25100834;

There is a line of scholarship that addresses the issue of over-crowded prison populations and the "community-to-prison pipelines" we see today as modern slavery propped up by the 13th Amendment to the Constitution. Michelle Alexander argues this point in her book The New Jim Crow, see generally. June 19th, 1865 has been celebrated by various African communities in America as Juneteenth with June19th (or the closest Saturday to that date) has been traditionally passed down as a day of celebration ,mainly for Black folk on this side of the Diaspora.

[200] Please see FISHEL, L. (1993). The "Negro Question" at Mohonk: Microcosm, Mirage, and Message. *New York History, 74*(3), 277-314. Retrieved September 3, 2020, from http://www.jstor.org/stable/23182525 discussing how these were the only two post Reconstruction conferences convened to address newly "freed" Africans held in Lake Mohonk, NY; the Negro Question was ultimately framed as what was the settler state ever going to do with us as chattel slavery ended.

Africans approached that question on completely different level and framework as groups like the organizations like the Afro-American League (1890) spearheaded by Timothy Thomas Fortune after calls for this League had fizzled out in 1887 and 1888—the initial conference called for the establishment of a Black bank, a lobbying and legislative action arm, and an emigration bureau to assist Blacks engaged in the Great Migration, see Fishel and Quarles The Negro American; Op.Cit. pp. 325;

The National Association of Colored Women (1896) formed as a result of the merger between the National Federation of Afro-American Women and the Colored Women's League and selected Mary Church Terrell as its founding President and the organization continued to publish the *Women's Era* which engaged in various topics including those of particular interest Black women in America, see Logan's Betrayal of the Negro; Op.Cit. pp. 336;

The National Negro Business League (1900) founded by Booker T. Washington to serve as the national Black Chamber of Commerce and create space for Black business leaders to share ideas, network, and support each other's business interests, see Quarles' The Negro in the Making of America; Op.Cit. pp.169;

Sigma Pi Phi (the "Boule") in 1904 (the first Black Greek lettered fraternity) by design was set up to keep information strictly within its group, if you can get a copy (I had a photocopy once) of Charles Harris Wesley's history of the organization, it provides great insight into what Henry McKee Minton was thinking when he called for the creation of the organization;

And the Niagara Movement (1905) (which followed a possible détente between Washington and DuBois in 1904) was led in large part by DuBois and William Monroe Trotter in reaction to the "Tuskegee Model". This Movement called for social and political advances for Black folks in America and had to meet on the Canadian side of the Falls as no hotel in New York would rent them rooms. This organization, along with the Springfield race riot in 1908, was largely created with setting the stage for the founding of the NAACP in 1909; please Aptheker's Afro-American History in the Modern Era for analysis of the Washington-DuBois Conference and the Niagara Movement.

These organizations were all constructed, in varying degrees, to offer answers to how newly freed Africans were going to account for themselves. There are volumes written on these various organizations, well except maybe the Boule, and are relatively easy to find. I would recommend that readers begin with Aptheker's Afro-American History, Fishel and Quarles' The Negro American, Quarles' The Negro in the Making of America; Logan's Betrayal of the Negro; generally for documentary and summary analysis of these groups and the roles they played in advancing African interests at the turn of the twentieth-century.

13th Amendment (1864)[201]

SECTION 1

Neither slavery nor involuntary servitude, except as a punishment for crime whereof the party shall have been duly convicted, shall exist within the United States, or any place subject to their jurisdiction.

SECTION 2

Congress shall have power to enforce this article by appropriate legislation.

14 Amendment (1868)[202]

SECTION 1

All persons born or naturalized in the United States and subject to the jurisdiction thereof, are citizens of the United States and of the State wherein they reside. No State shall make or enforce any law which shall abridge the privileges or immunities of citizens of the United States; nor shall any State deprive any person of life, liberty, or property, without due process of law; nor deny to any person within its jurisdiction the equal protection of the laws.

SECTION 2

Representatives shall be apportioned among the several States according to their respective numbers, counting the whole number of persons in each State, excluding Indians not taxed. But when the right to vote at any election for the choice of electors for President and Vice President of the United States, Representatives in Congress,

---

[201] U.S. Const. amend XIII, See also Bascom, J. (1906). The Three Amendments. *The Annals of the American Academy of Political and Social Science, 27*, 135-147. Retrieved July 29, 2020, from www.jstor.org/stable/1010516; see also Pillsbury, A. (1909) "The War Amendments" *The North American Review, 189*(642), 740-751. Retrieved July 29, 2020, from www.jstor.org/stable/25106358

[202] U.S. Const. amend XIV

the Executive and Judicial officers of a State, or the members of the Legislature thereof, is denied to any of the male inhabitants of such State, being twenty-one years of age, and citizens of the United States, or in any way abridged, except for participation in rebellion, or other crime, the basis of representation therein shall be reduced in the proportion which the number of such male citizens shall bear to the whole number of male citizens twenty-one years of age in such State.

SECTION 3

No person shall be a Senator or Representative in Congress, or elector of President and Vice President, or hold any office, civil or military, under the United States, or under any State, who, having previously taken an oath, as a member of Congress, or as an officer of the United States, or as a member of any State legislature, or as an executive or judicial officer of any State, to support the Constitution of the United States, shall have engaged in insurrection or rebellion against the same, or given aid or comfort to the enemies thereof. But Congress may by a vote of two-thirds of each House, remove such disability.

SECTION 4

The validity of the public debt of the United States, authorized by law, including debts incurred for payment of pensions and bounties for services in suppressing insurrection or rebellion, shall not be questioned. But neither the United States nor any State shall assume or pay any debt or obligation incurred in aid of insurrection or rebellion against the United States, or any claim for the loss or emancipation of any slave; but all such debts, obligations and claims shall be held illegal and void.

SECTION 5

The Congress shall have power to enforce, by appropriate legislation, the provisions of this article.

15th Amendment (1870)[203]

SECTION 1

The right of citizens of the United States to vote shall not be denied or abridged by the United States or by any State on account of race, color, or previous condition of servitude.

SECTION 2

The Congress shall have power to enforce this article by appropriate legislation.

Black Codes (1865-66)

"I should expect in Louisiana, as in the whole Southern country, that the withdrawal of the Freedman's Bureau would be followed by a condition of anarchy and bloodshed"
Testimony of Thomas Conway, to the Joint Commission on Reconstruction; February 22 1866[204]

As the settler state began to snap back into place after its bloody convulsion known as the Civil War, White supremacy and anti-Blackness returned to their seats of prominence in the form of the Southern Black codes; mostly because there was no way that the South was going to implement, overnight, a "free labor" system and open economy for newly "freed" Africans.[205]

The South instituted sets of laws referred to as "Black Codes" or "Black laws" with the express purpose of reinstituting slavery in every way except the physical control of African bodies and torture.[206]

---

[203] U.S. Const. amend XV

[204] Fishel, Leslie et.al ; <u>The American Negro</u>; Op.Cit. pp.266-71. ; Op.Cit. pp.266-71.
[205] Klarman, <u>From Jim Crow to Civil Rights</u> Op.Cit. pp.71-2.

[206] Ibid.

Some of these laws were hallmarked by focusing on long-term work contracts, peonage, vagrancy laws, criminal surety and non-solicitation agreements between the planters, discriminatory apprenticeships, laws barring Africans from work outside of agriculture or domesticated jobs, convict lease laws, and segregated residential districts.[207] These laws developed out of a sense of comfort and convenience for sure, but they were driven by Whiteness, White supremacy, and anti-Blackness, especially fear of Black political participation.[208]

The Virginia legislature passed a "tough on crime" anti-vagrancy law, in an attempt to restore some of the pattlerollers antebellum stature and powers. This law authorized any random White person to be able to "stop and frisk" anyone who doesn't show the obvious signs of being able to take care of themselves, but the Whites could make the defendants "work" for up to three months. Sally Hedden points out that these laws were almost exclusively executed on African people as a way to shuffle them right back into *de facto* bondage.[209]

South Carolina enacted its Black Codes in 1865 when Governor Benjamin E. Perry declared that "militia organizations would continue to act like militias and patrols, and that they would be charged with the police duty." This as a way to enforce the news laws passed with the hopes of confining the newly "freed" Africans; those laws focused on peonage and vagrancy and were specifically meant to funnel Africans in that state right back to the death farms; or prison.[210]

---

[207] Ibid.

[208] Ibid. Stephenson, G. (1909) "The Separation of The Races in Public Conveyances" *The American Political Science Review*, 3(2), 180-204. doi:10.2307/1944727; see also Richardson, J. (1969) "Florida Black Codes "*The Florida Historical Quarterly*, 47(4), 365-379. Retrieved July 29, 2020, from www.jstor.org/stable/30140241.

[209] Please see Hadden, Slave Patrols; Op.Cit. pp.200

[210] Ibid.

Civil Rights Act of 1866[211]

"I have lived among Negroes, all my life, and I am for this Government with slavery under the Constitution as it is. I am for the Government of my fathers with Negroes, I am for it without Negroes. Before I would see this Government destroyed, I would send every Negro back to Africa, disintegrated and blotted out of space...If the institution of slavery denies the Government the right of agitation and seeks to overthrow it, then the Government has a clear right to destroy it"
Andrew Johnson (17) 1863, at a three-hour union speech in Indianapolis, IN[212]

The *Civil Rights Act of 1866* was passed, over the veto of President Andrew Johnson (17), to protect certain rights of newly unburdened Africans on these shores by declaring that all people born in the United States were U.S. citizens with certain inalienable rights, including the right to make contracts, to own property, to sue in court, and to enjoy the full protection of federal law.

The act gave the U.S. district courts exclusive jurisdiction over criminal cases related to violations of the act, and concurrent jurisdiction, along with the U.S. circuit courts, of all civil and criminal cases affecting those who were unable to enforce in state court the rights guaranteed by the act. This *Civil Rights Act* began a gradual transformation of the federal courts into the primary forums for individuals to enforce their constitutional and statutory rights.[213]

---

[211] P.L. 14 Stat. 27-30

[212] Trefousse, Hans L. Andrew Johnson: A Biography (New York: W.W. Norton, 1989) pp.166-67.
[213] There was also a very short-lived *Civil Rights Act of 1875*, and while most of the key provisions like the call for fully integrated schools, integrated cemeteries, and a prohibition against segregated public facilities, public transportation, public modalities, and public amusement, it would ninety years later before these eventualities came to pass. As Reconstruction came to an end it was essentially deemed unconstitutional by the *Court* in the 1883 *Civil Rights Cases* (109 U.S. 3). These provisions pre-empted *Brown* and the *Civil Rights Acts* of the 60's discussed *below*. Please see the speech by Rev. Richard Harvey Cain of Mother Emmanuel AME Church in Charleston, SC in support of the *Act* in The Negro American: A Documentary History; Op.Cit. pp.283-89.

The quote from Johnson (17) occurred while he found himself on a speaking tour, of sorts, defending his positions that a) the East TN region should be exempted from the Emancipation Proclamation because it's only the rest of the state that is in open revolt from the United States, b) the Southern rebels had always wanted to secede and cannot be negotiated with, and c) like Lincoln (16), he doesn't have any particularly special or heartfelt love for African people in America and if the Union could be saved by deporting us then so be it.[214]

It was that spirit of negligent ambivalence and conscious indifference, expressed by the Court, the federal government, and other White defenders of the settler state that helped set the stage for the emergence of American Al Qaeda and the generational reign of terror it visited upon the sons and daughters of Africa, newly released from bondage or "freeborn" alike. It was in this cauldron that the newborn Knights of the Ku Klux Klan became American Al Qaeda.

Klavern circa 1920 (Public Domain)
LukaSvanidze / CC BY-SA (https://creativecommons.org/licenses/by-sa/4.0)

---

[214] Trefousee, Hans Andrew Johnson: A Biography; Op.Cit. pp.166

Klu Klux Klan "America First Rally" Binghamton, NY 1920's (Public Domain)

Replica of the famous sign hung outside of the NAACP Headquarters in the 1920s Mliu92 (talk · contribs) (Public Domain)

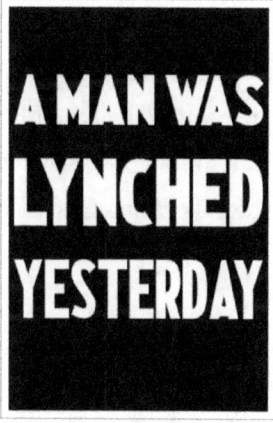

Rise of the KKK (1866)-American Al Qaeda

"An article published on August 12, 1868, in the Upcountry Edgefield Examiner suggests how depictions of Klu-Klux violence were absorbed into and shaped local ideas of violence. It was one of the few early articles that described specific attacks and the one it described was not a small attack on an individual home, but a massive Klu-Klux mobilization against a jail: the mid-July abduction and lynching of a Black man named William Gustine in Franklin, TN. The article claimed that Gustine had outraced a White girl and had been subsequently jailed"
Incident reported in the Edgefield County, SC *Edgefield Examiner*[215]

Pulaski Six, founders of the Klu Klux Klan; Pulaski, TN 1866 (Public Domain)

As the world turned and Southern Whites were forced to confront the changing demographics of their day (not much unlike the Trump (45)'s #MAGA crowd), a small group turned to their Scottish roots and formed a Klan, the Klu Klux Klan (KKK); which eventually morphed into one of the most ardent White nationalist civilian armies this the settler state ever produced.[216] One of the best works on the history of the various rises and falls of the Klan is Klu Klux: The Birth of the Klan during Reconstruction is by Elaine Frantz Parsons.[217]

---

[215]Parsons, Elaine Frantz, Ku Klux: The Birth of the Klan Reconstruction (Chapel Hill: University of North Carolina Press, 2015). pp.267

[216]Ian Lilley and Neil Oliver put out a documentary which traces the Scottish connection to the KKK in 2018 called "Who Put the Klan into Ku Klux Klan".

[217]Parsons, Elaine Frantz, Ku Klux: The Birth of the Klan Reconstruction Op.Cit.

The KKK, while founded in Pulaski, TN in 1866, had hopes and plans to reestablish Whiteness, White supremacy, and anti-Blackness as primary ideological frameworks and watch them spread like a virus across the Mid-South, Midwest, and Deep South and within 60 years, they had become one of the major political forces in the whole settler state.[218]

And as such, the Klan was able to infiltrate and influence public offices across the states and in the federal government, including the Supreme Court, and from those lofty perches committed decades of open, unflinching terrorism against African populations, including night raids, lynchings, murder, assault, arson, rape, and had their blood-soaked hands involved in several of the highlighted incidents throughout the remainder of this work.[219]

---

[218] Ibid. Op.Cit. pp.1 Klan violence raged in moments and then waned, depending on a multitude of factors including Reconstruction, Post-Reconstruction, Prohibition, the Great Depression, World Wars, the expanded Civil Rights Movement, Multi-Culturalism, for over 150 years until very recently, etc. The early Klan scored a coup by recruiting former Confederate General Nathan Bedford Forrest to its ranks.

[219] Ibid. Op.Cit. Frantz also examines the various roles and needs that cross-dressing played in the Klan formation, for example she notes it was done "as a way to reassert male identity through contrast and projection", pp. 95-7.

This need to reassert White manhood also comes up some of the more heinous lynching rituals, where the mobs' most prized possession is the hacked off genitalia of the "conquered Black brute", in fact, Louise Wood recounts that after the 1916 lynching of Jesse Washington in Waco, TX (images of which are in this text) NAACP investigator , Elizabeth Freeman, reported that one White townsperson was actually carrying around Washington's penis like a souvenir so he could literally possess "that sexual power" he found so fearful and despicable. Wood, Lynching and Spectacle, Op Cit. pp. 99.

Note the archived edition of the Pittsburgh-Post Gazette's award winning article dated September 13, 1937 which exposes Supreme Court Justice Hugo Black, drafter of the opinion in *Korematsu v. United States*, 323 U.S. 214 (1944) which upheld the internment of Japanese-Americans during WWII, as a former Klansmen. The article imprint can be found at the following link here: https://pgdigs.tumblr.com/image/3086908730; Klarman also notes that the Senate had a relatively easy time confirming Black to the Court despite the rumors of his past Klan membership which were confirmed shortly after his confirmation to the bench; please see Klarman, From Jim Crow to Civil Rights; Op.Cit. pp.116.

Pittsburgh Post-Gazette, article exposing longtime U.S. Associate Supreme Court Justice, Hugo Lafayette Black as a Klansman; Black served on the Court for thirty-four years, (fifth longest term), all of which after this expose' was published. (Public Domain)

They turned then from carnival barkers into American Al Qaeda relatively quickly and without any trouble at all.[220] And that meteoric rise and *"red record"* caught the attention of federal legislators who in 1871 passed the Klu Klux Klan Act, discussed below.

As the Klan rose in prominence and began to move from the margins of genteel White society towards the mainstream, they entered a mainstream that already began to question itself but also the newfound freedoms that our ancestors were somewhat marginally granted. These questions started to lead to the legal challenges of the "war amendments" themselves, analyzed below.

Civil Rights Act of 1871

"The Klu Klux were bands of men who had joined themselves together for the purpose of regulating the conduct of the coloured people, especially with the object of preventing the members of the race from exercising any influence in politics. They corresponded somewhat to the "patrollers" of whom I used to hear a great deal during the days of slavery."
Booker Taliaferro Washington, 1901[221]

Also known as the Enforcement Act of 1871 and the Klu Klux Klan Act of 1871, which allows the President of the United States to suspend habeas corpus to specifically combat the Klu Klux Klan and other White nationalist organizations. Congress passed the Act, on April 20, 1871, at the behest of Ulysses S. Grant as the last of the Reconstruction Era Enforcement Acts passed by Congress from 1870-71.[222]

---

[220] Sally Hadden, in her book Slave Patrols notes that there were at least three predecessor thrusts that also feed into the founding of the Klan, 1) White only mutual aid and agricultural associations, 2) White only gun clubs, and 3) other vigilante groups; please see Hadden, Slave Patrols; Op.Cit. 205-6.
[221] Washington, Booker T. Up From Slavery (New York: Viking Penguin Publishing, 1986) pp.77-8.
[222] P.L. 42-22, please also see Bullitt, W. (1924) "THE SUPREME COURT AND UNCONSTITUTIONAL LEGISLATION" *American Bar Association Journal*, *10*(6), 419-425. Retrieved August 25, 2020, from http://www.jstor.org/stable/25711622. Incidentally, this *Act* initially allowed for citizens to present claims against government officials, including

Grant had been receiving reports out of South Carolina and across the rest of the Deep South about Klan violence from General Alfred H. Terry and wanted to get some flexibility in targeting this terrorist organization, to the extent that he wanted to "make an example out of the Klan."[223]

One of the longest standing parts of the Act is codified as 42 U.S.C. § 1983: *Civil action for deprivation of rights*. Oddly enough, this is a preferred code that civil rights attorneys who often use it to present claims against local governments when law enforcement mistreats their clients and questions of "qualified immunity" arise.[224]

The signature case coming out of this Act was *United States v. Harris*, 106 U.S. 629 (1883), or the *Ku Klux Case*.[225] In that case, Sheriff R. G. Harris and 19 others dragged four African men out an unlocked jail cell, beat the men, and killed one. The four men were beaten, and one was killed. A deputy sheriff tried to prevent the act but failed. Here the Court held that the Fourteenth Amendment only authorized Congress to enact remedies against inviolate state action, not state inaction or acts of individual private parties. Sheriff Harris did not commit state action and was acting in his individual capacity.[226]

---

members of law enforcement but as we will discuss *below*, the Court had decidedly moved against this type of legal action. Black's Law Dictionary defines habeus corpus as: "Lat. (You have the body.) The name given to a variety of writs,(of which these were anciently the emphatic words,) having for their object to bring a party before a court or judge. In common usage, and whenever these words are used alone, they are understood to mean the habeas corpus ad subjiciendum".

[223] See Hadden, Slave Patrols; Op.Cit. pp.216

[224] 42 U.S.C. § 1983; see also

[225] *United States v. Harris*, 106 U.S. 629 (1883); Bullitt, W. (1924) "THE SUPREME COURT AND UNCONSTITUTIONAL LEGISLATION" *American Bar Association Journal*, 10(6), 419-425. Retrieved August 25, 2020, from http://www.jstor.org/stable/25711622

[226] Ibid.

Slaughterhouse Cases 83 U.S. 36 (1873)[227]

"Of the privileges and immunities of the citizen of the United States, and of the privileges and immunities of the citizen of the State, and what they respectively are, we will presently consider; but we wish to state here that it is only the former which are placed by this clause under the protection of the Federal Constitution, and that the latter, whatever they may be, are not intended to have any additional protection by this paragraph of the amendment."
Supreme Court Justice Samuel Freeman Miller, (razor-thin) majority opinion

The Slaughterhouse consolidated cases were presented by a group of butchers who were challenging a Louisiana law which limited the butchering of animals in New Orleans to a single, chartered corporation, the Crescent City Live Stock Landing and Slaughterhouse Company, for twenty-five years.

The petitioners argued that the law banned the slaughtering of animals anywhere else in the city. Because all of the other slaughterhouses were closed, this law created a monopoly that denied them their ability to earn a living through their trade and made them indentured servants in violation of the thirteenth Amendment. They further argued that this monopoly abridged their privileges and immunities, and deprived them of equal protection under the law, and deprived them of both the right to liberty and property without due process under the Fourteenth Amendment as well.[228]

The Court ultimately ruled against the Butchers' reasoning that the fourteenth Amendment only (narrowly) banned states from denying Africans equal rights and did not guarantee that everyone should receive equal economic privileges by the state. Still, this case stands for the preposition that the Constitution only protects federal citizenship as enumerated, but not state citizenship. As such, citizens should seek equal protection under the law from the state they reside in. This was a literal death sentence for vast numbers of Africans and their children in America who were

---

[227] *Slaughterhouse Cases* 83 U.S. 36 (1873)

[228] U.S. Const. amend Art. IV § 2

brutalized in the same states they were now formally condemned to seek recourse and protection.

And while this decision set the framework for a line of cases to follow, including the next one to be examined, Justice Stephen Johnson's dissent calls for a more expansive view of the Fourteenth Amendment, which future cases would follow.

KKK firebomb lynching of Vernon Dahmer, Forrest County, MS NAACP Leader January 10, 1966, Photo Credits FBI Images, https://multimedia.fbi.gov/?q=civil%20rights&perpage=50&page=1&searchType=image

United States v. Cruikshank 92 U.S. 542 (1876)[229]

"The second and tenth counts are equally defective. The right there specified is that of 'bearing arms for a lawful purpose.' This is not a right granted by the Constitution. Neither is it in any manner dependent upon that instrument for its existence. The second amendment declares that it shall not be infringed; but this, as has been seen, means no more than that it shall not be infringed by Congress. This is one of the amendments that has no other effect than to restrict the powers of the national government, leaving the people to look for their protection against any violation by their fellow-citizens of the rights it recognizes, to what is called, ...the 'powers which relate to merely municipal legislation, or what was, perhaps, more properly called internal police,' 'not surrendered or restrained' by the Constitution of the United States".
U.S. Supreme Court Chief Justice Morrison Remick Waite[230]

At the tail end of Reconstruction, the Court heard another string of consolidated cases (called the *"Civil Rights* Cases") challenging the *Civil Rights Act of 1875's* affirmation of the equality of enjoyment of persons in public facilities, including inns, public transportation, theaters, and other public places of amusement.

In these 5 cases, Africans were denied the same accommodations of Whites, and *Cruikshank* is one of the most dispositive cases in regards to the lynching of African-

---

[229] *United States v. Cruikshank* 92 U.S. 542 (1876); note that two short years after this decision came down, the continent of Africa was being set up for its next apocalypse (borrowing the phraseology from Gerald Horne) as the Berlin Congress of 1878, which was designed to address the fate of the Balkans, the Ottoman Empire, and piecemeal dispositions of landholdings on the Continent but clearly set the stage for the devastating "West Africa Conference" beginning in Berlin, Germany on Saturday, November 15 1884.

This first round, attended by nineteen diplomats and fifteen assistants representing fourteen nations including Germany, the UK, France, Russia, Austria, and a participating "non-participant from America named "General" Henry Shelton Sanford, Lincoln (16)'s ambassador to Belgium.

Sanford was not a military man *per se,* he earned that nickname as a gun runner for the Union army during the Civil War. Old lying Leopold II convened the conference with the claim that the assembled would work together to "carry into the interior of Africa new ideas of law, order, humanity, and protection of the natives" (according to an editorial in The *Daily Telegraph* on October 12, 1884) but by the time the Conference adjourned on February 25, 1885 the Continent had been carved up like a Christmas goose and a new phase of Colonialism was set to blast off. Volumes have been written on this topic over the decades, but Thomas Pakenham specifically makes the linkages between 1878 and 1884 and the background on Sanford in his massive work; please see Pakenham, Thomas The Scramble for Africa: 1876-1912 (London: Abacus, 1992) pp.239-55.
[230] 92 U.S. 542 at 553

Americans as it effectively sent the victims of American terror to seek redress from the various state and local courts that were heavily influenced by the terrorists themselves.

Here, the Court found that the state is virtually powerless to correct private acts of racial discrimination.

In 1872, the Louisiana gubernatorial election went down to the very wire; subsequently, a race riot ensued, and dozens of Africans were lynched, and a handful of Whites were killed. Federal charges were brought in to put down the members of the mob under the *Enforcement Act of 1870*, which prohibited mob activity designed to deprive anyone of their constitutional rights. Charges including abridging the Africans First Amendment right to free assembly and the Second Amendment right to bear arms.

Chef Justice Morrison Waite penned the majority opinion, he overturned the convictions, as the Court held that the Africans (plaintiffs) had to go to the State courts for any protection. The Court failed to find any State action sufficient to implicate any Constitutional violations at all (freedom to assemble, right to bear arms, equal protection, or due process).

This bare-knuckled ruling left Africans across the settler state wholly exposed, but especially in the South, and at the mercy of the White nationalist state and local controlled systems and entities, remnants of which are seen in Tulsa, Ok in 1921 and Neshoba County, MS as we discuss them below.[231]

---

[231] Ibid at 542.

This case began a string of cases that nullified the Reconstruction laws that provided the criminal penalty for Disenfranchisement.[232] The lines of cases stemming from the Court's decisions in both the *Slaughter House* cases and *Cruikshank* legally set the stage for what was heading African's people way in just a few short years, the formal end of post-Civil War Reconstruction and the renewed terror that was visited upon African in America, as a result, will be analyzed below.

Hayes-Tilden Compromise (1877)

"The last decade of the nineteenth century and the opening of the twentieth century marked the *nadir* of the Negro's status in American society"
Rayford Logan, 1954[233]

The deadly deal between the two political parties to decide the highly contested presidential election of 1876 resulted in removing all federal troops from the South in exchange for allowing Rutherford B. Hayes to become the nineteenth president of the United States. Rayford Logan, former chair of the Howard University History Department, argues that this deadly deal virtually dragged Blacks into the "nadir" or our darkest hour in this country as it effectively ended the post-war Reconstruction period.[234] And when it came to the Court specifically, Logan argued that "all the relevant decisions during Reconstruction to the end of the nineteenth century

---

[232] See F. R. (1874) "Circuit Court of the United States. District of Louisiana. *The United States v. Cruikshank et al*" The American Law Register (1852-1891), 22(10), 630-644. doi:10.2307/3303600. Also see The Jurisdiction of the Federal Courts in Cases of Conspiracy against Persons of African Descent. (1907). *The Yale Law Journal,* 16(3), 200-202. doi:10.2307/783978

[233] Logan, Rayford Betrayal of the Negro: From Rutherford B. Hayes to Woodrow Wilson (Cambridge: Da Capo Press, 1997), pp.52

[234]Ibid. Merriam Webster's online dictionary defines *nadir* as the lowest point. The next several pages of this work will show some of the evidence of Logan's contention, along with the lynchings, there was rampant intimidation, another rise of the Klan, disenfranchisement, American Apartheid we called Jim Crow, etc. Please see the link to the dictionary definition here: https://www.merriam-webster.com/dictionary/nadir?src=search-dict-box

nullified or curtailed the rights of Negroes that many "Radical" Republicans thought they had written into laws and the Constitution."[235]

Logan further blamed the Court for its recoil in the areas of equal access and protection under the law in terms of segregation, privileges and immunities, peonage, service of jury duty, and accused these various decisions in providing legal cover for the establishment of second-class citizenship for Blacks.[236] The lynchings kept right coming. Jelani Favors notes that in 1889 "there were twenty-five known Black Mississippians who fell victim to lynch mobs, a state record for lynching at that point that was well ahead of the national average."[237]

---

[235] Ibid. pp.97.

[236] Ibid. 97-116, Logan lays bare his stinging critique of the Court in Chapter of 6, "The Supreme Court and the Negro". Logan's analysis should be juxtaposed with the truncated Marxist analysis offered by C.L.R. James in <u>A History of Pan-African Revolt</u> (Oakland: PM Press, 2012).pp. 55-63. The issue with James's analysis here is that by swiftly glossing over the roles of Whiteness, White supremacy, and anti-Blackness, played in fostering the "nadir", James merely praises the successes of enfranchised Africans during Reconstruction but fails to show how those limited gains were almost immediately wiped away.

[237] Favors, Jelani, <u>Shelter In a Time of Storm: How Black Colleges Fostered Generations of Leadership and Activism</u> (Chapel Hill: The University of North Carolina Press, 2019). pp.50 Favors offers a detailed analysis of the historical role that HBCU's played as a refuge for young (now elders ancestors) activists from the Jim Crow era through the expanded Civil Rights Movement while at times propelling them to feed and lead that very movement.

Oddly enough, Favors points out an earlier lynching, the 1871 lynching of Octavius Catto in the streets of Philadelphia, PA, as a seminal moment in the history of African education in the U.S. Catto was a popular "professor" at the Institute for Colored Youth (ICY) and a fiery defender of the 13th and 14th Amendments, especially as applied to the liberation of Black folks; and for that he was lynched, shot dead by a pattleroller (deputy) in full view of several witnesses including another member of law enforcement. Catto's killer, an Irishman named Frank Kelly was eventually acquitted like so many of his professional descendants. pp.18-9.

Posse Comitatus Act (18 U.S.C. § 1385) (initially enacted in 1878)[238]

"Those who would integrate our schools at any price are still among us. They have seized upon the present situation to promote and foment concern and discontent, because of the temporary closing of the schools. They have spread wild rumors and attempted to organize demonstrations. These are the same people and the same forces who have all along been opposed to the majority will of the people of Little Rock and Arkansas"
Arkansas Governor Orval Eugene Faubus, 1958 in a speech threatening to turn the closed schools in Little Rock, AR, into private schools to avoid integrating them.[239]

The *Posse Comitatus Act* is a United States federal law enacted on June 18, 1878, by President Rutherford B. Hayes (19), limiting the powers of the federal government in the use of federal military personnel to enforce domestic policies within the United States. The Act was passed as an amendment to an army appropriation bill following the end of Reconstruction and has been amended and enacted over the years since it hit the books.

This law deals with the use of the military in a law enforcement function and strictly applies to the Army, Air Force, Navy, and Marines. In fact, according to the Rand Corporation, a longstanding think tank for the defense contractor industry, "the *Posse Comitatus Act*, 18 U.S. Code, Section 1385, the original intent of which was to end the use of federal troops to police state elections in former Confederate states, prescribes the role of the Army and Air Force in executing civil laws and states.[240]

---

[238] 18 U.S.C. 1385, originally codified as P.L. 20 Stat. 152.

[239] University of Arkansas Libraries, Special Collections Department has archived a copy of the speech in a document and made it available on this link: https://libraries.uark.edu/specialcollections/research/lessonplans/FaubusSpeechLessonPlan.pdf (2008)

[240] Please see The Rand Company's "Overview of the Posse Comitatus Act" in its report Preparing the U.S. Army for Homeland Security: Concepts, Issues, and Opinions by Eric E. Larsen and John E. Peters (2001); pp. 243-45. The link to the Appendix D is located here: https://www.rand.org/content/dam/rand/pubs/monograph_reports/MR1251/MR1251.AppD.pdf

The Act was used as an exception on September 24, 1957, to dispatch the 101st Airborne Division to Little Rock, AR, to help walk Daisy Bates and the NAACP "Little Rock Nine" (Minnijean Brown, Elizabeth Eckford, Ernest Green, Thelma Mothershed, Melba Patillo, Gloria Ray, Terrence Roberts, Jefferson Thomas, and Carlotta Walls, into class, after Arkansas Governor Roy Faubus activated the national guard to stop them.

Again, given the general #BLM strike and protests during the early summer of 2020 in direct response to the lynching of George Floyd, the presence of federal law enforcement and national armed services actively engaging civilians in the hostile manner that categorized the overall law enforcement response should give residents pause. And Trump's order to tear gas protestors in Lafayette Park on June 1, 2020, so he could hold a propaganda stunt complete with the military props makes sense for this law to be analyzed in the lynching context.[241]

Hanging African Man, Late nineteenth Century
Loewenthall Collection of African-American Photography
Cornel University Library, Rare Collection Department

Lynching of Will Brown in front of the Omaha, NB courthouse September 28, 1919. (Public Domain)

---

[241] Trump was accompanied on this brazen photo op by Joint Chiefs Chairman Mark Milley and Acting Department of Defense Secretary Mark Esper. This was a major news story captured around the world and struck yet another blow against the lie of "American exceptionalism", especially since the federal police agency originally lied about gassing the protestors then had to publicly backtrack. Alex Ward, New York: *Vox*, June 5, 2020 located here: https://www.vox.com/2020/6/5/21281604/lafayette-square-White-house-tear-gas-protest.

Anonymous Lynching, 1905 Trenton, GA (Public Domain)

Niagara Movement National Meeting, 1907 (Public Domain)

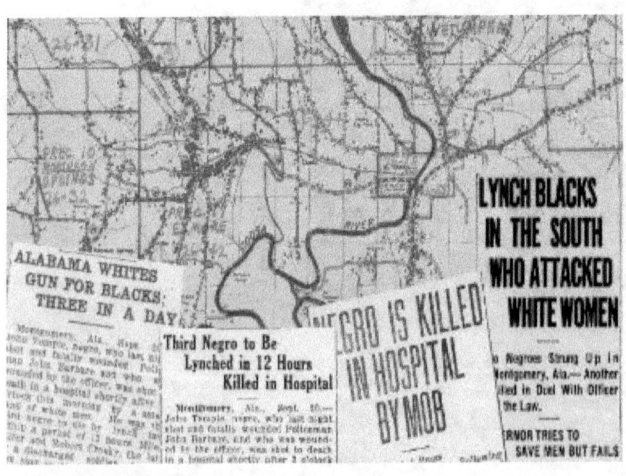

1919 Lynching in Montgomery, Alabama
- File:1950 Census Enumeration District Maps - Alabama - Elmore County - Elmore County - ED AL 26-1 to 46 - NARA - 7551239.jpg

Harrisburg Telegraph. September 30, 1919, Image 1
- Rock Island Argus., September 30, 1919, Image 1
- Evening Capital news., September 30, 1919, Image 1

- 169 -

- Hickory Daily record. September 30, 1919, Image 1 (Public Domain)

https://commons.wikimedia.org/wiki/File:1919_Lynching_in_Montgomery_Alabama.png

George Meadows, January 15, 1889
Jefferson County, AL
Credits: L. Horgan, Jr.

Chapter 5

American Jurisprudence and American Terrorism from Jim Crow through the Civil Rights Movement of the 1960s

Plessy v. Ferguson 163 U.S. 537 (1896)[242]

> *"The object of the amendment was undoubtedly to enforce the absolute equality of the two races before the law, but, in the nature of things, it could not have been intended to abolish distinctions based upon color, or to enforce social, as distinguished from political, equality, or a commingling of the two races upon terms unsatisfactory to either. Laws permitting, and even requiring, their separation, in places where they are liable to be brought into contact, do not necessarily imply the inferiority of either race to the other, and have been generally, if not universally, recognized as within the competency of the state legislatures in the exercise of their police power. The most common instance of this is connected with the establishment of separate schools for White and colored children, which have been held to be a valid exercise of the legislative power even by courts of states where the political rights of the colored race have been longest and most earnestly enforced".*

Supreme Court Justice Henry Billings Brown, majority opinion

As Reconstruction ended, the curtain was raised on the settler project next act, Rayford Logan's "nadir," the second rise of the Knights of Ku Klux Klan terror network, and the dehumanizing *Jim Crow* Apartheid laws across the South all raged simultaneously, African people entered a new, bolder, bloodier phase of American Terrorism while manning the see-saw of American Jurisprudence [243]. The Springfield

---

[242] 163 U.S. 537 (1896), six short years before this Court decision came down Congress passed a second version of the Morrill Act (1890) and thereby established eighteen Black land grant universities, the Association of Public Land Grant Universities (APLU) offers a concise history of this act in a report presented by John Michael Lee, Jr. et.al titled <u>Land Grant but Unequal: State Match One to One Match Funding for 1890 Land Grant Universities</u> located here: https://www.aplu.org/library/land-grant-but-unequal-state-one-to-one-match-funding-for-1890-land-grant universities/file#:~:text=A%20second%20Morrill%20Act%20was,institution%20for%20pe rsons%20of%20color; also see Eugene Anderson's thoughts on the leading role that 1890 HBCUS still play in producing Africans in America in fields related to healthcare, engineering, agricultural sciences, etc., in an article published to the online edition of *Diverse Issues in Higher Education* titled "*Land Grant HBCU's Celebrating the 130th Anniversary of the 1890 Morrill Act*" on August 27, 2020 by Autumn A. Arnett located here: https://diverseeducation.com/article/188838/

[243] One of the numerous and more dehumanizing outgrowths of the maturing system of American Apartheid post-Reconstruction was the genesis of the "sundown town". These cities, towns, and suburbs had unwritten rules where our ancestors were "not allowed after

(Massachusetts) *Weekly Republican* set the tone as it published an editorial in 1896 stating that "the noble and valiant Anglo-Saxon of Manatee County, FL are engaged just now in demonstrating the superiority of the race" as the lede in the retelling of an extended mass lynching.[244]

The story stems from a fistfight between the son of the local sheriff and an African man, where the African man prevailed, and the sheriff and his armed posse show up at his home to collect him. The man and his father get into a shootout with the posse, killing the sheriff. The posse retreats, regroup and returns with reinforcements. Like a gang of wicked Yosemite Sams, they "were going about the county firing into the cabins of innocent and defenseless Blacks, burning up the homes of some, killing others and ordering a general exodus of Negroes; a vicious precursor to the Greenwood Massacre in Tulsa in 1921 and the Rosewood, FL massacre in 1923.[245]

---

dark" were sprinkled throughout the country and word was getting out, not much unlike the "Green Books" which were distributed amongst future generations. Refer to Cameron, <u>A Time for Terror</u> pp. 140, discussed in the notes.

[244] Ginzburg, Ralph <u>100 Years of Lynchings</u>, pp.9-10.

[245] Ibid. The Greenwood Massacre will be revisited in detail *below* and the Rosewood Massacre was retold in a fictionalized account in the 1997 John Singleton film *Rosewood* starring Esther Rolle, Ving Rhames, and the coolest Black man on the planet, Don Cheadle. When the mob gets going, they are relentless.

Another example of this occurred in March 16, 1901 near Nashville, TN, an African woman named Ballie Crutchfield got lynched, because her brother, who was accused of theft, was taken from the jail and escaped the mob. Out for blood and vengeance, the mob turned to William Crutchfield's sister and dragged her from her home, took her to a bridge over Rock Lick Creek, shot her in the head and dropped her dead body off the bridge. Ginzburg, Ralph <u>100 Years of Lynchings</u>, pp. 38.

It got so bad, that even the "Wizard of Tuskegee", Booker Taliaferro Washington who got roasted by folks like DuBois, Trotter, and other for not doing enough to openly "dignify" the race had to publish a leap year op-ed in the *New York Tribune* on February 29, 1904 condemning the lynching and burning of three Africans within the same week; one of which was an African woman. pp.64-5.

The major Supreme Court decision of the day came down in *Plessy v. Ferguson* (163 US 537, 1896). This case stood for the preposition that states could allow for the use of "separate but equal" rules for public accommodations for individuals, essentially concretizing American Apartheid.[246]

Homer Plessy presented the legal issue and his challenge to a Louisiana state law, which forced railway cars to stay segregated. The Supreme Court voted to uphold the law by a 7-1 vote and found that the Louisiana state violated neither the thirteenth Amendment's prohibition of chattel slavery nor the fourteenth Amendment's Equal Protection Clause.[247]

Three short years after this shameful decision, African people were rocked by one of the most brutal and symbolically impactful lynchings ever recorded, the lynching of Sam Hose.

---

[246]*Plessy v. Ferguson* (163 US 537, 1869). In his lone dissent, Justice Harlan Marshall resurrected the ghosts of Chief Justice Taney in his *Dred Scott* opinion, where he stated that "I do not deem it necessary to review the decisions of state courts to which reference was made in argument. Some, and the most important, of them, are wholly inapplicable, because rendered prior to the adoption of the last amendments of the constitution when colored people had very few rights which the dominant race felt obliged to respect". Plessy v. Ferguson, 163 U.S. 537, 16 S.Ct. 1138, 41 L.Ed. 256 (1896) at 563.

Please also see "Supreme Court of the United States: Plessy v. Ferguson" May 18, 1896. (1896). *The Virginia Law Register, 2*(5), 327-347. doi:10.2307/1099065 and refer to W. E. Burghardt Du Bois. (1898). The Study of the Negro Problems. *The Annals of the American Academy of Political and Social Science, 11,* 1-23. Retrieved July 28, 2020, from www.jstor.org/stable/1009474 for more historical context.

[247]Ibid. Also see Michael J. Klarman, From Jim Crow to Civil Rights (Oxford: Oxford University Press, 2004) pp. 18-19. Here, Klarman argues that the plain text of the 14th amendment does not provide any concrete answers to the question as it does not specifically ban the use and implementation of "racial classifications" and "equal protection of the laws" does not specifically ban the use and implementation of facilities separated based on race. This argument sets the stage for the legal jui-jitsu a future Court (The Warren Court) will employ to integrate public schools.

American Al Qaeda
Hooded Ku Klux Klan members share a stage with members of the Royal Riders of the Red Robe, a Klan auxiliary for foreign-born White Protestants Portland, OR, 1922
Credits: Oregon Historical Society (Public Domain)

The lynching of Jessie Washington; May 15, 1916, Waco, TX (Public Domain)

Sam Hose Lynching (1899)

"One cannot be a calm, cool, and detached social scientist while Negroes were lynched, murdered, and starved."[248]
William Edward Burghardt DuBois, 1899 upon hearing of the lynching of Sam Hose

The lynching of Sam Hose, whose birth name was Tom Wilkes, occurred in a multi-layered and toxic atmosphere based on White fear, White supremacy, political gamesmanship, media hype and framing, and blood lust.[249] On April 12, 1899, in

---

[248] Lewis, David Levering, W.E.B. DuBois: Biography of a Race 1868-1919 (New York: Owl Book Company Henry Holt and Company, LLC 1993) pp. 227. DuBois was an intellectual giant, and his accolades alone could fill a chapter, yet he was rocked to his very core at the sight of Sam Hose's knuckles, chopped off, and pickled in that jar in that storefront window. DuBois certainly suffered from that trauma DeGruy warned us about. Yet, it did not stop him from any of his missions, activist or intellectual.

Other relevant treatments of the lynching phenomena near the turn of the 20th century can also be found in Mary Church Terrell's 1904 essay *"Lynching from a Negro's Point of View" The North American Review, 178*(571), 853-868. Retrieved July 28, 2020, from www.jstor.org/stable/25150991; Pillsbury, A. (1902) "A Brief Inquiry into a Federal Remedy for Lynching" *Harvard Law Review, 15*(9), 707-713. doi:10.2307/1323748 and Vernier, C. (1912) "Local Sentiment and Lynching in Pennsylvania" *Journal of the American Institute of Criminal Law and Criminology, 3*(2), 171-173. Retrieved July 28, 2020, from www.jstor.org/stable/1133019.

[249] Franklin, John Hope, "Propaganda as History" pp. 10–23 in <u>Race and History: Selected Essays 1938–1988</u> (Louisiana State University Press, 1989); first published in *The Massachusetts Review*, 1979.

A year after this tragic event, a widely read book entitled <u>Negro a Beast</u> was published by Charles Carroll followed by a string of other polemics directed at African people, including The <u>Tempter of Eve</u> (and expansion of Thomas Dixon, Jr's <u>The Clansman</u> (the inspiration for the 1915 film *Birth of a Nation* discussed below), <u>The Caucasian and the Negro</u> in the United States by William P. Calhoun in 1902, and <u>The Negro: a Menace to American Civilization</u> by Robert W. Shufeldt in 1907, among others.

Franklin's work will be revisited and his critique of the history, as a disciplined reformed and published as "propaganda" will be analyzed *below*. Incidentally, the National Association for the Advancement of Colored People (NAACP) was founded a year later in direct response to a massive race riot in Springfield, IL in 1908, one of the oldest Civil Rights organizations still around and one that spent a lot of time, focus, energy, and resources in its earliest days to stop the practice of lynching especially the brutal lynchings of African people; especially highlighted by their push for the federal Anti-lynching legislation discussed *below*.

Newnan, GA (about 40 miles southwest of Atlanta), Hose was tortured, lynched, and desecrated after a fateful incident occurred where Hose killed his employer, Alfred Cranford, days earlier, in self-defense.[250]

See Markovitz, Legacies of Lynching; pp.5 where Markovitz also offers a brief history of the Commission of Interracial Cooperation (CIC) which was made up of a coalition of multi-racial ministers ultimately funded by the Laura Spelman Rockefeller Memorial foundation, Southern ministers dedicated to eradicating racialized lynching and the underlying stereotypes which fueled lynching phenomena. Markovitz also discusses the relatively short lived Association of Sothern Women for the Prevention of Lynching (ASWPL), a group of mostly White women, who understood that the chauvinistic use of the concepts of "chivalry" and "White womanhood" were used as much to control them and their bodies as they were used to justify the brutality of men, mostly African men; this group also understood the potential their message, which was shared by other anti-lynchers, could have for being received differently because of their own race and class. In other words, they felt that this message would be impactful having come from White women of means. pp.17.

See also, Benjamin Quarles and his book, The Negro and the making of America (London: Collier Books, 1969) pp. 199. African women would address this directly with White women themselves, for example Cecilia Eggleston, a Howard University graduate and Washington, D.C. public school teacher, offered a stinging critique and deconstruction of systemic White supremacy and the structural challenges her "imaginary child" would have to overcome if she had one and raised it in the settler state in her 1938 article published in the White facing magazine *The Forum and Century*. Hebert Aptheker, A Documentary History of the Negro People in the United States, Vol. IV, pp.291-97.

Also see Anna Julia Cooper's earth shattering collection of essays A Voice From the South and her essay titled "Has America a Race Problem: If so How Can it Be Solved?" where she offers one of the clearest, most brutal deconstructions of this settler project coming out of the nineteenth century. Cooper's main thrust in this essay is that "this nation (the U.S.) was foreordained to conflict from its incipiency...and its elements were predestined from their birth to in an irrepressible clash with the stable equilibrium of opposition. Exclusive possession belongs to none. There never was a point in (U.S.) history when it did" pp. 78; also see Gines, Kathryn T., "Anna Julia Cooper", *The Stanford Encyclopedia of Philosophy* (Summer 2015 Edition), Edward N. Zalta (ed.), URL = <https://plato.stanford.edu/archives/sum2015/entries/anna-julia-cooper/>. https://plato.stanford.edu/entries/anna-julia-cooper/

[250]Donald Matthews offers a painstakingly detailed account of this incident from multiple angles in his excellent accounting, At The Altar of Lynching: Burning Sam Hose in the American South (New York: Cambridge University Press, 2018) pp. 139-40. Matthews spent considerable time making the case that because Jesus of Nazareth was lynched, the Christian observers of lynchings would have "to rethink their understanding of lynching within the ethos of the Cross". Ibid. pp.266. Also see the pamphlet by Ida B. Wells-Barnett titled Lynch law in Georgia : a six-weeks' record in the center of southern civilization, as faithfully chronicled by the "Atlanta journal" and the "Atlanta constitution" : also the full report of Louis P. Le Vin, the Chicago detective sent to investigate the burning of Samuel Hose, the torture and hanging

The issue between Hose and Cranford was a simple employee-employer conflict that quickly escalated into a matter of life and death. Hose asked Cranford for wages owed, and Cranford flew off the handle, pulled a pistol on Hose, and by all accounts, Hose threw his ax and killed Cranford on the spot.[251] Once the rumors of the incident spread the story morphed. The retelling had Hose sneaking up behind Cranford, killing his employer in cold blood as he sat at the dinner table.

Hose then reportedly tossed Cranford's infant child on the floor and made Mrs. Mattie Cranford gather household valuables. Hose and then raped her in the blood, guts, and brains of her newly deceased husband. He finished his nasty business, taunted Mrs. Cranford, and slunk back of into the shadows of the night.[252] This story was fueled by and focused on the falsity of the rape of Mattie Cranford and goes a long way to explain what was eventually done to Hose's body.[253]

Hose goes into hiding, the Whites are on fire in the search and pursuit of Hose, and the inflammatory and exaggerated stories are appearing in the pages of the *Atlanta Journal Constitution* are steadily pouring literary kerosene on the situation not much unlike members of the mob would pour actual kerosene on the tortured body of Sam Hose.[254] Hose was finally captured while trying to board a train to Macon, GA, and

---

of Elijah Strickland, the colored preacher, and the lynching of nine men for alleged arson located in the U.S. Library of Congress at the following link: https://www.loc.gov/resource/lcrbmrp.t1612/?st=gallery.

[251] Ibid. 140-141, Hose had merely asked Cranford for time off and money so that he could travel to go see his sick mother. Cranford, who was known for having a quick temper was enraged at Hose's audacity (uppitiness) to dare assume that a White man, let alone Cranford, even owed Hose dignity or respect let alone money.

[252] Ibid.

[253] Ibid.

[254] Ibid. pp.146, the stories of innocent Africans being harassed and captured in the wake of the massive, multi-state hunt for Sam Hose is heartbreaking. The fear factor kicked in as the Whites were constantly worried about Denmark Vesey styled conspiracy and plan for massive African rebellion. In fact, one of the local African ministers who was accused of stirring up

after some horse-trading between the mob and the local sheriff, it was decided to lynch him in Newnan, GA, after the mob was able to extract Hose from the county jail.²⁵⁵

The lynching itself took on a "carnival" like atmosphere as Hose was paraded through town, past local shops, and screaming crowds (estimated to be upwards of over two-thousand people, including men, women, children, and former judges and a former Governor.²⁵⁶

The lynching of Sam Hose, April 12, 1899, Newman, GA (Public Domain)

---

unrest among the Africans after the lynching was J.W. Thorpe, a Methodist, and he had to be secreted out of town with the help of Bishop Henry McNeal Turner of the African Methodist Episcopal Church. pp.143. For days, the *Constitution* ran stories playing up the need to protect the sanctity of White women and the Southern landscape being littered with marauding Africans hell bent on mayhem and destruction.

²⁵⁵ Ibid. pp.155; also see Ida B. Wells-Barnett in Lynch Law in Georgia, where she offers three reports of lynchings occurring in that State in 1899, including a report on the Sam Hose lynching. Barnett's accounts are both harrowing and detailed and should be analyzed for their contributions to preserving the historical record. It is amazing to read the accounts of the investigator that the "colored citizens of Chicago" sent to look into the details around Sam Hose, Louis Pe Le Vin found facts to support Hose's self-defense narrative and failed to find any facts suggesting that Hose assaulted Mrs. Cranford, see pp. 31-42.

²⁵⁶ Ibid.

William Edward Burghardt DuBois, Boston, MA; Summer of 1907 (Public Domain)

Several times, the procession would stop, and Hose would be hoisted up above the adoring crowd like a trophy being shown off at a championship parade or like the parading floats stop and preen during Mardi Gras.[257] When it was finally all said and done, they had ravaged Sam Hose, chopped off parts of his body that the mob sadists fought fiercely over the bits of flesh like Mardi Gras beads, and even sold some (like the set of knuckles that traumatized young DuBois) for .$25 apiece, they poured kerosene on his body. They lit him ablaze as he would scream out in agony until his painful, gruesome death.[258]

---

[257] Ibid. 159. Mathews offers a deep dive into this symbolic parade of the conquered "Black savage" frog marched on his way to his pre-ordained doom. He describes a party like atmosphere full of revelry and cheer. pp.164.

[258] Ibid. 166-69. The descriptions of the torture are horrifying, but Matthews handles it deftly while pulling no punches. And it should come as no surprise that Hose's genitalia where some of the most prized souvenirs.

News of the lynching of Sam Hose spread far beyond the Georgia-Alabama border and likely had a profound impact on all who even heard about it. One of those it deeply impacted was William Edward Burghardt DuBois. He was working as a researcher at Atlanta University at the time of the lynching.[259] DuBois was actually on his way to meet with *Constitution* editor-in-chief Joel Chandler Harris when he found out that Hose had been barbecued and his chopped off knuckles were on display in White storefront owner's shop window down the street. The dismayed Dubois at this point turned away from his work and declared, "One cannot be a calm, cool, and detached social scientist while Negroes were lynched, murdered, and starved."[260]

Africans, still dealing with the trauma of over 300 years of oppression in general and the weight of the Sam Hose lynching, barely had enough time to catch their breath before the devastating piece of glorified American terrorist propaganda, *Birth of a Nation,* hit the movie screens.

---

[259] Lewis, Biography of a Race Op Cit. pp.227

[260] Ibid. Lewis does a masterful job in explaining how this tragic event deeply, deeply impacted Dubois and shaped the scope of his work from that point forward; See also Terrell, M. (1904) "Lynching from a Negro's Point of View" *The North American Review, 178*(571), 853-868. Retrieved August 1, 2020, from www.jstor.org/stable/25150991 to help solidify the point that the Sam Hose served as a bit of a turning point for Africans forced to deal with this brutality, pp. 859.

Anna Julia Cooper, from her 1892 essay collection "A Voice from The South."(Public Domain)

- 181 -

June 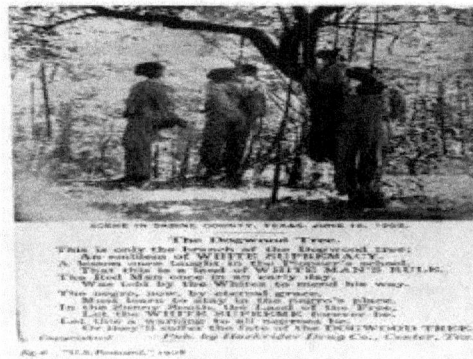 J15, 1905 Postcard; Sanine County, TX 1905 "The Dogwood Tree" (Public Domain)

Birth of a Nation (1915)

"White men were roused by a mere instinct of preservation. Until at last there had sprung into existence a great Ku Klux Klan, a veritable empire of the South to protect the Southern country"
Woodrow Wilson (28), after a screening of the movie in the White House East Room, February 18, 1915. [261]

The Capture of Gus
Birth of a Nation
David W. Griffith, 1915 (Public Domain)

Debuting during the *Great African Migration* from Southern states to Northern states, David W. Griffith's silent film melodrama is heralded as a triumph in movie making. Still, it was equally more triumphant in transfixing the myths of Whiteness, White

---

[261] Please See Benbow, Mark (2010) "Birth of a Quotation: Woodrow Wilson and Like Writing History with Lightning". *The Journal of the Gilded Age and Progressive Era*, 9(4), 509-533. Retrieved August 3, 2020, from www.jstor.org/stable/20799409, here Benbow clarifies that Birth of a Nation was not the first film actually screened at the White House (as another film had been shown earlier in 1914) and despite the shared senses of White nationalism and anti-Blackness between Wilson (28), Thomas Dixon, Jr., and D.W. Griffith, Benbow makes the case that Wilson (28) likely did not actually state the quote that has been famously attached to him concerning the film, namely that "this is history written in lightening and unfortunately true" but it was clear that he gave the quote heading this summary; pp.513-19.

supremacy, and Anti-Blackness indelibly in the imagination of the settler state.[262] Essentially the story is a familiar trope. If given half a chance, unfettered Africans enter the halls of government and other aspects of genteel, White society, and wreak absolute havoc. And following every dehumanizing Black stereotype imaginable, "free" and unfettered Black's wreck Congress, the economy, society, and engage in every trespass up to and most notably including the rape and ravishing of helpless White women.

---

[262] Franklin, "The Birth of a Nation: Propaganda as History" pp.10-23. In this essay, Franklin walks through the detailed history from Thomas Dixon Jr.'s The Clansman play and novella and his work entitled The Leopard Spots, Griffith's borrowing from that work and use of the title for his initial showing, the changing of the name, and the phenomenal commercial success including the private White House screening with avowed White nationalist POTUS Woodrow Wilson (28) and then sets about deconstructing the entire effort, pretty much frame by frame; also see Ibram X. Kendi, as he succinctly traces Dixon's ahistorical and perverted view of Reconstruction to none other than William Archibald Dunning and the school of Reconstruction History named after him at Columbia University; Dunning was considered the American progenitor of using an "objective, scientific method" in the study of humanities like history and literature. Kendi, states that along with Dixon another snarling racist sycophant of Dunning's to claim fame at the time was native Georgian Ulrich Bonnel Phillips due to his well-regarded but clearly off book, American Negro Slavery,

See Kendi, Stamped From the Very Beginning, Op.Cit. pp.287. Despite the White nationalists dressing up as scholars and artists, Franklin highlights, however, that Africans were some of the loudest voices out there condemning Dixon and his work, in fact, then Howard University president Kelly Miller lambasted Dixon in personal correspondence by telling him that "your teachings subvert foundations of law and established order. You are the high priest of lawlessness, the prophet of anarchy" as an example of a line of African (or at least African facing) critiques lodged at Dixon and his life's work by the likes of Francis J. Grimke, Francis Hackett, the NAACP, etc. This critique continued even after Dixon conceded and convinced Griffith to add a reel to *Birth of a Nation* congratulating the industrial training accomplishments of the Hampton Normal Institute. pp.15-8.

An excellent history of Hampton, VA and (now) Hampton University can be found in Colita Nichols Fairfax's Black America Series: Hampton Virginia (Charleston: Arcadia Publishing 2005). This work is critical, as Fairfax combines a concise, detailed history of the town and university viewed through lens of gentrification, industrialization, and settler colonialism with a review of primary documents and rare photos.

And the only organization ready, willing, and able to stop the "marauding" Black horde is the Ku Klux Klan.[263] Large numbers of Whites loved this. They ate this up like Aunt Jemima pancakes. These tropes played out on-screen electrified their sense of White nationalism, reinforced their beliefs in White supremacy, and justified their anti-Blackness. Meanwhile, the imagery enraged equally large numbers of Whites who were as horrified as the castigated Blacks that the stereotypes were meant to demean.[264]

John Hope Franklin notes that the same year *Birth of Nation* hit the big screen, in the wake of the lynching of Jewish businessman Leo Frank mentioned *above*, saw a

---

[263]Ibid. See also Wiggins, W. (1988). Boxing's Sambo Twins: Racial Stereotypes in Jack Johnson and Joe Louis Newspaper Cartoons, 1908 to 1938. *Journal of Sport History*, 15(3), 242-254. Retrieved August 1, 2020, from www.jstor.org/stable/43609224 for a fascinating look at the brutal caricatures of Jack Johnson and Joe Louis littered throughout the nations newspapers in the lead up to some of their bigger championship fights. This article laid bare historical examples of modern sentiments telling LeBron James to shut up and dribble or calling kneeling Black pro football players "sons of bitches"; it shows that for some, despite the heights and achievement talented African's are able to reach, our sole and acceptable role in and contribution to this society is to entertain Whites regardless of anything and everything else.

Gerald Horne strikes a similar chord about African-Mexican solidarity in his book Dawning of the Apocalypse where he is notes that Mexico had boasted of having a African-Indian president in the seventeenth century; please see Horne The Dawning of the Apocalypse; pp. 208.

The naked racism of those articles and cartoons were, at times, equally matched by sentiments found in the halls of high office, for example on February 6, 1914 Congressman James K. Vardaman (D-MS) delivered one of the most vehemently and viciously White supremacist, anti-African speeches on the House Floor; and this speech hit all the familiar, Hegelian tropes of African savagery and the carving out of ancient Egypt away from the continent, general Black backwardness, glorification of Black "mammies", even admitting that "God almighty never intended that the negro would share in the government of this country", etc. The text of this is recorded in The Congressional record, 63rd Cong., 2nd sess. (Feb. 6, 1914), 3036, 3038, and 3040 and is cited from Fishel, Jr. et. al, The Negro American: A Documentary History, pp.378-82.

[264] Franklin, John "Propaganda as History" Op. Cit. pp. 10-23.

rebirth of the Klan in Atlanta, GA, in direct response as well as a rise in anti-Klan sentiment.[265]

None of that stopped the Klan, however, as William J. Simmons and dozens of men, including original Klansmen from 1866 and a former member of the Georgia State legislature, ascended Stone Mountain, GA on Thanksgiving Eve, lit a cross, and held a secret ritual thereby reigniting American Al-Qaeda, otherwise known as the Knights of the Ku Klux Klan.[266] The text of the Klu Klux Kreed as read aloud during its second rise is as follows:

> We, the Order of the Knights of the Ku Klux Klan, reverentially acknowledge the majesty and supremacy of the Divine Being, recognize the goodness and providence of the same. We Recognize our relationship to the Government of the United States of America, the Supremacy of its Constitution, the Union of States thereunder, and the Constitutional Laws thereof, and we shall be ever devoted to the sublime principles of a pure Americanism and valiant in the defense of its ideals and institutions. We avow The distinction between the races of mankind as same as has been decreed by the Creator, and shall ever be true in the faithful maintenance of White supremacy, and will strenuously oppose any compromise thereof in any and all things. We Appreciate the intrinsic value of a real practical fraternal relationship among men of kindred thought, purpose, and ideals and infinite benefits accruable therefrom, and

---

[265] Ibid. pp.21.
[266] Ibid. pp.21, See also the Ian Lilley and Neil Oliver 2018 documentary "Who Put the Klan into Ku Klux Klan" mentioned *above*.

shall faithfully devote ourselves to the practice of an honorable Klanishness that the life and living of each may be a constant blessing to others.[267]

This single movie help set the tone for this bloody age of lynching in the first of the twentieth century. The "Red Summer of 1919" is a perfect example of how lynching had become an almost default, reactionary mechanism as opposed to an extremely rare event.

The lynching of Jessie Washington; May 15, 1916, Waco, TX (Public Domain)

---

[267]The text of the KKK creed can be found in <u>The Negro American: A Documentary History</u> (ed. Leslie Fisher and Benjamin Quarles) Op. Cit. pp. 426-27.

Red Summer Lynchings (1919)

"It was not long before the Negroes were back, coming from the North with others of their race. Then began a series of attacks and retreats, counterattacks, and stone throwing"
John Harris, the fifteen-year old whose friend's murder at the 25th Street Beach sparked a riot in Chicago, IL, July 27, 1919

A table listed in the *Journal of the American Institute of Criminal Law and Criminology* in 1918 lists a few of the recorded lynchings of enslaved Africans during bondage, according to the Abolitionist paper, the *Liberator*. Still, it shows that approximately 2,735 Africans had been lynched between 1885-1915, according to a study done by the *New York Times*.[268]

The kindling had been stacking at this point for almost four hundred years by January 1919 and was lit and set ablaze by that May.[269] In June 1919, the settler state had been rocked by at least ten full-blown race riots, dozens of minor racially motivated incidents, and almost 100 lynchings, all across the land with an official death toll of well over 150, mostly African women, men, and children.[270]

During these incidents, it was said that time and time again that while Whites would instigate the situation, often under the color of law and with full knowledge and

---

[268] Lynching Statistics. (1918). *Journal of the American Institute of Criminal Law and Criminology, 9*(1), 144-146. Retrieved July 28, 2020, from www.jstor.org/stable/1133750 pp. 144-45. *The Liberator* was William Lloyd Garrison's paper published in Boston from 1831-1865.

[269] Krugler, David, 1919, The Year of Racial Violence: How African-Americans Fought Back (New York: Cambridge University Press, 2015) pp.2-3. Krugler's book is powerful because he purposely places the resisting Africans at the center of the story, which is a stark difference from the modern mainstream corporate media obsession with framing Black victimhood and the dead bodies as the primary focus and our lynchings on a twenty-four hour Black snuff film loop.

[270] Ibid.3.

assistance from law enforcement, our ancestors refused to back down.[271] One of the main issues was that these Africans had either returned from the front lines of World War I, or lost limbs or loved ones on the battlefields in Europe, only to be returned to the settler state and subjected to second-class citizenship, Jim Crow, and lynchings; the other issue was that these Africans were often armed and were trained how to use those arms. [272]

The fed-up Africans primarily fought this war on three fronts, 1) self-defense, 2) taking the truth about the incidents viral, especially the cause of the riots, the lynchings, and the brutality, and 3) justice.[273]

The forces and defenders of White supremacy were met with equal force and measure; in the sentiment captured brilliantly by W.E.B. DuBois in an essay entitled "Returning Soldiers" where he ends stating, "We return from the slavery of uniform which the world's madness demanded us to don to the freedom of civil garb. We stand again to look America squarely in the face and call a spade a spade. We sing This country of ours, despite all its better souls, has done and dreamed, is yet a shameful land...We *return*. We *return from fighting*. We return *fighting*".[274]

Eventually, the violence died down, and some Africans were expectedly charged for their roles in the riots while the Whites tended to escape prosecution. A study of the fierce debates and fissures that emerged throughout the Black community through

---

[271] Ibid.

[272] Ibid.

[273] Ibid. 3-5. Again, see John Harris and Ida B. Wells Barnett (Narrated by Acie Cargill) <u>Red Summer Race Riot Chicago 1919</u> (2019). Review the eyewitness accounts of both Harris and Wells for some perspective.

[274] Ibid. pp.2

the press and pulpit are worthy of study. Hubert Harrison and the Blood Brotherhood, DuBois, Ida B. Wells Barnett, Marcus Garvey, Claude McKay, William H. Ferris, James Weldon Johnson, and the other "New Negro" amplifiers would loudly condemn the "Old Negro" speakers and their calls and pleas for Africans to stand down. Claude McKay's famous poem "If We Must die" was published in September 1919, mainly in response to the race riots and subsequent lynchings.[275]

While the communists and socialists were blamed for all the rabble-rousing, there are valuable lessons for African people to learn from revisiting the Red Summer of 1919 and the ways, means, and levels of resistance to the lynching and brutality that the White supremacists, and supporters of White supremacy, waged against our ancestors at that time. One of the clearest examples of the brutality of the White nationalists and defenders of the settler state occurred two years later, in the Greenwood section of Tulsa, OK, otherwise known as "Black Wall Street."

---

[275] *The Negro World, the Chicago Defender, the Crisis, the Cleveland-Gazette* and others would not only lead the charge in the truth-telling phase of attack, but in a brilliant emption of William Patterson, El hajj Malik el Shabazz, Martin Luther King, Jr. and Kwame Ture, etc., they also lead way in beginning to inter-connect the struggle for African liberation in America with other, larger international struggles around the world.

East St. Louis Race Riot 1917 (Public Domain)

Washington, DC Race Riot 1919-Red Summer Lynchings (Public Domain)

Chicago Race War 1919-Red Summer Lynchings

By Grand Forks herald. July 29, 1919The Richmond palladium and sun-telegram. July 29, 1919The Bemidji daily pioneer. July 29, 1919File: Map of 1919 Chicago Race Riot Hot Spots extending over the Black Belt.jpgFile: Chicago race riot, five police officers, and one soldier.jpg - Grand Forks herald. July 29, 1919The Richmond palladium and sun-telegram. July 29, 1919The Bemidji daily pioneer. July 29, 1919File: Map of 1919 Chicago Race Riot Hot Spots extending over the Black Belt.jpgFile: Chicago race riot, five policemen and one soldier.jpg, Public Domain,
https://commons.wikimedia.org/w/index.php?curid=92654007

Greenwood Massacre, Tulsa Race Riot (1921)

"NEGRO SECTION ABOLISHED BY CITY ORDER. Thirty-five blocks south of Standpipe Hill now in ruins following the fire Wednesday morning. Greenwood will never again be a Negro quarter but will become a wholesale and industrial center".
June 7, 1921 headline from the *Tulsa Tribune*

The Greenwood Section of Tulsa Oklahoma, still ablaze
June 1, 1921 (Public Domain)

It's always good to remember that this occurred because a small group of armed and determined Black folk (like their ancestors at Stono) dared to protect one of its own and deny the mob its pound of Black flesh to desecrate.

For years, the stories of "Black Wall Street" and what happened to those Africans starting on May 31, 1921, were a mere whisper, often loosely spoken in nationalist or Pan-Africanist circles. Now it appears that more interest has been generated in finding out what happened and what was destroyed. Several books have been written on this tragedy, but I will mostly rely on Tim

Madigan's The Burning: Massacre, Destruction, and the Tulsa Race Riot of 1921 (New York: Thomas Dunne Books, 2001).[276] This is a story of the chicanery of villains and African resistance to it.

By 1921, Tulsa, OK, had transformed from a sleepy outpost in Indigenous (Indian) country to a booming oil town. The Africans in segregated Tulsa built a thriving community across the railroad tracks from the Whites. There were numbers of highly successful professionals like the famous Dr. Andrew C. Jackson, O.W. Gurley, and the Mann Brothers, regular everyday Black folk, like Mamie and Dick Rowland, were able to hammer out a solidly middle-class existence by working in the service industry and earning money on the disposable income of the nouveau riche Whites.[277]

The trouble started with the aforementioned Dick Rowland and his alleged minor transgression against a White woman named Sarah Page. It was said that the flashy

---

[276] Madigan, Tim The Burning: Massacre, Destruction, and the Tulsa Race Riot of 1921 (New York: Thomas Dunne Books, 2001). This tragedy occurred at a time when one of the greatest Pan-African movements the world has ever seen was at its absolute height, the Universal Negro Improvement Association and African Communities League (UNIA), which boasted millions of members from across the African world and its journal *The Negro World* boasted massive readership united under the single banner of "One God, One Aim, One Destiny". For example, Umoja informs us that the largest concentration of Garveyites were in deeply segregated Mississippi and one of the strongest Garveyites, Queen Mother Audley Moore (maa kheru) out of New Iberia, LA. Please see Umoja, We Will Shoot Back; Op.Cit pp.18 for the discussion of the UNIA in Mississippi.

Literal volumes have been written on the UNIA and its leader, Marcus Mosiah Garvey, the rise and fall, those that were inspired, the doubters, the settler state responses, etc. Tony Martin's Race First is likely the easiest place to get a solid introduction to the UNIA. Martin, Tony, Race First: The Ideological and Organizational Struggle of Marcus Garvey and the Universal Negro Improvement Association (Dover: Majority Press, 1976). It should also be noted that African resistance during this period was not always as flamboyant as seen with the UNIA, often it was much subtle but just as direct.

Returning to Klarman, he notes how in a growing Black middle class in 1920 Jacksonville, FL used its burgeoning economic clout to effect when thousands of them cancelled insurance policies when it was discovered that their insurance agents led a lynch mob (woke capitalism indeed). Klarman, Michael Jim Crow to Civil Rights; pp. 102.
[277]Ibid.

Rowland, who worked at an office building as a nicely paid shoeshine boy, accidentally bumped into Page while she was working the elevator at the office building; Page became incensed, and eventually, the story turned into an assault and rape.[278]

The key villains of the story, like Richard Lloyd Jones, who at one point helped salvage Abraham Lincoln (16)'s Kentucky's birthplace, as the editor-in-chief of the *Tulsa Tribune,* did everything he could to inflame, instigate, and amplify the alleged crime and the call for the need to lynch Dick Rowland after months and months of referring to Greenwood as "Niggertown" and "Little Africa" in the pages of his paper.[279] The other villains were the Klan, the "hidden hand" that pulled many strings in Tulsa at that time. Through its control of the "Tulsa Benevolent Association."[280]

After the repeated calls for Rowland's arrest, the county Sherriff William McCullough had bravely promised Rowland once in custody that the mob would not get him; likely because he was haunted by the memory of having to escort a prisoner to the gallows for a murder that likely hadn't even been committed.[281] As expected and as if on cue, the mob assembled demanding Rowland's release to them and their warped sense of justice. Fatefully word had reached the African community, and the armed *"Defenders of Greenwood"* showed up and shut the mob down, led by men like WWI

---

[278]Ibid. pp.52-3.

[279]Ibid. pp.31. See also pp. 140.

[280]Ibid. 233-4, See pp. 44-5 to get an example of the type of power the Klan-. Madigan notes that Klan amassed as they were able to shield Lloyd from criminal charges for lewd behavior even after the married family Lloyd had gotten caught dead to rights engaged in a sexual tryst with his assistant, the Klan was able to get the local prosecutor to drop the warrants and the charges. pp. 43.

[281]Ibid. pp.73.

vet O.B. Mann, O.W. Gurley, Andrew J. Smitherman, John, and Bill Williams, and others.[282]

The violent skirmishes started that night, and the Whites were thoroughly beaten off, but after emptying the sporting goods stores in Tulsa, they waged war right after midnight.[283] The battle raged for less than seventy-two hours. Still, the devastation of Greenwood was beyond massive, and the National Guard was activated by its order and launched planes to drop bombs (nods to Tulsa's own GAP Band); the block by block warfare was intense, filled with the looting of Black homes and businesses, and deadly.[284]

As the clouds finally cleared and the dust settled, the death tolls and damage estimates have been contested. The Red Cross at the time estimated that they treated five hundred thirty-one people during the week after the massacre, with only forty-eight Whites among the wounded. In 1971 the retiring chief of the Tulsa Police Academy found a tabulation in old files that listed two hundred fifty casualties. However, the stories of bodies being dumped in the river and unknown, unmarked, missing mass graves are still rampant.[285]

Greenwood's commercial area was utterly destroyed. The mounting losses included over one hundred ninety-one businesses, like the Gurley's theater, office building, and sweet shop, John Stratford's hotel, the First Baptist Church. The Red Cross

---

[282] Ibid.

[283] Ibid. pp. 119.

[284] Ibid. 125-44. The GAP Band brothers Charlie, Ronnie, and Robert Wilson are from Tulsa and their band is named after Greenwood Avenue, Archer Ave, and Pine Street, which was the heart of the Greenwood section.

[285] Ibid. 224, Bill Willbanks was the chief who found the notes. See pp.266-8 for details about the missing dead of Greenwood.

reported that at least one thousand, one hundred fifteen houses were burned, and another three hundred fourteen were looted. There were an estimated one and a half million dollars in real estate damage and seven hundred fifty thousand in personal property damage. Over one million, eight hundred thousand dollars in claims related to the riots was filed against the City of Tulsa in 1922. These numbers equate to twenty-six million four hundred ninety-two thousand one hundred sixty-four dollars and ninety-two cents in commercial and personal damages in 2020 dollars. And twenty-three million eight hundred forty-two thousand nine hundred forty-eight dollars and forty-five cents property damages claims filed in 2020 dollars.[286]

In the immediate aftermath, the City of Tulsa washed its hands of the whole incident, mostly blamed the African resistance, and sought to condemn the burned-out properties and, in almost unlawful "eminent-domain" like fashion, planned to relocate the Blacks and turn Greenwood into a wholesale and commercial section.[287]

Through the decades of subverted trauma, the fights for truth, reconciliation, and reparations continue for the Greenwood survivors and their descendants to this very day, primarily through the *Reparations for Greenwood* organization. In a tragically ironic

---

[286]Ibid. pp. 221. The financial estimates are pulled from the record of the Oklahoma Commission (published on February 28, 2001, as its Final Report, Oklahoma Commission to Study the Tulsa Race Riot of 1921, Tulsa Oklahoma (retrieved archive on July 29, 2020 and recalculated for 2020 equivalency). See also Rosser, L. (1921). "The Illegal Enforcement of Criminal Law" *American Bar Association Journal,* 7(10), 519-524. Retrieved July 28, 2020, from www.jstor.org/stable/25710665.

[287]Legal justification for eminent domain actions by the state is found in the "takings" clause in the 5th Amendment, which reads in part *"Nor shall private property be taken for public use, without just compensation"*. In understanding the provision, we both agree that it is helpful to keep in mind the reasons behind it".

The main issue here is that the City of Tulsa not only failed to offer any real compensation to the burned out victims it turned around changed the building codes in such a way as to hamper the Blacks ability to rebuild, which encouraged the White capitalists to swoop and buy up all the property for "pennies on the dollar". Madigan, The Burning Op.Cit. pp.226-28.

twist, Dr. Tiffany Crutcher, a member of the organization, is a great grand-daughter of massacre survivor-now ancestor Rebecca Brown Crutcher, also lost her brother Terrance Crutcher to a "lynching by law enforcement" on September 16, 2016, at the hands of Tulsa Police Department officers Betty Shelby and Tyler Turnbough.[288] We explore instances where members of law enforcement have flat out lynched African men, women, and children in this country, often without any type of apology (formal or otherwise), let alone justice; there are likely just as many times as the very law itself lynches those same Africans.

Legal Lynchings

"Forrest County Justice of the Peace T.C. Hobby recommended a $500 fine for the illegal possession of liquor and a $100 fine for reckless driving, two weeks later the judge found Kennard guilty on both charges after stating that he had not known another case where the State proved more clearly the guilt of the defendant"
Yashuhiro Katagiri, 2001

As we saw with the John Punch case *above*, there is a deep and painful history between Black folk and American law on every level. And in some cases, Black folk got lynched by the law itself.

Take the heartbreaking case of Clyde Kennard, the one-time University of Chicago political science major who was denied admission to the lily-White campus of Mississippi Southern College (now Southern Mississippi University) in 1956, 1958,

---

[288] The Reparations for Greenwood website is full of information and contact details on how to support the effort and is located at this link: https://www.greenwoodreparations.com/about-us; Please see Neile Jones's article posted to the ABC 8 website discussing Shelby's new Deputy Sherriff job in neighboring Rogers County, Oklahoma after getting acquitted for killing that "big, Black dude" Terrance Crutcher at https://ktul.com/news/local/betty-shelby-talks-about-starting-over-one-year-after-her-acquittal.

and again in1959.[289] Kennard was an Army vet and decided to return to his native Mississippi after completing his first two years of college to help with the family farm.[290]

It was during that time of transition that Kennard decided to enroll at Mississippi Southern College, thereby becoming the first Black person to integrate the school. Not only were the school officials not having it, but neither was the Mississippi State Sovereign Commission; the post-Brown government spy agency set up to clandestinely keep tabs on, and subvert if need be, individuals and organizations attempting to break Jim Crow's back anywhere in that state.[291]

The Commission kept tabs on Kennard, even setting up a meeting between him and Governor James Plemon "J.P." Coleman, where Kennard was offered admission into a "Negro school" or an "integrated school back up North" in exchange for dropping his now well-known attempts to integrate Mississippi Southern College.[292]

Another meeting was set up with the head of Mississippi Southern on September 15, 1959. The school rejected Kennard yet again. And after being escorted out of the office after his third and final time, Kennard saw two police officers waiting for him at his car, Forrest County Constable's Charlie Ward and Lee Daniels. They subsequently arrested Kennard for speeding through campus and, during the arrest,

---

[289]Bowers, Rick Spies of Mississippi (Washington, D.C.: National Geographic Society, 2010) pp. 32.

[290]Ibid.
[291]Ibid. 28-31. The Mississippi Sovereign Commission will be discussed more at length *below*.

[292]Ibid. pp. 2-98. Kennard, in his dignified frustration had written an op-ed in the *Hattiesburg American*, where he openly mocked American Apartheid and asked "Are we to assume that two sets of hospitals are to be built for two groups of doctors? Are we to build two bridges to cross the same stream to give equal opportunity to two groups of engineers? Are we to have to courts of law to give both groups of lawyers the same chance to demonstrate their skills? Are we two have two legislatures for those politically inclined, and of course two Governors?"

planted five bottles of liquor in his car. With Mississippi being a "dry state" at the time, Kennard was later charged with possession and reckless driving.[293]

The State of Mississippi was not through with Clyde Kennard, however, not by a long shot. Kennard was subsequently named an accomplice to the theft of twenty-five dollars' worth of chicken feed from the Forrest County Cooperative Warehouse. The burglary was committed by a nineteen-year-old White man named Johnny Lee Roberts, an employee of the Co-op who left a door unlocked after his shift was over one evening. When the cops caught up to Lee, he implicated Kennard in the crime. This was a felony charge, and at trial, the all-White jury gave Roberts a suspended sentence and convicted Kennard. Kennard's sentence, the full seven years, was to be served at the notorious Parchman Farm, the Mississippi state penitentiary [294].

Kennard contracted cancer earlier during his sentence, but neither Governor Plemon nor then-current Governor Ross Barnett considered commuting his sentence despite the deteriorating condition, until the lynching of Medgar Evers on June 12, 1963. Kennard, a political prisoner, held on trumped charges backed by earlier trumped-up charges, was released from custody on July 4th, 1963, and died from cancer two months later after having left Mississippi and returned to Chicago, IL.[295]

---

[293]Ibid. pp.31-2. Also see Katagiri's book, The Mississippi State Sovereignty Commission where he highlights some of the financial pressure applied to Kennard as the Commission started to squeeze him, the bank foreclosed on the family farm, the insurance company canceled his auto insurance, etc. all within the weeks before his meeting with McCain, pp. 59. Also note that the Chief of Highway Patrol B.S. Hood and an Inspector Gray were to be set up in an adjacent room to listen in on the discussion to see if anything arose so that they could arrest Kennard right then and there and there was also an order for all of the cops involved in the street takedown to be at their posts by 8:00 am. This incident was hard wired from the top on down.

[294]Ibid. pp. 44-46, Kennard enlisted the aid of the NAACP in filing appeals and highlighting his plight but to no avail.

[295] Ibid. pp. 76-7, 105-06. In 2006, after Roberts finally recanted his trial testimony at the behest of a group of students at Lincolnshire High School in IL and the Center for Wrongful Convictions at Northwestern University School of Law, and the judge in the same court that

This was a legal lynching. It would have taken that all-White jury longer to boil a pot of water than it did to convict Kennard, and the judge turned right around and hit him with everything he could, all for trying to integrate a public college.

This page was last revised on September 15, 2019. It was originally submitted on June 15, 2018, Photo Credits: Cajun Scrambler of Assumption, Louisiana. (Public Domain)

One of the famous lines of legal lynching cases to hit the Court, however, was sorted out a generation before the Clyde Kennard case and came to be known collectively as the "Interwar cases," perhaps the most famous of which involved the "Scottsboro Boys."[296]

Michael Klarman's From Jim Crow to Civil Rights: The Supreme Court and the Struggle for Racial Equality analyzes the various cases, *Moore v. Dempsey*, 261 U.S. 86 (1923), *Powell v. Alabama*, 287 U.S. 45 (1932), *Norris v. Alabama*, 294 U.S. 587 (1935) and *Brown v. Mississippi* 297 U.S. 278 (1936).[297]

---

convicted Clyde Kennard back in 1960, vacated his sentence. And as a half-hearted apology to its role in this legal lynching, the University of Southern Mississippi (formerly Mississippi Southern College) has named its student services building after Clyde Kennard
[296] Klarman, From Jim Crow to Civil Rights; pp.117-21

[297]Ibid. See also *Moore v. Dempsey*, 261 U.S. 86 (1923), *Powell v. Alabama*, 287 U.S. 45 (1932), *Norris v. Alabama*, 294 U.S. 587 (1935) and *Brown v. Mississippi* 297 U.S. 278 (1936)

Here Klarman makes the succinct argument that in each of these cases, with *Powell* and *Norris*, being known officially as the "Scottsboro Boys" cases, you find poor and illiterate Blacks accused of either outright killing White men or raping White women, railroaded in court in hastily slapped together trials simply to appease the mobs gathering on the courthouse steps.[298]

While these cases stood for many things, like the unlawful exclusion of Blacks from jury duty, due process prevention of coerced confessions, Court review of criminal state cases on grounds established in the Bill of Rights (like the sixth-amendment right to counsel), the main takeaway is that Whites across the South were relying on "kangaroo trials" and other legal lynchings that often carried steep prison sentences to supplement the "off-the-books" lynchings and burnings they had grown so accustomed to in their recent past.[299] The Whites honestly thought that this was a "great step forward" and were deeply offended that they were so heavily criticized due to this practice.

Every lynching, whether they took place in a courtroom, public square, or dusty field somewhere each had a driving force behind it; one of those main forces was fear. For some, this was a deep-seated fear of what the changing world (and demographics) of forced integration would look like. Well, in *Brown,* the Court delivered a moment of reckoning to those poor, fearful souls and delivered a much needed shot in the arm to the movement for Civil Rights for Africa's daughters and sons here in America.

---

[298] Ibid.

[299] See U.S. Const. amend VI, see also generally *Gideon v. Wainwright*, 372 U.S. 335 (1963) where the sixth-amendment right to counsel in federal prosecutions was finally applied to State felony prosecutions where defendants cannot afford to hire counsel.

Brown v. Board of Education of Topeka, 347 U.S. 483 (1954)[300]

"Segregation of White and Negro children in the public schools of a State solely on the basis of race, pursuant to state laws permitting or requiring such segregation, denies to Negro children the equal protection of the laws guaranteed by the Fourteenth Amendment -- even though the physical facilities and other "tangible" factors of White and Negro schools may be equal"
Supreme Court Chief Justice Earl Warren, unanimous decision

There was a sea change in settler state popular culture on April 15, 1947, when young Jack Roosevelt Robinson, Army Second Lieutenant whose refusal to move to the back of a bus on Ft. Hood base in El Paso, TX eventually led to his discharge, broke the color barrier of America's other great pastime, major league baseball, by making his debut with the Brooklyn Dodgers.[301]

---

[300] *Brown v. Board*, 347 U.S. 483 (1954)

[301] Suzanne Bileyu, "1947: Jackie Robinson Integrates Baseball: Long before the Civil Rights Movement Took Center Stage, Baseball's Color Barrier Fell When Robinson Joined the Brooklyn Dodgers", *New York Times Upfront* Vol. 139, No.2 April 2, 2007. This is an excellent article that walks through the historical backdrop around Robinson's move, history in the National Negro Leagues, and the impact down the road. The story of Robinson's refusal to cow tow to that White nationalist bus driver is recounted by Charles E. Cobb, Jr. in This Non Violent Stuff'll Get You Killed: How Guns Made the Civil Rights Movement Possible (Durham: Duke University Press, 2014) pp. 91.

The decision in *Brown*, which Whites across the territories assumed would cause an insurgency of "uppity niggers" to start making all kinds of unseemly demands came down roughly two years after the Kenyan struggle for Independence began and was elevated through the formation of the Kenya Land Freedom Army (KLFA) (widely known as the Mau Mau) and escalated by legendary freedom fighter Dedan Kimathi wa Wacuiri, destined to help lead a true insurgency that not only demanded but fought, tooth and nail, for the liberation of its people. Please see Maina wa Kinyatti and his edited work, Kenya's Freedom Struggle: The Dedan Kimathi Papers (www.BookSurge.com, 2009).

This compilation of correspondence is primarily made up of field reports, Kimathi ordered from the Field Generals, so the true story of the masses of Kenyan people struggling for their liberation and the KLFA they formed could accurately and fully be told. The British colonizers, with the help of traitors, discovered the bulk of the correspondence, studied it, catalogued it, and then destroyed. This book claims to be some of the field notes that were salvaged, hidden among the people, and eventually smuggled out; also see Ngugi wa Thiongi an Micere Githae Mugo's play entitled the Trial of Dedan Kimathi (Portsmouth: Heinemann Educational Books, 1976).

His story is well known and has been excellently retold in television, film, and countless stories and articles. And congruently, another sea change in the law and settler state-society occurred roughly seven years later on May 16, 1954, when the Court decided *Brown v. Board* finding the following:

> Segregation of White and Negro children in the public schools of a State solely on the basis of race, pursuant to state laws permitting or requiring such segregation, denies to Negro children the equal protection of the laws guaranteed by the Fourteenth Amendment -- even though the physical facilities and other "tangible" factors of White and Negro schools may be equal. pp. 486-496.
>
> (a) The history of the Fourteenth Amendment is inconclusive as to its intended effect on public education. pp. 489-490.
>
> (b) The question presented in these cases must be determined not on the basis of conditions existing when the Fourteenth Amendment was adopted, but in the light of the full development of public education and its present place in American life throughout the Nation. pp. 492-493.
>
> (c) Where a State has undertaken to provide an opportunity for an education in its public schools, such an opportunity is a right which must be made available to all on equal terms. p. 493.
>
> (d) Segregation of children in public schools solely on the basis of race deprives children of the minority group of equal educational opportunities, even though the

physical facilities and other "tangible" factors may be equal. pp. 493-494.

(e) The "separate but equal" doctrine adopted in *Plessy v. Ferguson,* 163 U.S. 537, has no place in the field of public education. P. 495

There were numerous direct and indirect outcomes and manifestations with the changes in the law. This decision unleashed, beginning with the massive overturning of *Plessy v. Ferguson*. As Black folks in all areas and walks of life began to use equal protection arguments in a string of post-*Brown* cases, as is often the case, our use of this case is highlighted because of the equally massive backlash, especially as this watershed moment is viewed, incorrectly in my opinion, as the birth of the "Civil Rights Movement."[302]

---

[302]Michael Klarman reminds us that most Court commentators view this decision as the single most important decision published by the Court. From Jim Crow to Civil Rights, Op.Cit. 344. See Also, Henderson, L. (2004) "Brown v. Board of Education at 50: The Multiple Legacies for Policy and Administration" *Public Administration Review,* 64(3), 270-274. Retrieved July 28, 2020, from www.jstor.org/stable/3542592,

The crumbling of "American Apartheid" represented in this case spurred Africans in all walks of life forward with a new found confidence in the use of legal action as a weapon, one such string of incidents occurred in Delray Beach, FL and Tallahassee, FL. In late Fall 1954, an organization known as the Negro Civic League, formed by various Africans who were sometimes armed and prepared to defend themselves, who had been thwarted in earlier efforts to either get access to the City of Delray Beach's pool, access to the City's beach, or get their own pool, filed a suit against the City based on the precedent set in *Brown* and two students at Florida Agricultural & Mechanical University (FAMU, where I spent my freshman year in college) named Wilhelmina Jakes and Carrie Patterson, refused to leave the "Whites only section" of a Tallahassee, FL thereby setting off the Tallassee bus boycott. These tales are recounted in Derrick White's historical analysis of Black College Football and the life and times of legendary football coach Jake Gaither, entitled Blood, Sweat, and Tears: Jake Gaither, Florida A & M, and the History of Black College Football (Chapel Hill: University of North Carolina Press, 2019) pp. 101-03.

High School student from Little Rock Central punching a lynched African in effigy during a school integration protest. Little Rock, AR 1957 (Public Domain)

But even during the most seemingly magnanimous moments, the settler state seems always to manage to deliver a bucket of ice water to the burning embers that slowly flicker in the hearts and minds of Black folk still longing to be free; in this case, the Court decided to hear further arguments around the details of integration of public schools, timelines, and address plans for rules of implementation. Remedies for State non-compliance in the very next session, as the decision in *Brown,* left all of those issues still on the table.

The Court heard arguments in 1955, and its decision came to be known as *Brown II*; here, the court held that implementing programs to achieve desegregation in public schools belongs to the schools and states themselves. [303]

And after dumping that bucket of ice water on those hopeful observers watching the matter closely, the Court threw the empty bucket at them by remanding (the cases) to "the District Courts to take such proceedings and enter such orders and decrees

---

[303] 349 U.S. 294 1955

consistent with this opinion as are necessary and proper to admit to public schools on a racially nondiscriminatory basis with *all deliberate speed.*"[304]

This amorphous, wishy-washy non-direct, directive allowed the champions of Whiteness, White supremacy, and Anti-blackness to assert its war footing as we will soon see *below*. An early test of the *Brown* and *Brown II* decisions was the case of the Little Rock Nine mentioned *above* in regards to Eisenhower (34) using the *Posse Comitatus Act* exception to deploy the 101st Airborne Division to escort those African babies on their first day of school as protection from the hate-filled mob on September 24, 1957.[305]

Michael Klarman crystallizes the critical questions of the White lash when he asks: "To what extent did desegregation rulings mobilize Southern White resistance, radicalize White politics, and encourage violence, which ultimately produced a national backlash in favor of civil rights legislation? How much did *Brown* create concrete opportunities for violent confrontation, which influenced national opinion in favor of civil rights?"[306] In this steaming gumbo pot of fear, contempt, false pride, illiteracy, and poverty, you see Citizens Councils, the Klan, and White nationalist

---

[304]Ibid at 301.

[305] Please see note 241 *above*.

[306]Klarman, From Jim Crow to Civil Rights; Op.Cit. pp.364. Klarman aptly argues that *Brown* may have influenced the violent defenders of Whiteness and White nationalism more than it actually inspired the direct-action mobilizers that the movement has come to be known for. Also see The Southern Poverty's Law Center History of the Klan in its report "Ku Klux Klan: A History of Racism" report for a brief history of the second rise of the Klan in direct and deadly response the extended Civil Rights Movement. Find the link here: https://www.splcenter.org/20110228/ku-klux-klan-history-racism.

Sheriffs, Judges, Bankers ladled out into bowls of an ever-changing society. And the grumbling from those forces was growing louder and louder.[307]

One of the more prophetic Southern voices to predict the reaction from the affronted Whites, and the fate of Emmett Till and so many others sacrificed on the altars of White nationalism and White supremacy like him, was Mississippi Supreme Court Justice Thomas Pickens Brady in a book published shortly after *Brown* entitled Black Monday, as he projected that "the supercilious, glib young negro, who has sojourned in Chicago or New York, and who considers the council of his elders archaic, will perform an obscene act, or make an obscene remark or vile overture or assault upon some White girl."[308] Prophetic, indeed.

African-American boy looks on as angry Whites march to protest the admission of the "Little Rock Nine" to Central High School in Little Rock, AR. Photo Credits: John T. Bledsoe, Library of Congress Prints and Photographs Division (Public Domain)

---

[307]Ibid. 385-442, Klarman craftily analyzes the defiance of sheriffs operating under the "color of law" like Bull Connor, the lynching of Medgar Evers, the Freedom Summer lynchings, the 16th Street bombings, etc.

[308]Anderson, Devery Emmett Till: The Murder That Shocked the World and Propelled the Civil Rights Movement (Jackson: University Press of Mississippi, 2015) pp.25. We will explore the lynching of Emmett Till and this tragedies deep impact on the expanded Civil Rights Movement immediately below, the cite for Till's love of baseball can be found on pp.18.

Emmett Louis "Bo" Till
July 25, 1941
August 28, 1955 (Public Domain)

Emmett Till Lynching (1955)

"Oh yes, we're going to open the casket. No let the people see what I've seen. I want the world to see what I see, because there is no way I can tell the story and give them the visual picture of what my son looked like"
Mamie Carthan Till-Mobley, speaking to Chicago mortician Ahmed A. Rayner in 1955[309]

In April 1955, the African World family was abuzz with news from the Bandung Conference and the overall push for decolonization on the continent and across Asia.

---

[309]Ibid. pp.56. Till-Mobley was a brave woman and showed a lot of courage in defending her son, our ancestors were lynched for showing such courage; for instance Mary Conley was dragged out of her jail cell near Arlington, GA on October 4, 1916 after defending her son, Sam Conley, who was getting yelled at by his "bossman". The bossman, E.M. Melvin, was taken aback and slapped Mary Conley and "tussled" with her and Sam Conley killed him on the spot (as should have been expected). The family runs, the son escapes but Mary Conley got caught, jailed, and eventually lynched. Please see Ginzberg, <u>100 Years of Lynchings</u>, Op.Cit.pp.110. Sometimes our ancestors were spared, Please see Cobb Jr., Charles E. <u>This Nonviolent Stuff'll Get You Killed</u>; Op.Cit. pp.93-4 where he recounts stories of Lou Ella Townsend, mother of Fannie Lou Hamer-Mississippi luminary, and the ways she used to run lustful White nationalists clean off her property and never to be bothered by the same ones twice.

Still, that family was rocked just four short months later with the lynching of Emmet Louis "Bo or "BoBo" Till in Money, MS, on August 28, 1955.[310]

In the week before Till arrived in Mississippi, Black political activist Lamar "Ditney" Smith was lynched in front of the Lincoln County courthouse in Brookhaven, MS, while he was working a voter-registration drive. And just four months later, Rosa Louise McCauley Parks would make her courageous, yet organized stand against White oppression in the form of Apartheid busses in Montgomery, AL.[311] This is the tinder box atmosphere in which Mamie Carthan Till-Mobley sent her only child into.

Emmett Till was a mischievous fourteen-year-old when he convinced his mother to leave Chicago on a visit to Mississippi with his great uncle Moses "Mose" Wright

---

[310]Gerald Horne draws a brief connection between these two global phenomena in his treatment of Claude Barnett entitled The Rise and Fall of the Associated Negro press: Claude Barnett's Pan-African News and the Jim Crow Paradox, (Champagne: University of Illinois Board of Trustees, 2017) pp.146.

Horne describes in vivid detail how Barnett was able to weave his life, and life's work, into the lives of so many of our luminary ancestors and elders, from Booker T. Washington, Marcus Garvey, The DuBois', Paul Robeson, Zora Neale Hurston, Sekou Toure', Gamel Abdel Nasser, Ralph Bunche, Marian Anderson, and others; a lot of times these legends actually provided copy for the ANP news gathering service, sometimes Barnett developed personal relationships with them. The Bandung Conference took place between April 18th-24th, 1955 and had over 29 countries represented, where the attendees emerged with a 10-point plan which encouraged mutual corporation and assistance among the newly emerging, independent states.

[311]Anderson, Devery Emmett Till; Op.Cit. pp.25. Anderson offers an intricately detailed and thorough account of the events leading up to the lynching of Emmett Till and the role his tragic death played in electrifying the awareness of the sleeping Black giant, ready to resume the fight of resistance and advancement. See Also, the documentary The Untold Story of Emmett Till (2005) directed by Keith Beauchamp. It should also be noted that the defiant African spirit Till showed in the face of White oppression was also on full display as the nation of Ghana asserted its independence from its colonizing oppressor less than two years later Ghana achieved its independence from the United Kingdom on March 6, 1957.

with some of his cousins Wheeler Parker and Curtis Jones.[312] Till arrived in Money, MS on August 24, 1955, and after being warned about the ways of that world, was found dead, having been lynched four days later on August 28, 1955, and finally fished out of the Tallahatchie River on August 31, 1955[313].

The story, as recounted by the eyewitnesses, is that Till and his friend and cousins were dropped off at a general store, which served mostly Black locals in the Money business district. The Bryant family operated this store, and it was here that Till had his initial encounter with his accuser, twenty-one-year-old Carolyn Bryant.[314]

The remains of Bryant's Grocery and (Meat) Market, the store that Emmett Till walked into in Money, Mississippi, and crossed paths with Carolyn Bryant. WhisperToMe / Public domain

Till was egged on by one of the group of boys to go and flirt with the young, White Woman that worked the cash register. Till, being a rambunctious teenager (probably not much unlike other teenagers, or pre-teens like Tamir Rice or Trayvon Martin) entered the store and, depending on whom you believe, touched Bryant's hand as he was paying for a purchase, left the store and said "bye" or "bye, ma'am," and then

---

[312]Ibid. pp. 11-3, 18-9. Till's father Louis had been lynched by military law while serving in the U.S. Army in Italy for "willful misconduct", Till moved around a bit in his childhood but had settled in Chicago in the time before his lynching, also Till had been able to manage a bout with Polio.
[313]A picture of that murky graveyard adorns the cover of this book.

[314]Ibid. 24-31, Bryant apparently admitted to embellishing her story at the behest of family members and Anderson recounts this on pp.30-1.

sealed his fate as he is "wolf-whistled" at Bryant in public as she subsequently left the store.[315]

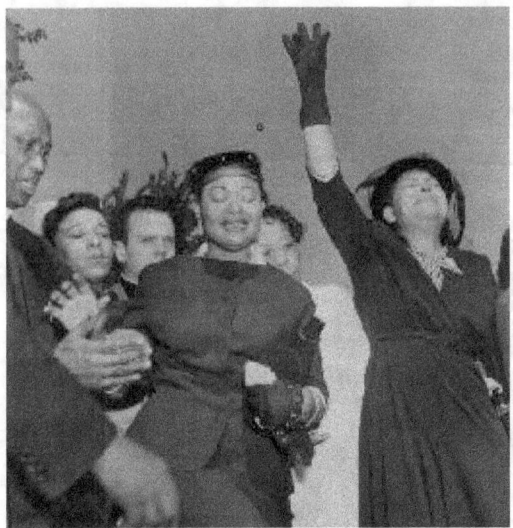

Mamie Elizabeth Till-Mobley, September 6, 1955
Smithsonian Institution Accession No. 2013.92 NMAAHC-2013_92_003
(Public Domain).

Years later, Bryant would admit that her husband and in-laws coerced her to come up with a story, and she exaggerated parts of her testimony.

Saturday, August 27, 1955, Roy Bryant, Carolyn Bryant's husband, his half-brother J.W. Milam, and a Black assailant, Leroy "Too Tight" Collins, showed up at Uncle Mose's house to get the boy who "did that smart talk up at Money."[316] The lynch mob barged into the home and made their way to the back of the house until they

---

[315] Ibid. 32-3.
[316] Ibid. pp.36.

found Till, awoke him out of his sleep, and marched him straight out of the house and to a waiting vehicle.[317]

The family honestly expected Till to be returned after receiving a "whooping" and likely being scared to death, none of them had any clue that Till was on his way to meet his death.[318] The facts played out that Till was taken to the Sheridan Plantation, on J.W. Milam's property, and was brutalized, castrated, had his teeth knocked out, his eyes almost poked out, his tongue pushed back in his skull, an ear lopped off, beaten to a pulp, and then shot. His body was found in the Tallahatchie strapped to a seventy-pound cotton gin with barbed wire, by seventeen-year-old Robert Hodges, who just so happened to be out fishing a few days later.[319]

Uncle Mose identified the body, Bryant and Milam had offered partial confessions and were released. Till's body was shipped back to Chicago amid a media whirlwind, including the iconic pictures splashed across the pages of Black print media throughout the African World family and the rest of the globe.[320]

Roy Bryant and J.W. Milam were eventually acquitted for the murder and no-billed on the kidnapping on September 23, 1955, after readily confessing to the sheriff.[321] Protected by double jeopardy, they admitted to the lynching as being the result of a drunken rage after strenuous negotiation and multiple offers of payment, in an interview with *Look* magazine published in an article on January 10, 1956, written by

---

[317] Ibid. pp. 35-8.
[318] Ibid. pp.36-7, the searing image of Uncle Mose just standing on his porch staring off into the darkness is heart breaking. The family begged Bryant and Milam just to go punish Till, they even offered to pay them for "damages".

[319] Ibid. pp. 37-45.

[320] Ibid. pp.46-56.

[321] A No-Bill verdict means that the Grand Jury refused to issue an indictment in a case.

William Bradford Huie. The best part of the article is the show of bravery and defiance; it displays young Till with until the very end; Bryant and Milam said they just meant to whip the child (like he was back in bondage), but "they were drunk and got out of hand."[322] Till had that defiant African spirit we see throughout this work.[323]

Deisenbe / CC BY-SA (https://creativecommons.org/licenses/by-sa/4.0)
Sign identifying the site of J.W. Milam's farm near Glendora Gin, MS.

After some great work and contributions from countless sources, the Emmett Till lynching case was reopened by the U.S. Department of Justice and was reportedly

---

[322]Ibid. 224-37, There are a lot of questions around the fact that these "confessions" were paid for and Anderson does a tremendous job sorting through the all the details, politics, infighting, etc. The archived copy of the article can be found on the Public Broadcasting Services link posted at: https://www.pbs.org/wgbh/americanexperience/features/till-killers-confession/. Carolyn Bryant, who avoided prosecution early on had long been suspected and accused of lying, ultimately admitted to exaggerating her tale as well, see Note 162 *above*.

[323]In 2006, the Tallahatchie County, MS Board of Supervisors, led by Jerome G. Little the first Black president of the Board, launched the Emmet till Memorial Commission. In 2007, the EMTC offered a formal public apology to the Till family and its efforts eventually led the opening of the Emmett Till Interpretive Center.

Here recently, the EMIC has had to replace the sign commemorating the lynching at the scene of the crime with a new bulletproof sign as the older ones have become frequent shooting targets of White nationalists and others. The ETIC website is located at this link: https://www.emmett-till.org/visit-the-museum; please see Levenson, Eric "Emmett Till Memorial sign In Mississippi Now Protected By Bullet Proof Glass" *CNN* October 20, 2019 located here: https://www.cnn.com/2019/10/20/us/emmett-till-memorial-bulletproof-trnd/index.html.

nearing completion in the spring of 2020. This case and the fact that something so gruesome and wicked could happen to a mere fourteen-year-old kid captured the imagination of observers across the world, but especially Africans in this part of the Diaspora who had become so emboldened in the years after *Brown*.[324]

But just as we saw with the lynching of Tamir Rice in 2014, in the immortal words of that Bay Area poet Earl Stevens (E-40), "anybody can get it," and as we will see shortly, babies often get caught up in the madness.[325]

---

[324]Five years later, on February 1, 1960 four students from the Historically Black land-grant institution, North Carolina Agricultural and Technical College (A&T) jump started another high-water mark when they refused to move from a "Whites only" lunch counter at a F.W. Woolworth store in downtown Greensboro, NC. Clayborne Carson makes the historical connection between the Woolworth Sit-in and the activation of the student "shock troops" into the epic battle for African liberation in America in the 60's; Carson In Struggle; pp.9; and again for a meticulously detailed analysis of the role HBCU's played in activating other shock troops, see generally A&T's own, Jelani Favors and his book Shelter in a Time of Storm.

[325]Twelve-year old Tamir Rice was lynched in the Cleveland, OH streets just before Thanksgiving Day on November 22, 2014 by Cleveland Police Department (CPD) pattleroller Timothy Loehmann. Rice was near a park playing with a toy gun, within seconds of arriving on the scene Loehmann gunned him down, and it was later discovered that the shooter had several disciplinary actions and complaints from other law enforcement jobs and should not have been allowed to "patrol" the streets of Cleveland at all and certainly not armed with a gun and a badge. Please see Eric Heiseg, "Tamir Rice Shooting: A Breakdown of the Events that lead to the 12 year Old's Death", *Cleveland.com* January 13, 2017.

Stevens, 2003 track #9

16th Street Church Bombing (1963)

"I felt numb. What am I supposed to do now? Do churches get bombed and children get killed, and then we all go on living life as usual? Is this just another day in the lives of Black people in Birmingham? Days passed, then weeks, and we simply walked through our same routines—predictable schedules disturbed only briefly that Sunday morning. No one asked me "Carolyn, are you okay?" "Carolyn, do you miss your friends?" "Carolyn, are you afraid" "Do you want to talk about what happened at church?" Nothing was said—not at home and not at school".

Carolyn Maul Mckinstry, a survivor of the 16th Street Church bombing in the aftermath of losing her friends, including her best friend in 1963

Addie Mae Collins (14), Carole Robertson (14), Cynthia Wesley (14), and Carol Denise McNair (11) Photo Credits: The Southern Poverty Law Center

The record of "non-violence" as both a deeply committed way of life and tactical strategy adopted, adapted, and deployed by civil rights organizations throughout the 1950s and 1960s is told and retold through the tales of organizations like the Southern Christian Leadership Conference (SCLC), the Student Non-Violent Coordinating Committee (SNCC), the Congress of Racial Equality (CORE), and the NAACP and their battalions of organizers, volunteers, and leaders. Still, there were groups within those organizations, and outside of those organizations that felt

African people had the right to protect themselves in the face of naked *American Terrorism.*[326]

One such group was the local Monroe, Union County, NC chapter of the NAACP, in 1961 led by U.S. Marine Corps vet Robert F. Williams.[327] The very quick story is that while that NAACP chapter was engaging in direct action to integrate the local swimming pool or force the authorities to build a new, all-black pool; members of the group were fired upon by members of the Klan and had the audacity (and guns) to stand their ground. Williams and his group did not subscribe to the non-violent philosophy and organized to defend themselves and had armed confrontations with Whites as far back as 1957.[328] This latest skirmish was the last straw for the authorities. Williams ultimately ended up on the Federal Bureau of Investigation's "Most Wanted List" and quickly made his way to Cuba with his family in tow.[329]

This case is shown to highlight some of the stark realities African people faced in that era. Whether they chose to defend themselves with equal force or turn the other cheek, the brutality they were met with was one of the few constants they knew and could consistently count on.

---

[326] Volumes has been written on the Civil Rights Movement, its ebbs and flows and would have various leaders and phases; the entire list itself would be far too many to exhaust here but the key players involved in the Birmingham bombing and the Freedom Summer lynchings will be discussed within the context of those incidents.

[327] Williams recounts this story in his account of the incident in question can be found in Negroes With Guns (Mansfield Center: Martino Publishing, 2013 ed.) originally broadcast as an interview while Williams was exiled in Cuba on May 31, 1962. This book is a compilation from that interview and other interviews and articles Williams had granted and written throughout 1962.

[328] Ibid. pp.47-58.

[329] Ibid.

This was painfully, tearfully, traumatically brought to the forefront of their collective memory on September 16, 1963. Less than three weeks after the historic 1963 March on Washington, the world thought America was building a shining new bridge of humanity, racial conciliation, and peace, Africans across the world would awake that morning to see that so-called bridge reduced to a smoldering heap of hate, bricks, window glass, and dead babies. All of this from a bomb planted by Klan cowards Robert Edward Chambliss, Thomas Edwin Blanton, Bobby Frank Cherry, and Herman Frank Cash.[330]

Angels turned ancestors, Addie Mae Collins (14), Carole Robertson (14), Cynthia Wesley (14), and Carol Denise McNair (11), were roughly all the same age as Emmett Till (save one) when they got lynched, and this bitterly traumatic tale starts as innocently as Till's did.

16th Street Baptist Church, Birmingham Civil Rights Institute, Birmingham, Alabama. Credit: The George F. Landegger Collection of Alabama Photographs in Carol M. Highsmith's America, Library of Congress, Prints and Photographs Division [LC-DIG-highsm-050.

---

[330]This deeply traumatic event has been written about and recorded numerous times over the last fifty plus years, I will heavily rely on the autobiographical account of survivor, Carolyn Maul McKinstry entitled While The World Watched (Carol Stream: Tyndale House Publishers, 2011).

McKistry was not only a precocious fourteen-year-old, but she was best friends with Cynthia Wesley. Although traumatized, young McKistry was angry too; angry enough to defy her drill-sergeant father and join the first of what came to be known as the "Children's March" on May 3, 1963. A picture of her and her defiant courage was captured by Civil Rights photographer Charles Moore and is in his book entitled, Powerful Day: The Civil Rights Photography of Charles Moore.[331] Those young people faced the snarling attack dogs and high powered hoses from deputies on orders from snarling racist, Sherriff Eugene "Bull" Connor.[332]

The aftermath of this lynching was far more impactful than the terrorist act itself. The FBI conducted and concluded an investigation that wrapped up in 1965 without a single indictment. The first formal arrest of any of those Klansmen did not occur until "Dynamite" Bob Chambliss was convicted of the murder of eleven-year-old Carol Denise McNair, the very youngest victim. Between the years of 2001 and 2002, current (at the time of drafting this), U.S. Senator Doug Jones (D-AL) successfully prosecuted Thomas Edwin Blanton, Jr. and Bobby Cherry. The last of the despicable cowards, Herman Cash, died in 1994 and never was charged for alleged involvement in the deadly bombing.[333]

---

[331] Ibid. 124-30. McKinstry is a hero and took part in the very first organizational meeting for what came to be known as the "Children's March" and was held at the church, which was personally attended by Martin Luther King, Jr., Ralph Abernathy, Jessie L. Jackson, Sr., and Andrew Young; she also stared down "Eugene "Bull" Conner at the march and was spared an attack from the snarling dogs but did get blasted and injured from a high-powered firehose. All told, over 2,500 people got arrested because of their march participation with over 2,000 of them being children, even as young as four years old.

The really stinging part of the saga is that in 2009, the City of Birmingham merely issued "pardons" for the misdemeanors and wiped away the fines; those elders and ancestors clearly should have their records totally expunged. Mckistry's picture, according to her, is on pg. 99 of Moore's book and she describes her reunion with Moore in 1996 on a visit he made to Birmingham, where he presented her with an autographed copy of the book.

[332] Ibid.

[333] Ibid. 198-228.

In the short run, Connor lost his job after seven terms as county sheriff. King and the SCLC were able to flood American homes with the TV images of kids singing and walking the streets while vicious and snarling four-legged and two-legged dogs brutally attacked them and the powered water hoses and Billy-clubs were unleased.

For Martin Luther King, Jr. and the SCLC, this was precisely the outcome they gambled on and was able to use put the screws to Kennedy (35) and push for federal civil rights legislation, which we will discuss below. It was timely as this was just six months before Kennedy got gunned down on the streets of downtown Dallas, TX, later, that fall.[334]

All the killing in 1963 would tragically spill over into 1964, and one of the bloodiest episodes of that year in what came to be known as the "Freedom Summer Lynchings" served as yet another turning point in the Civil Rights Movement.

FBI Special Agent In-Charge, A. Rosen's request for an FBI investigation of the Chicago cop lynching of Fred Hampton and Mark Clark on December 4, 1969.

---

[334]John F. Kennedy was lynched by gunshot on November 22, 1963 by Lee Harvey Oswald even though this murder has been the subject of conspiracy theories for the fifty plus years since it went down.

Ella Josephine Baker, 1964 (Public Domain)

Young African Man guarding a campaign sign during the 1966 Countywide elections, Lowndes County, AL (Public Domain)

Freedom Summers Lynchings (1964)

"You have been slaves too long. We can help you help yourselves. Meet us here, so we can train you to qualify to vote."
Mickey Schwerner, Memorial Day 1964 recruiting folks at the Mount Zion Methodist Church

Michael Schwerner, James Chaney, and Andrew Goodman; 1964 (Public Domain)

The long struggle against the lynching of African people in American history has seen its fair share of White allies, like the public Abolitionists who gave lofty speeches and ran newspapers, the secret Abolitionists who would hide escaped enslaved ancestors from the catchers and pattlerollers, the benevolent Whites who spared James Cameron, numerous sheriffs and deputies like the one who saved Dick Rowland, or like the White women who petitioned for Lige Lane not to receive a death sentence after being accused of the murder of another White woman in Clinch County, GA, in 1913; the ranks of White allies even included, at one-time a "First Lady."[335]

The same has to be said of Freedom Summer COFO organizer Andrew Goodman and Congress of Racial Equality (CORE) organizers Michael Schwerner and James

---

[335] Ginzburg, <u>100 Years of Lynching</u>; pp. 88 originally published in the *Birmingham News* on September 4, 1913; Kendi notes that Eleanor Roosevelt, wife of Franklin Delano Roosevelt (32), was a public supporter of the passage of Anti-Lynching legislation, she was a fan of Black popular culture, and a friend of world renowned school teacher and activist Mary McCleod Bethune and the aforementioned Walter White; see Kendi <u>Stamped from the Very Beginning</u> Op.Cit. pp.338.

Cheney; the lynching of the young White men Schwerner and Goodman served as turning points in the push for new Civil Rights legislation which had been the goal of organizations since before the 1963 March on Washington.[336]

Throughout the history of *American Terrorism,* it was often perilous for Whites to befriend Blacks, especially when it came to White women and Black men. Such was the case of Joan Rivers, a nineteen-year-old White woman, in 1934 Newton, TX. Young Ms. Rivers spent a full week in the county jail on a vagrancy charge. Her boyfriend, twenty-year-old John Criggs, had been jailed on the serious charge of "associating" with a White woman; this could not stand. As local Sheriff T. S. Hughes ordered deputies to get Criggs out of town, the mob gathered up strength and intercepted the squad car about twenty-seven miles across the city limit. The heavily armed mob opened the door to the chagrin of the deputies and fastened a

---

[336] Mitchell, Don Freedom Summer Murders (New York: Scholastic Press, 2014) pp. 29-32. Mitchell offers an easy to read yet fairly detailed history of the lynching of the three CORE organizers that arguably led to the future passage of the Civil Rights Act of 1964; see also Charles Rivers Editors, The Mississippi Burning Case: The History and Legacy of the Freedom Summer Murders at the Height of the Civil Rights Movement (San Bernardino: Charles Rivers Editors, 2020).

This short retelling of the events is important for some of the images it offers. Clayborne Carson, in his definitive history of SNCC, highlights the organic tension between the young African organizers on the ground and the White organizers who were eventually parachuted in, because as Carson notes "the ambivalence of black staff members working with White volunteers was complicated by the staff's awareness that that only further violence—against the volunteers rather than black Mississippians-would prompt forceful federal intervention" Please Carson, Clayborne, In Struggle (Cambridge: Harvard University Press, 1995), pp. 114.

This idea was bolstered by the fact that SNCC researchers had highlighted "over 150 incidents of violence and intimidation" of Black organizers in Mississippi since SNCC began which did not garner so much as a stern look from the feds. Carson also briefly addresses the Mississippi Case here as well. Charles Cobb, Jr. makes the point that this lynching was likely a motivating factor for Louisiana CORE becoming tighter and tighter with the Deacons for Defense; please see Cobb Jr., Charles This Non Violent Stuff'll Get you Killed; Op.Cit. pp. 214.

noose around the victim's neck, dragged him out by the noose. He was later found strung up and shot full of holes.[337]

White professionals, who also happened to be allies, were indeed targets as well. Acclaimed "civil rights" lawyer Clarence Darrow was run off a podium in Mobile, AL, during a speaking engagement; the mob sent word after he hightailed it out of the City that it would be in his best interest to hop the train back to Chicago by noon the next day.[338]

Darrow's unforgivable crime, he dared speak to Whites in one session and Africans in another, preaching a message of mutual tolerance, temperance, and understanding and condemning lynchings and mob activity; it appears those lofty words fell on deaf ears.[339] Again, White allies took on tremendous risk throughout this often bloody history.

The risk for the three lynched organizers began in the early morning hours of June 17, 1964, when the "sixty-five-year-old" Mount Zion Methodist Church was set ablaze near Philadelphia, MS.[340] Word of this vicious act triggered Schwerner, who had just spoken there a few weeks earlier and pleaded with the congregation about using the location as a *Freedom Summer School* focusing on training Black folk to prepare for the literacy test they would need to pass to qualify to register to vote. After learning of the church burning, Schwerner decided to leave a Freedom Summer

---

[337]Ginzburg, Ralph <u>100 Years of Lynching</u>; Op.Cit. pp. 217-18. The details of the ages of the two were sketchy as so ages have them older, and it was not clear whether they worked together or were college classmates.

[338]Ginzburg, Ralph, 100 Years of <u>Lynching</u>; Op.Cit. pp.178-79.

[339] Ibid.

[340] Mitchell, Don <u>Freedom Summer Murders</u>; Op.Cit. pp. 18.

training up in Oxford, OH, and travel back to Longdale, MS, to investigate; fatefully, he brought MS native James Cheney and new organizer Andrew Goodman on the roughly six-hundred sixty-three-mile long trek.[341]

The White Knights of the Ku Klux Klan formed in 1963 and a year later became the most dominant and lethal Klan faction in the state, boasting over 5,000 members.[342] The terror cell was responsible for the lynching. It was significantly aided by receiving an Agent X, possibly R.L. Bolden, future vice president of the Mississippi NAACP, who provided the Mississippi Sovereignty Commission minute details about this particular mission down to the make, model, and license plate number of the vehicle the organizers would be driving down to Neshoba County, a 1963 Blue Ford Fairlane station wagon, license plate number: H25503.[343]

---

[341] Ibid. pp. 11. Freedom Summer was a massive voter registration effort spearheaded by the Council of Federated Organizations (COFO) a coalition of civil rights organizations operating in Mississippi and occurred in 1964. This lynching went down in Neshoba County, MS which was oddly enough the home of WWII vet Buford Posey, the first White person to join the NAACP in Mississippi. Charles Rivers Editors lists sections of the problems on the literacy tests where Blacks are asked to cite clause of the MS constitution, right a "reasonable interpretation" of the above cited section, and to set a statements explaining the duties and obligations of a citizen under a constitutional form of government; which would be virtually impossible for most Mississippians in general at that time; please see Charles Rivers Editors The Mississippi Burning Case, Op.Cit. The meeting took place at the then Western College for Women, a leading seminary for women, now it's called the Western Campus of the University of Miami, still located in Oxford, OH.; see also Don Bowers, Spies of Mississippi; Op. Cit. pp.85.

[342] Ibid.

[343] Ibid. pp. 89-90. Some Agent X's worked for the Day Detective Agency, one of the main contractors for the Mississippi Soverignty Committee, and convinced COFO to hire him onto staff as a seasoned MS organizer so he could train the Freedom Summer organizers. An Agent X wound up sending in a two-thousand-page report with intimate details about the plans for Freedom Summer, possible locations for Freedom Summer schools, voter registration plans with goals on running slates of candidates, even congressional candidates, etc. The Commission and their Citizen Council and Klan cohorts would put this information to deadly use.

The boys made it to Meridian, MS, okay on the morning of June 21, 1964, they even had a chance to service the COFO station wagon they drove down in, and Schwerner got a haircut while in town.[344] The trio told folk in town that they should be back by 4:00 p.m., but by 10:00 pm they hadn't shown back, and the local newscasts were reporting them missing.[345]

---

[344] Cobb Jr., Charles This Nonviolent Stuff'll Get you Killed; Op.Cit. pp. 214. Here Cobb notes that two new station wagons had been donated to CORE that summer for use by COFO, one for Louisiana and the one for Mississippi was driven by the lynched organizers. The Congress on Racial Equality (CORE) was
[345] Mitchell, Don Freedom Summer Murders; Op.Cit. pp. 27.

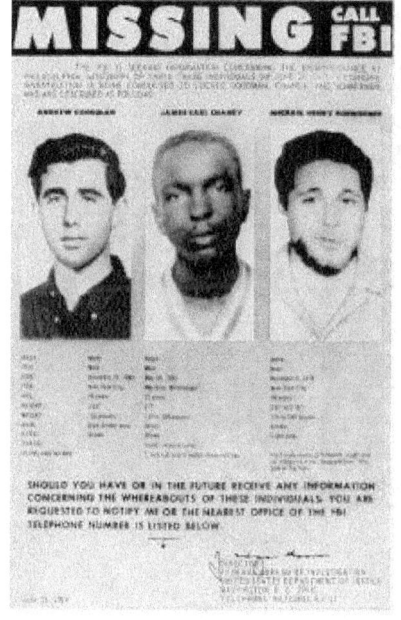

FBI Missing Poster seeking information on the COFO organizers, July 1964. Once the Feds posted the $25,000 reward, the tips started rolling in. (Public Domain)

KKK Lynch Mob Mugshots, December 10, 1964 (Public Domain)

Undated Klu Klux Klan Cross Burning, Phot Credits: FBI Website (Public Domain)

The Blue Ford Fairlaine COFO station wagon, license plate no. H25503. June 23, 1964, the COFO Station wagon is found in a creek near Bogue Chitto swamp in Neshoba County, MS (Public Domain).

Multiple Klansmen were involved in the lynching, including Neshoba County Sheriff Lawrence A. Rainey, Rev. Edgar Ray Killen, Horace Doyle Barnett, Olen Burrage, James Jordan, and Samuel Bowers, the Grand Dragon of the White Knights of the Ku Klux Klan.[346] The organizers were picked up by sheriff's deputies and sitting in the country jail by 5:30 pm. A plan had been hatched to murder and bury the trio upon their release from jail, and that was precisely what happened. Deputy Cecil Price was key to the plot as he was the one who let the boys out of jail and convinced them that he would safely escort them out of Neshoba County in the middle of the night.[347]

Price followed the organizers, and once he saw the signal, he pulled the boys over, ordered them to his car, and let the phalanx overtake them on that dark, country

---

[346] Ibid. 29-31. The FBI was able to get confessions from participants after the fact, and James Jordan was the one who laid out the "planning and organizing role" Rev. Killen played in the lynching. It was long understood that the Sheriff and the Deputy Sheriff were in the Klan.
[347] Ibid. pp.30

road. While the lynchers disputed the exact details of who pulled which trigger, the gist of the story is that the boys were dragged out of Price's car "one by one starting with the *nigger lovers* first leaving the *nigger* last," according to Barnette's eye witness testimony.[348]

The group was then led by Olen Burrage, to a damn on his property called Old Jolly Farm, where a bulldozer was waiting to bury the bodies; once that deed was done, Burrage torched the station wagon.[349] Once the word got out, luminaries like James Farmer, George Raymond, Dick Gregory, and recently transitioned John Lewis met in Meridian, MS, to get to the bottom of the case.[350]

Rita Schwerner led a media onslaught to find out what happened to her husband and the others and eventually got in touch with President Lyndon B. Johnson (36). The Federal Bureau of Investigation (FBI) launched an investigation into the disappearance of the organizers and named the case "Mississippi Burning" or "MIBURN."[351]

A massive search party was conducted, and the station wagon located near the Boggo Chitto swamp in Philadelphia, MS, but no bodies were found.[352] Not until August 4, 1964.

---

[348] Ibid. pp.31-3

[349] Ibid. pp.32-3

[350] Ibid. pp.97. Farmer was the head of CORE, Raymond was CORE's MS field secretary, Baba Dick was a well-known activist and entertainer in the mold of Paul Robeson and Harry Belafonte, Jr. And Congressman John Lewis (D-GA) made his transition on July 17, 2020. Dr. King and a contingent of the SCLC made it over to Neshoba County in July 1964.
[351] Ibid. pp.102-3. See also pp. 106.

[352] Ibid.

The bodies of Chaney, Goodman, and Schwerner, August 4, 1964 (Public Domain)

That was the day the organizers' bodies were found after massive interest in New York City, as Schwerner and Goodman were from the "City" not to mention they were young White men who got lynched working in the interest of African people and the FBI's "Missing" posters became iconic pictures of this stage of the Civil Rights Movement.[353] And that poster turned out to be critical, as the FBI finally got tips on where the bodies were located after a $30,000 reward were attached to the search and an anonymous caller finally gave up the information.[354]

Federal charges were eventually brought against multiple defendants—October 7, 1967, *United States v. Cecil Price et al.*, in the federal courthouse in Meridian, MS presided over by staunch anti-Civil Rights jurist William Harold Cox. An all-White jury was empaneled and oversaw a dramatic trial, which ended in the first-ever convictions in Mississippi for the lynchings of any Civil Rights organizers. Among

---

[353]Ibid. pp.99-101. The FBI missing posted is embedded in this work.

[354]This tidbit was noted in the Charles Rivers Editors pamphlet, The Mississippi Burning Case, no pp. listed.

the guilty were Deputy Cecil Price, Imperial Wizard Samuel Bowers, Billy Wayne Posey, Horace Barnette, Jimmy Arledge, and Jimmy Snowden; Rev. Edgar Ray Killen and Sheriff Rainey were no-billed, which meant they free to be retried; sentences for the mob ranged from three to ten years and the first of which started serving their sentences in 1970.[355]

Rev. Killen was retried for the Mississippi Burning lynchings on June 13, 2005, and was eventually convicted on three charges of manslaughter forty-one years to the day of the lynchings, June 21, 2005, and he got a sixty-year sentence—twenty years for each organizer to run consecutively.[356]

As noted earlier, the lynching of Michael Henry Schwerner, James Earl Chaney, and Andrew Goodman was tragically instrumental in the passage of the *Civil Rights Act of 1964* and the *Voting Rights Act of 1965*.[357]

---

[355]Ibid. pp. 142-47. All those defendants were out of prison by 1977. Please also *United States v. Cecil Price*, et. al 383 U.S. 787 (1966)

[356]Ibid. 169-175.

[357]Ibid. Charles Cobb, Jr. and Akinyele Umoja resoundingly make the point that the Freedom Movement as it played out in Mississippi however was driven by and protected by armed Africans in Mississippi who became legends, take this poem written about farmer Hartman Turnbow by a young Freedom School participant Lorenzo Wesley for example "I know a man who has no foe, His name is Mr. Turnbow, He is about five feet six, Every time you see him he has a gun or a brick, If you want to keep your head, Then you better not come tipping around his bead, When he talks to you, His fingers talk too, Some people might not understand, But Mr. Turnbow is a good old man"; see Umoja's <u>They Will Shoot Back</u>; Op.Cit. pp. 104-05.

Martin Luther King, Jr. and Lyndon Baines Johnson (36) at the signing of the Civil Rights Act of 1964, The White House, Washington, D.C. (Public Domain)

Civil Rights Act of 1964[358]

The first of the *Civil Rights Acts* passed in the immediate aftermath of the 16th Street Church Bombing, the 1963 March on Washington, and the Freedom Summer Lynchings, this next installment of the settler state generational shell game prohibits discrimination based on race, color, religion, sex, and national origin by federal and state governments as well as some public places. The Act has been amended to include protections for disability status, age, and, most recently, sexual orientation protections.[359] The Act is broken down as follows:

Title I-Voting Rights
Title II-Public Accommodations
Title III-Desegregation of Public Facilities
Title IV-Desegregation of Public Education
Title V-Commission on Civil Rights

---

[358] P.L. 88-352 (1964)
[359] Please see this link to a report posted by the U.S. Department of Justice, Civil Rights Division, Disability Rights Section discussing the added protections for the disabled to the VRA of 1965; you can find the report here: https://www.ada.gov/ada_voting/ada_voting_ta.htm.

Title VI-Nondiscrimination in Federally Assisted Programs
Title VII-Equal Employment Opportunity
Title VIII-Registration and Voting Statistics
Title IX-Community Relations Service
Title X-Miscellaneous

Picking up where the *Civil Rights Act of 1964* left off, the *Voting Rights Act of 1965* delivered the Franchise to African people in this South for the first time since the end of Reconstruction.

Voting Rights Act of 1965[360]

Prohibits racial discrimination in voting.
1. Provisions
    1.1. General provisions
        1.1.1. General prohibition of discriminatory voting laws
        1.1.2. Specific prohibitions
        1.1.3. Bail-in
    1.2. Special provisions
        1.2.1. Coverage formula
        1.2.2. Preclearance requirement
        1.2.3. Federal examiners and observers
        1.2.4. Bailout
        1.2.5. Bilingual election requirements
2. Impact
3. Constitutionality
    3.1. Voter eligibility provisions
    3.2. Section 2 results test
    3.3. Coverage formula and preclearance
    3.4. Racial gerrymandering

But just like we saw in *Brown* and *Brown II*, whenever African people in this country (collectively speaking) turn to the law to spark some embers within their souls, the Court hovers above the scene like some rogue prankster with that bucket of ice water

---

[360]P.L. 89-110 (1965)

of theirs. In this case, the ice water meant to cool the heels of the fired-up Black masses came down in the razor-thin *Holder v. Shelby County* decision.[361]

This case essentially addressed whether the covered electoral districts, like Shelby County, Alabama, still had to seek permission from the U.S. Department of Justice or D.C. District Court before implementing changes to "election laws and procedures." In the 5-4, published by Chief Justice John G. Roberts, Jr., the Court found the sections of the 1965 Voting Rights Act implicated in this scheme, namely Section 4, to be unconstitutional as the majority found that neither constraints that the Section of the Act imposed on the covered districts, those that had a history of using state action to suppress Black participation in the electoral process, nor the need for federal review was needed any longer in the post-racial Shangri La.[362]

The problem with this judicial short-sightedness almost immediately reared its ugly head in the closely contested gubernatorial races in Florida and Georgia in 2018, especially in Georgia, where Gov. Brian P. Kemp had been credibly accused of "rigging" that election in his own favor and capacity as Georgia Secretary of State in charge of "running" the overall election for office while simultaneously campaigning for that very same office.[363]

That was a shameful turn of events.

---

[361] 570 U.S. 579 (2013)
[362] Ibid.
[363] Please see Kushbu Sha in an article entitled "Textbook Voter Suppression: A Battle Years in the Making" *The Guardian* November 10, 2018 located here: https://www.theguardian.com/us-news/2018/nov/10/georgia-election-recount-stacey-abrams-brian-kemp to get a sense of the accusations, allegations, and ultimately litigation which was filed in this matter.

Civil Rights Act of 1968[364]

Provides for the applicability of the certain parts of the Bill of Rights to Indigenous Nations within U.S. borders, prohibits discrimination in housing based on race, color, religion, sex, and national origin. And like the *Civil Rights Act of 1964, above*, this Act has been amended to include protections for disability, age, and sexual orientation.[365]

1. Parts
    1.1. Title I: Hate crimes
    1.2. Title II–VII: Indian Civil Rights Act
    1.3. Title VIII–IX: Fair Housing Act
    1.4. Title X: Anti-Riot Act
2. Titles
    2.1. Title I—Interference with Federally Protected Activities
    2.2. Title II—Rights of Indians
    2.3. Title III—Model Code Governing Courts of Indian Offenses
    2.4. Title IV—Jurisdiction Over Criminal and Civil Actions
    2.5. Title V—Offenses Within Indian Country
    2.6. Title VI—Employment of Legal Counsel
    2.7. Title VII—Materials Relating to Constitutional Rights of Indians
    2.8. Title VIII—Fair Housing
    2.9. Title IX—Prevention of Intimidation in Fair Housing Cases
    2.10. Title X—Civil Obedience

---

[364]P.L. 909-284 (1968)

[365]Schill, Michael H and Samantha Friedman, "The Fair Housing Act of 1988: The First Decade", Cityscape: A Journal of Policy Development and Research, Vol.4, No.3 (1999). This is journal publication of the U.S. Department of Housing and Urban Development-Office of Policy Development and Research.

The arrest of a young African man during the Watts Riots, August 12, 1965.
New York World-Telegram / Public domain

The legendary Billie Holiday (born Eleanora Fagan) and her beloved Boxer Mister
Ms. Holiday's 1939 rendition of the song "Strange Fruit," the quintessential Anti-lynching anthem, was later named song of the twentieth century by Time Magazine in 1999.
Portrait of Billie Holiday and Mister, Downbeat(?), New York, N.Y., ca. June 1946
William P. Gottlieb Collection, Library of Congress (Public Domain)

The Lynchings of Fred Hampton and Mark Clark (1969)

"If you don't want no revolutionary act, I don't want myself on your mind"
Fred Hampton, IL Chairman of the Black Panther Party for Self Defense

While the Klan led the physical lynch mobs of the South during the mid-twentieth century, law enforcement assumed the position of lynch mob leaders in other parts of the settler state. Bruce Lee's 1973 classic film *Enter the Dragon* captures the essence of this dynamic brilliantly during a scene involving martial arts legend Jim Kelly.[366]

In the scene called "Williams v. the Cops," Williams (played by Kelly) is walking alone in a dark alley and accosted by racist cops (pattlerollers). After rousting Kelly and checking his papers, the cops find a ticket to Hong Kong via Hawaii. One of the jealous cops says, "Hey, this jig's got a passport," and before the cops can assault Williams, he quickly (and easily) dispatches them and drives off in the cop car. This scene is just a minute long, but it is one of the most powerful points in the film. And it is a perfect example of how *American Terrorism* plays itself out on these American streets every day. An innocent Black man, minding his own business and in his own space, encounters some random White person who refuses to mind their own business. Things worked out beautifully for Williams in that situation.

Hollywood wrote the perfect script for Jim Kelly, John Saxon, and Bruce Lee to shine in their roles. Jim Kelly was able to give a brilliant performance. While it echoed the emerging "Blaxploitation" movie genre, he was still able to share a snapshot of the daily *Terror* Black folk faces in America at the hands of those still "walking beats" after all these generations.

Lynch mobbing cops have always been on the vanguard of White supremacy and *American Terrorism*. Our comedians, like Dick Gregory, Richard Pryor, and Dave

---

[366] Enter the Dragon, 1973 Dir. Robert Clouse; Golden Harvest/Warner Bros

Chapelle, helped ease the trauma through laughter. Musicians like Billie Holiday, O'Shea "Ice Cube" Jackson, and Carlton "Chuck D:" Ridenhour gave voice to our trauma and rebellion. Without question, Lawrence "KRS-One" Parker's classic anthem "Bo Bo Bo" tells the whole story as he would say "in three minutes and some seconds." No matter how we tell them, though, whether couched in comedic genius or over elemental beats and wordplay, those stories never end well for us. One of the tragically glaring examples of this is the cop lynching of Illinois Black Panther Party leaders Fred Hampton, Sr. and Mark Clark.[367]

Gunshots rang out on October 4, 1969, and a brief firefight broke out between members of the Black Panther Party in Chicago, IL, and unknown assailants who shot up the group's office. Law enforcement arrived on the scene and was as heavy-handed as usual as far as the Panthers were concerned.[368] According to Jeffrey Haas, in his book The Assassination of Fred Hampton, the police violence that ensued was

---

[367] Parker, Lawrence "Kris" (1989) track 10

[368]This account of the events leading up to the lynching come from the e-book version of Jeffrey Haas' The Assassination of Fred Hampton: How the FBI and the Chicago Police Murdered a Black Panther (Chicago: Lawrence Hill Books, 2010). The Black Panther Party for Self Defense was originally founded in 1966 in Oakland, CA, borrowing the name and iconography from SNCC field secretary (and future comrade) Stokely Carmichael and the Lowndes County Freedom Organization (LFCO).

The BPP was a Marxist organization and postured itself as a revolutionary organization, it came to be known for its defiant stance on armed self-defense in the mold of Robert Williams as opposed to the quiet self-defense of King and the SCLC. The Panthers were effective organizers through the clarity of their ten-point program, community programs (leading to the adoption of federal programs like Head Start, Healthy Start, and WIC), and their ability to influence the creation of international chapters of the BPP. Volumes have been written and produced on the BPP, for ease of access generally see Bobby Seale's Seize The Time: The Story of the Black Panther Party and Huey P. Newton (Baltimore: Black Classic Press, 1991).

Peniel Joseph offers a thorough biography on Kwame Ture (Stokely Carmichael) including his Black Power days on the frontlines of SNCC in bloody Lowndes County, MS and his brief stint with the Panthers in his book Stokely: A Life (New York: Basic*Civitas* Books, 2014), see Chapter Fourteen—spanning the years from December 11, 1967 through April 3, 1968 and Ture's time with the Panthers for a great perspective on that history. See pp. 231-51.

the typical response that Chicago Panthers had grown accustomed to during those days.[369]

Fred Hampton, the fiery young state and national leader of the organization, drew the ire of the Chicago P.D. along [370]with the attention of the Federal Bureau of Investigation. It made sense, primarily because the Chicago Panthers were effective organizers through their community programs and their rhetoric. Hampton proclaimed that "you kill one pig, you get some satisfaction, you kill all the pigs, you get all the satisfaction." The cops took statements like that personally. So did the Federal Bureau of Investigation.

Hampton, right around this time, moved into a new apartment at 2337 W. Monroe street that was close enough to the Panther office that it turned into a regular hangout spot for members of the group. Yet, despite the rhetoric, gunplay, and law enforcement attention, the Panthers did not have top-level security at either location.[371] The apartment was near the Henry Horner Homes public housing project, the scene of yet another cop lynching of unarmed African men.[372]

---

[369] Ibid. pp. 78-9, Haas describes how the cops "kicked in the door, rushed inside, and started pushing everyone down the front steps. Panthers were met by the cops and were beaten, especially a member named Terry Watson, who the cops said "fit the description" of a man on the roof of the building with a shotgun. The cops beat Watson relentlessly, bystanders thought that he was going to get beaten to death.

[370]Ibid. pp. 80.

[371] Ibid.pp.80-1.

[372] Ibid. pp 81, note that Haas titles Chapter 12 of his book "A Northern Lynching"; so even without access to the expanded definition it is clear to any objective observers that Hampton and Clark were lynched by law enforcement and that bloody scene could have transpired in any region of the settler state or any century since Black folk been here fighting and rebelling.

> **Black Panther Party for Self Defense Ten Point Platform**
>
> We want freedom. We want power to determine the destiny of our Black Community.
>
> We want full employment for our people.
>
> We want an end to the robbery by the Capitalists of our Black Community.
>
> We want decent housing, fit for shelter of human beings.
>
> We want education for our people that exposes the true nature of this decadent American society. We want education that teaches us our true history and our role in the present day society.
>
> We want all Black men to be exempt from military service.
>
> We want an immediate end to POLICE BRUTALITY and MURDER of Black people.
>
> We want freedom for all Black men held in federal, state, county and city prisons and jails.
>
> We want all Black people when brought to trial to be tried in court by a jury of their peer group or people from their Black Communities, as defined by the Constitution of the United States.
>
> We want land, bread, housing, education, clothing, justice and peace.

This time it was the Soto brothers, John and Michael. John Soto was a teenage community group leader lobbying to install traffic lights after motorists in the neighborhood had accidentally killed some kids. John Soto organized some protests in September of 1969, and his brother Michael, who was on leave from Vietnam, had joined him. On October 5, 1969, a Chicago cop lynched John Soto by "accidentally" shooting him in the back of the head during an attempted arrest or detainment.[373]

The streets began to heat up, and Michael Soto extended his leave to attend his younger brother's funeral. On October 10, 1969, Chicago PD lynched Michael Soto by gunshot as well. And just like John's lynching, Michael's lynching was highly controversial, and the facts of that case were equally disputed.[374] Here eyewitnesses stated that the cops tried to "pit maneuver" Soto and some friends as they walked

---

[373] Ibid. pp.81. The account of this highly controversial event is disputed, as the official police report state it was an accident while eyewitnesses stated that there was no scuffle during the attempted arrest and the lynch mob cops were totally unprovoked.

[374] Ibid.

down the street. The men got to their feet and took off running with the cops now giving pursuit.

The cops confronted Michael on the Horner Homes building's second floor and shot him. The cops said that Michael pulled a gun. Eyewitnesses said that Michael was unarmed and lynched like his younger brother.[375]

Given the Panthers "revolutionary" posture, explosive rhetoric, the systemic White supremacist attitudes and culture rampant in the Chicago PD members "patrolling" the neighborhood, and the justified rage in the community, the Panthers were in the crosshairs, and someone was bound to get lynched, likely Hampton. That stage was effectively set in late November 1969. The Illinois appellate court upheld a trumped-up robbery conviction based on an incident that occurred in the summer of 1968, and his appeal bond was getting revoked in ten days.[376] There was a suspicion that Hampton would head underground or overseas like some of his Panther comrades.[377]

Haas assessed that those suspicions were unfounded. Hampton announced at a meeting that enough money was raised for the Panthers to buy the building that held their offices. Also, Haas offered his legal assistance in closing the purchase *pro bono*. The details of the early morning lynching are heavily contested, but there is agreement on one critical point, however. Edward Hanrahan, the Cook County

---

[375] Ibid.

[376] Ibid. pp.65-6. This incident involved an ice cream vendor who identified Hampton as the individual who entered his truck, knocked him to the floor, and handed out ice cream bars to kids in the Maywood section of town. Hampton had always denied this charge, and According to Haas another man named Thomas Blair admitted to the crime personally during a meeting decades later.

[377] Ibid. pp.85-6.

State's Attorney, and Fred Hampton foil assembled and dispatched the lynch mob. Hanrahan's mob showed up at 2337 West Monroe Street in Chicago, IL, guns blazing at 4:00 am on December 4. 1967. By 4:45 am, the heavily armed lynch mob got Mark Clark as he died instantly, taking a bullet to the chest. The mob also got Fred Hampton as he lay in bed with this pregnant fiancée Deborah Johnson.[378]

Over 5,000 people attended Hampton's funeral, but the story of the lynched Panther's didn't end there.[379] The FBI had a well-placed informant in the ranks, William O'Neal, who not only supplied a floor plan of Hampton's apartment but was present on the scene and had drugged Hampton earlier in the evening. This is the type of action that showed how intricate the connections were between local law enforcement, the state legal apparatus, and the federal government. There were commissions formed, inquests and investigations, and several press conferences.

In the immediate aftermath, the surviving Panthers had been arrested and released on bond by the end of the month; Fred Hampton, Jr. was born on December 18, 1969.[380] After that, members of the lynch mob began to get summarily exonerated, beginning with the Chicago PD Internal Investigation Division (IID).[381] The coroner's inquest found that Hampton and Clark were murdered by "justifiable homicide" based on a couple of police accounts. The Civil Rights community met both the inquest determination and IID ruling with deep skepticism.[382] The pressure

---

[378] Again, Haas offers a birds-eye view of the incident as one of the attorneys on the ground representing the Panthers during this time.

[379] Ibid. pp.127, Jesse Jackson and Ralph Abernathy eulogized Hampton, with Jackson stating that "the police attack on Fred Hampton was an attack on the entire Black community".
[380] Ibid. pp.127.

[381] Ibid. pp.127, Haas makes note that this division asked the mob members three questions and supplied the answers. This smacks of a color of law lynching and legal lynching rolled into one wicked event.

[382] Ibid. pp. 127

began to mount to the point where the U.S. Justice Department announced that a federal grand jury would be called in response to the demand for further investigations. The panel began hearing evidence in January 1970.[383]

A Cook County grand jury, empaneled by Hanrahan, to look at state-level prosecutions, returned charges of attempted murder, armed violence, and weapons violations against the surviving Panthers.[384] This led to a "People's Inquest," where the goal was to have Hanrahan and the lynch mob brought up on formal charges. The Panthers, to build community support, issued a statement laying out the facts of the lynching and called for the "decentralization" of the police so that the "people can get control of the pigs in our neighborhood, and the pigs won't just get to kill our youth."[385] The People's Inquest returned with an indictment of Edward Hanrahan and the lynch mob cops understanding that it was a mere symbolic gesture.

On May 8, 1970, the charges against the Panther survivors were dropped effectively with prejudice as the State would have been forced to reveal the identity of any informants if trial proceeded.[386] Later, the federal grand jury refused to issue any indictments. Despite the physical evidence to the contrary, it blamed the Panthers for the violence and passed on passing judgment on Hanrahan.[387] A special grand jury was convened and did indict Hanrahan, his assistant Richard Jalovec, the fourteen-member lynch mob, for their role in the lynching, and various Chicago PD investigators for their "obstruction of justice."[388]

---

[383]Ibid. pp. 127

[384]Ibid. pp.127-28.
[385] Ibid pp. 132-3. Africans in America have been calling to "Defund the Police" since the police have been brutalizing African-American communities.

[386] Ibid. pp.137

[387] Ibid. pp.140

[388] Ibid. pp.165.

Eventually, the Clark and Hampton families would file a civil suit in the Northern District of Illinois later in 1970 against the City of Chicago, Cook County, and the Federal Government for violating the Panther's civil rights. In 1971, federal judge J. Sam Perry, who, according to Haas, was extremely hostile to the complainant's positions, dismissed the civil suit primarily on "qualified immunity" grounds.[389] The survivors appealed the judge's ruling. In the meantime, the obstruction charges against the lynch mob leaders and executors were dismissed.[390]

A crack of light glimmered at the end of this long tunnel as the 7th Circuit Court of Appeals overturned Perry's ruling and remanded the case back to the District Court for retrial, the parties settled for $1.82 M on February 28, 1983.[391] This represented the largest civil rights settlement in U.S. history at the time and almost triple what the survivors of the Kent State lynchings had received.[392]

The lasting impact of the lynching of Fred Hampton and Mark Clark is the collective exposure of the FBI's Counter-Intelligence operation geared towards breaking the backs of the groups and individuals working to stop *America Terrorism* throughout the 1960s and 1970s. This program, code-named COINTELPRO, has been written about extensively in the decades since it has been unclassified and was one of the most effective coordinated campaigns to designed support the settler state's

---

[389] Ibid. pp.177-8. The legal construct "qualified immunity", which prohibits public employees from facing litigation as a result of actions they took in an "official capacity" will be discussed below.

[390] Ibid.

[391] Ibid.pp. 382. The Kent State Lynchings went down on May 4, 1970 and occurred when thirteen Kent State University student protestors were gunned down, in cold blood, by members of the Ohio National Guard.

[392] Ibid. pp.379.

dominance of organizations that challenged both the status quo and *American Terrorism*.

Poster Showing four women demonstrating for the release of six members of the BPP from the Niantic State Women's Farm in Connecticut.
They were published in Prop art/Gary Yanker. New. York: Darien House, 1972 Library of Congress

Yanker Poster Collection / Public domain

Chapter 6

American Law and Modern-Day American Terrorism

Sandy Speaks, for Sandra Bland—The Black Lives Matter street mural in Harlem, NY.
July 9, 2020
Jules Antonio from New York, NY, USA / CC BY-SA
(https://creativecommons.org/licenses/by-sa/2.0)
Artwork credit: Dianne Smith Art https://www.diannesmithart.com/#_=_

Sandra Bland was found asphyxiated in her cell in Waller County, TX, on July 13, 2015. The authorities ruled it a suicide, which is curious as "Sandy," as loved ones called her, was apparently excited about starting a job at Prairie View A&M University in August of that year and by all accounts had no reason to kill herself. There were questions about the pretextual nature of her traffic stop and the violent encounter with ex-State Trooper Brian Encina that led to her arrest.

The inauguration of Barack Hussein Obama (44) on January 20, 2009, seemingly ushered in a "post-racial" society. The facts unfolding on the ground showed that this historic inauguration, subsequent presidency, and eight-year administration utterly failed to the stem the tide of the latest round of American Terrorism on African people. And yet all American jurisprudence could offer was a smattering of arrested pattlerollers and a string of no-bills and acquittals; Black folk barely got the gratuitous "thoughts and prayers" let alone any real, lasting, final justice.

Lynching of nineteen-year-old Michael Donald on March 20, 1981, and strung up on Herndon Ave, in Mobile, AL.
Credits: Southern Poverty Law Center

Michael Donald Lynching (1981)/ KKK Trial 1980's

"A nigger ought to be hung by the neck until dead to put them in their place."
Convicted and eventually executed Klansmen, Henry Hays public statement at a Klan rally in response to suggesting that an almost all-Black jury may acquit an African man accused of killing a police sergeant.

While the modern Ku Klux Klan, "American Al-Qaeda," was soundly whipped and left hobbled and broken as a result of the lynching of Michael Donald and the litigation which followed, Laurence Leamer offers that "historically lynching had been one of the Klan's emblematic acts" and that by committing one was an attempt to "bring back the old days" when hooded night riders roamed the countryside looking to mete out Klan justice.[393]

Ibram X. Kendi would agree as he informs us that the Klan tripled its membership between 1971 and 1980, and in the state of Mississippi alone, there were at least twelve lynchings in 1980 alone.[394] The Klan was so bold and powerful at one point that it could lynch an African person for the slightest perceived action without any consequence. For example, there was a 1923 lynching of Dallas Sewell, hanging from a barn rafter according to "Klan Kode" for allegedly passing for White and associating with White women.[395]

---

[393] Leamer, The Lynching; pp.14. Leamer presents an immaculately detailed treatment of the lynching of Michael Donald and the successful lawsuits that were eventually leveled against the United Klans of America (UKA).

[394] Kendi, Stamped from the Very Beginning, Op.Cit. pp. 430

[395] Ginzburg, 100 Years of Lynchings; Op.Cit. pp.173. This report was published in the *St. Louis Argus* on November 9, 1923. This lynching, and the legendary litigation that followed turned out to be a key turning point in the war against American Al Qaeda. And as history plays often plays out it occurred just five short years after another key turning point in the African World Family's generational war against global White supremacy, namely the Soweto Uprising.

Soweto is a small town in South Africa, and in 1976, after months of protesting cultural eradication though the forcing of the sole use and implementation of Afrikaans, the language of their oppressor, and being inspired part by a trial testimony of radical freedom fighter, Steven "Bantu" Biko, thousands of Sowetan students took the streets in protest. The response of the South African White supremacist authorities mirrored Bull Connor's response in 1963 Birmingham, AL, it was swift, vicious, and widely condemned; upwards of four thousands of students were injured and death tolls range in the hundreds.

Gerald Horne notes how this uprising was critical to the International negotiation with the Union of South Africa (the other "USA") because it "made the nation incapable of governance" and actually helped paved the way for the future release political prisoners, like Nelson Rolihlahla Mandela in 1990. Gerald Horne, White Supremacy Confronted: U.S. Imperialism and Anti-Communist vs. the Liberation of Southern Africa, from Rhodes to Mandela (New York: International Publishers, 2019) pp.577

Also see Traci D. Wyatt for an analysis of radical "theology" of Steven Biko found in Steve Biko: The Radical Gospel of Black Consciousness. Here, in the published edition of her dissertation, Wyatt makes a provocative point that Biko shares a similarity with Jesus Christ

For Great Titan (and escaped convict) Bennie Jack Hays, leader of the Klavern 900 of the United Klans of America (UKA) in Theodore, AL, his ne'er do well son Henry. Fellow Klansman, seventeen-year-old James "Tiger" Knowles, the time for huffing and puffing about the "good old days" were over; for them, it was time for some action.[396]

Henry Hayes and Tiger Knowles were loose cannons, even for the American Al-Qaeda crowd. The night before the previous Klan meeting *above*, they kidnapped a gay man after purposefully meeting him and offering him a ride to a nightclub with the sole intent of causing him harm. Luckily that man was able to escape; their next targeted victim, a young African named Michael Donald, would not be so lucky.[397]

Gainesville, FL KKK Rally Early twentieth century.
National Archives via the FBI Website
(Public Domain)

---

in that the both preached liberating messages for the masses of their people, expected their disciples to be well trained (in Biko's case he was spreading the message of "Black consciousness"), and she further makes the point the that Biko himself was raised in the Christian traditions and likely would not have been able to realize the "journey for which he was called" without first having been steeped in that Christian tradition. Traci D. Wyatt, <u>Steve Biko: The Radical Gospel of Black Consciousness</u> (Meadville: Fulton Books, Inc., 2020); pp. 162-3.

[396] Leamer, <u>The Lynching</u>; Op.Cit. pp. 5-12. Bennie Hays was born Herman Otto Houston in rural Missouri in 1916 and after WWII was sent to prison for cattle rustling, check forgery, and escaped from a prison farm on a stolen only to re-emerge in Southwest Alabama with a new identity and newfound, evil purpose.

[397] Ibid. pp.11. Once in the car dastardly duo put a knife to man's throat, drove him to a secluded spot, made him strip, but then botched the job as they squabbled over what to do with the guy now, he ran off into the woods and the soon-to-be killers sped off back to town.

Klan Dress; Klu Klux Klan exhibit, Birmingham Civil Rights Institute, Birmingham, Alabama. Credit: The George F. Landegger Collection of Alabama Photographs in Carol M. Highsmith's America, Library of Congress, Prints and Photographs Division [LC-DIG-highsm-05074]

Henry and Tiger left that Klavern meeting, where they huddled up with Bennie afterward and, as a group, decided `to lynch a random Black person in response to Josephus Anderson. The trio decided that if Anderson did get off, then any African they could get their hands on "should be killed." Bennie suggested Herndon Ave, a prominent street in a central neighborhood, would be a perfect location; he was worried about a pending sale of some rental properties he was disposing of over there and did not want to scare off the prospective buyer.[398]

---

[398] Ibid.pp. 14; also see Ginzburg, <u>100 Years of Lynchings</u>; Op.Cit. pp. 141. The bloody history is actually chockfull of these types of stories as we have highlighted, Africans were routinely snatched from jails, snatched up after posting bail like in the tragic case of Roger Malcolm we will discuss *below*, snatched up after being acquitted, in fact in one instance in Tylertown, MS on November 23, 1920, an African man named Harry Jacobs, was on trial for capital murder of a White woman and was literally dragged from the courtroom by the mob, had a rope placed

Once Henry and Tiger got word that Bennie closed his real estate transaction, the duo borrowed a rope from a Klansman's mother, and Knowles tied a "thirteen-knot" noose which executioners used to inflict maximum damage; they also borrowed a pistol from another Klansman. They got in Henry's car and crept off.[399]

The "bosom buddies" weren't necessarily concerned about whom they were going to lynch, it could have been a baby, elder, man, woman, but as they were prowling around a Black neighborhood around 11:00 pm and low and behold, they happen upon 5'10", nineteen-year-old Michael Donald. The car pulls up, they ask Donald for directions, pull the gun on him, make him get in the backseat, and empty his pockets if he had any weapons. Donald complied. The killers drove Donald to roughly the same area as they had taken the gay man a few nights earlier and pulls over.[400]

After begging for his life seemingly to no avail, Donald's fight reflex kicks in (in some ways similar to how Emmett Till's did in the face of his lynching), and Donald was able to hold his own and knocked the killers down and slapped both the weapons out of their hands.[401] Henry and Tiger were able to turn the tables; however, despite being shocked that Donald was so strong and fierce and able to grab a tree limb and flail at them both, Leamer notes that they "had been brought up thinking that

---

around his neck with the other end tied to a rear axle of an automobile, and literally dragged again (this time through town) were he was tied to a tree and shot to pieces, his Swiss cheese like body left to dangle in the breeze like a bloody wind chime. This report was published in the *Atlanta Constitution*, on November 24, 1920.

[399]Leamer, The Lynching; pp. 11, like Henry was the son of a high Klan leader, Knowles was the son of proud Klan parents and had been radicalized as a young man, in fact he was went to the 1978 "Klanvocation" with his parents in 1978 and was awarded the first Klan youth charter in the state of Alabama.

[400]Ibid.pp. 17-20.

[401]Ibid, pp. 17-20; Knowles also had a textile blade on him.

African-Americans were a timid, lot who were terrified half to death of men riding through the night wearing night robes."[402]

Though scared, the killers were able to get the limb from Donald and beat him down to the ground with it; Henry went and retrieved the noose from his trunk, returned, slipped it over Donald's neck, and placed his foot over Donald's face (having the same impact as having a grown man's knee on the back of your neck) and pulled the rope as hard as he could hoping to strangle the young man. Yet, Donald arose to his feet once more (apparently that form of lynching takes eight minutes and forty-six seconds to carry out).[403]

The crew would take turns. One would beat Donald with the tree limb as hard as he could while the other would try to pull the rope as hard as possible; they would manage to switch off without allowing a chance for escape. And after several rounds of this back and forth, young Donald finally collapsed in a heap.[404] While on the ground, Henry kept pounding Donald with the tree limb while Tiger was able to finally to pull the rope as strong as he could one last time, drawing so tight that he cut Donald's skin and broke a bone in his neck, finishing the deed at long last.[405]

As they dragged the body to the trunk of the car, wondering aloud if he was dead, one of the killers grabbed the blade and slit Donald's throat just to make doubly sure.[406] The killers dusted themselves off, got back in the car, and made their way

---

[402] Ibid. pp. 19. Clearly these gentlemen never heard of Prosser, Vesey, Turner, Dessalines or Will the Executor, O.B. Mann, or "Crazy" Jim Evers, etc.

[403] Ibid.

[404] Ibid. pp.20.

[405] Ibid.

[406] Ibid.

over to Herndon Ave as planned. Once on the street, they couldn't find a suitable tree and wound up having to tie the body around the trunk of a less than suitable one and were barely able to hoist it off the ground; they didn't get the iconic photo they imagined but, as they did see later, the body could be viewed from a distance.[407] The killers went back to Henry's apartment and interrupted a card game and party with their clothes soaked in blood.[408]

Investigations ensued, and the first round of suspects was released as the authorities suspected that this was simply a random drug deal gone wrong. Still, Donald's mother, Beaulah Mae Donald, refused to accept that as an answer and kept the pressure on both the authorities and Black U.S. Assistant District Attorney, Thomas Figures out of Mobile, AL.[409] Eventually, Henry was charged, convicted of capital murder, sentenced to death, and executed in Alabama's electric chair, on June 5, 1997, at Holman State penitentiary.[410]

James "Tiger" Knowles, who was seventeen at the time of the lynching, was indicted by a federal grand jury in 1985 for violating the civil rights of Michael Donald and pled guilty to civil rights violations in the United States District Court for the Southern District of Alabama. Knowles avoided the death penalty by testifying against Hays, Cox, and other Klansmen at the trial and testified that the slaying was done "to show Klan strength in Alabama"; he ultimately received a life sentence parole eligibility after ten years.[411] Tiger ultimately served twenty-five years, at one

---

[407] Ibid. pp.20.

[408] Ibid.

[409] Ibid. pp.29.

[410] Ibid. pp.312, prior to dying Henry offered a death bed confession, corroborated much of Tiger's account, but said that Tiger was the one who slashed Donald's throat, not him. Tiger testified that it was Henry that did the throat slashing.
[411] Ibid. pp.67-8.

point granted a full-throated apology to the Donald family and did what he could to bring down the Klan, and was eventually granted parole.[412]

Benjamin Franklin Cox, Jr., the Klansman who provided the rope, was initially discharged by a trial judge in 1984, citing Alabama's 3-year statute of limitations for criminal conspiracy. Still, an Alabama grand jury re-indicted Cox for murder in 1987. Initially resulting in a mistrial in 1988, a second trial held on May 18, 1989, led to Cox's conviction for being an accomplice in Donald's killing, and he was sentenced to life in prison. Cox ultimately served eleven years on that charge.[413]

Bennie Jack Hays was also indicted for inciting the murder. His case took a while and several turns but ultimately ended in a mistrial when he suffered a heart attack during court proceedings. The judge declared a mistrial; Bennie later died before he could be retried.[414]

Typically, this would have been the end of the matter, but this is a landmark case, in many respects; and Beaulah Mae Donald and Civil rights attorney Morris Dees deserve all the credit. Through her undying pursuit of justice, she convinced Morris Dees, founder of the Southern Poverty Law Center (SPLC) in Montgomery, to bring a 10,000,000 dollar wrongful death suit against the United Klans of America in federal district court in the Southern District of Alabama in 1984; styled *Donald v. United Klans of America*.[415]

---

[412] Ibid. pp. 320, Morris Dees, discussed *below*, believed the sincerity of Tiger's apology and testimony and assisted him in getting parole.
[413] Ibid. 249-50, 306-9, and 319.

[414] Ibid. pp.310.

[415] Ibid. pp.233-34, Dees brought suit based on a novel theory that the UKA had an agency relationship with the local Klavern; please see *Donald v. United Klans of America* C.A. 84-0725 (S.D.Ala. Feb. 12, 1987)

Dees' relatively novel legal theory of the case was that the UKA was essentially a structured military organization headed by Imperial Wizard Robert Shelton whose "custom, practice, and policy" was to promote White supremacy through acts of violence. Further, Donald's lynching was the "natural consequence" of their stated goals and UKA officer Tiger Knowles, Klavern officer Henry Hays, and likely directed by Bennie Hays, Shelton's top Lieutenant in South Alabama. The latter jointly carried out the "violent philosophy and directives," which directly implicates the UKA in the lynching of Michael Donald.[416]

February 12, 1987, the UKA was found civilly liable by an all-White jury and sentenced to damages of $7 million in the wrongful-death verdict in the case, sending a jolt through some of the staunchest defenders or Whiteness, White supremacy, and Anti-Blackness the settler project ever produced. That judgment brought American Al Qaeda to its knees. The suit became a precedent for civil legal action against other racist hate groups in the United States.[417]

Renamed Herndon Ave is now Michael Donald Avenue, Mobile. AL (Public Domain)

---

[416] Ibid. The argument shows how these terrorist organizations work in concert with each other and how the titular head can have some agency over its localized parts, this supports the argument for rebranding the Klan as "American Al Qaeda".

[417] Ibid. pp.290-99.

This was a rather pathetic end to an organization that once boldly helped set in motion the sacking of African enclaves like "Black Wall Street" in the Greenwood section of Tulsa, OK; bombed the 16th Street Church in Birmingham, AL, infiltrated high offices and general society and committed atrocity after atrocity. Like the March 8, 1960, lynching of Felton Turner in Houston, TX. Turner, an African man, was found hanging from a tree by his heels with the letters "KKK" repeatedly carved across his chest and stomach, apparently in direct response to African students holding "sit-in" protests on the campus of the HBCU Texas Southern University a short time before the brutalized body was found. The Klan needed to pay for the years of naked pain and terror they visited upon the sons and daughters of Africa in America, and the other groups they terrorized.[418]

Payment of the judgment bankrupted the United Klans of America. It resulted in its "national headquarters" being sold for $51,875, the proceeds going to Beulah Mae Donald, which she used to purchase her first-ever home.[419]

Dees decided that the SPLC should build a Civil Rights Memorial in Montgomery, AL, which was completed and eventually dedicated in November 1989. Some of the speakers were Myrlie Evers, wife of slain civil rights activist Medgar Evers, Chris McNair, father of eleven-year-old Denise McNair, the youngest victim in the 16th Street Church Bombing, and Mamie Till-Mobley, mother of fourteen-year-old Emmett Till who was lynched by hate-filled goons in a drunken stupor all discussed

---

[418] Ginzburg, 100 Years of Lynchings; Op.Cit. pp. 245 originally published in the Birmingham (AL) News; March 8, 1960
[419] Ibid. pp.303

below.[420] In 2006, Donald's family members and local politicians renamed Herndon Avenue to Michael Donald Avenue.[421]

The fighting spirit of Beaulah Mae Donald that she passed on her to son Michael, and the legal mastery and skillfully effective advocacy of Morris Dees and the SPLC, together decapitated the vaunted KKK and have reduced them to carnival barkers, sideshow acts, and Cretans and creatures of a long bygone era relegated to obscure websites. However, they have found an ideological ally in the White nationalism of Trump (45).[422]

---

[420] Ibid. pp.304-5. Medgar Evers was the Mississippi leader of the NAACP, and was lynched by lone-wolf Byron De La Beckwith on June 12th, 1963. See Rick Bowers, Spies of Mississippi; Op. Cit. pp.71-3, 106 for an intimate description of this lynching; also pay attention to how De La Beckwith's defense sought and received assistance with the screening of eleven prospective jurors for the retrial after the first De La Beckwith trial ended in a hung jury, the Commission's assistance helped secure the second hung jury verdict. De La Beckwith was finally convicted in 1994 after the jury tampering in the second trial came to light, and that popular White supremacist died at the Parchman Farm in 2001;

Also see Carson, In Struggle; Op.Cit pp.97. In his amazing book on the commitment of the Africans of Mississippi and the grassroots organizing they inspired and organizers they courageously protected, Charles E. Cobb, Jr recounts a story of Medgar and his older brother Charles Evers, along with four friends, as they attempted to cast their ballots on election day, 1946 in Newton County, MS. The crew were WWII vets and often armed but were turned away from a mob of angry and armed Whites standing guard over the courthouse steps. Cobb notes that the differences in the way the brothers told the stories offers a sense of their different personalities. Cobb, Jr., Charles E. This Non-Violent Stuff'll Get You Killed: How Guns Made the Civil Rights Movement Possible Op.Cit. pp. 83-6.

And in keeping with the through line of this essay, the Evers brothers were deeply impacted by the lynching of family friend Willie Tingle, who the mob got a hold of for "eyeballing" a White woman. Tingle was apparently dragged through the streets, hung from a tree, used for target practice, and left to dangle, for all to see, including children like the Evers boys, who would have to pass his body on their way to school. Op.Cit. pp.92-3. Cobb also credits Amzie Moore, legendary organizer in his own right, for being one of the main individuals responsible for SNCC's presence and work in Mississippi in regards to "grassroots organizing for voting rights". pp.86-91.

[421] Ibid. pp.312.

[422] Please see Andrew Naughtie "Former KKK leader endorses Trump for President Again and Tucker Carlson for VP" July 9, 2020 *The Independent* located on the link to their website

New Cretans have primarily surpassed the Klan on all sides. The lynching responsibility has shifted back to disaffected members of law enforcement who need to be defunded, violent White nationalists (like Aryan Brotherhood, Aryan Brotherhood of Texas, Skinheads), and lone wolf #MAGA shooters for the most part; and the ideological responsibility has been taken up by the "Alt-Right," "Boogaloo Boys," "Proud Boys," and far right-wing pundits and politicos.[423]

James Byrd, Jr. Lynching (1998)

"We're starting the Turner Diaries early."
John "Bill" King, June 6, 1998

While Beulah Mae Donald and Morris Dees may have effectively ended this current iteration of the Klan's reign as American Al Qaeda, there are always other settler state born terrorist cells waiting in the wings to get right back to the mission of the indiscriminate lynching of Africans within these borders. Here lately, it's been members of law enforcement, but on the night of June 6, 1998, in Jasper, TX, it was a couple of neophyte members of the Aryan Brotherhood of Texas (ABT) White supremacist prison gang.[424]

On that fateful night, ABT members John "Bill" King, Lawrence Russell Brewer, and Shawn Berry offered a ride to an inebriated Black man Berry likely recognized

---

here: https://www.independent.co.uk/news/world/americas/kkk-trump-david-duke-tucker-carlson-election-2020-a9609491.html

[423] The SPLC keeps an updated report on White nationalist groups on its website, www.splc.org

[424] Founded in the 1980's, this offshoot of the California prison based Aryan Brotherhood, is one of the most notorious prison gangs in the Texas Department of Corrections (TDC). Like most prison gangs, this group is as concerned with its drug business and other prison rackets as it is to its ideological dedication to Whiteness, White supremacy and anti-Blackness. The Southern Poverty Law Center has a report on the ABT on its website located at https://www.splcenter.org/fighting-hate/extremist-files/group/aryan-brotherhood-texas.

by sight named James Byrd, Jr., 49-year-old father and grandfather, and let Byrd climb in the back of his "rickety" old 1982 Ford pickup. This act set King off as he yelled, "that's some ho ass shit, picking up a fucking nigger". The truck was driven to a closed convenience store, and the guys changed seats with Byrd climbing into the cab; traveled on to a secluded spot where the men pulled over, got out, and shared some beer and cigarettes; but before Byrd could finish his drink, he was jumped, beaten, urinated and defecated on, and eventually tied to the hitch of the truck with a 25-foot logging chain.[425]

Like Emmet Till and Michael Donald before him, though Byrd had chronic arthritis and was almost twenty years older than the lynch party, he put up a hell of a fight. He went down kicking, screaming, and praying; his fate was sealed when a disgusted and agitated King stepped away and yelled: "Fuck it, let's kill this nigger".[426] During the melee, the killers left evidence that was quickly traced back to them, including long neck beer bottles, cigarettes, a lighter with Zippo etched on the side, and a nut wrench with "Berry" etched on it.[427]

---

[425] Joyce King offers a detailed history of this event in her book Hate Crime: The Story of Dragging in Jasper, TX (New York: Pantheon Books, 2002).pp. 22-8. King makes the point that Byrd and Berry shared the same parole officer and may have seen each other in passing. Incidentally, Ms. King used to be a presenter to the *Wesleyan Innocence Project* during my first year of law school while I served as the night program team lead. See also, Jennifer Petersen's book Murder, the Media, and the Politics of Public Feelings: Remembering Matthew Shepard and James Byrd, Jr. (Bloomington: Indiana University Press, 2011).

Here, Petersen criticizes the mass corporate media and Black media alike for falling into the trap of playing into the age old tropes around framing and messaging, especially in its treatment of Bryd as a disabled, out-of-work, hitch hiking, troubled, transitory type and never really doing deeper dives involving him as a man, a family man, a sentient being, as the media tends to focus on what she calls "melodrama" to drive stories like this. Op.Cit. pp.92-112. Please note that Matthew Shepard was the White gay man that attended the University of Wyoming who was lynched the night of October 6, 1998, exactly four months after the lynching of James Byrd, Jr. pp.24.

[426] King, Joyce Hate Crime; Op.Cit. pp.24-5.
[427] Ibid. pp. 25.

Byrd was dragged for over 2 miles down a logging road.[428] When his remains were found the next day on Huff Creek Road, Sunday morning, his body had been ripped apart, he was conscious for almost half the time he was being dragged, and he had been decapitated, and his right arm was severed when he hit a culvert in the road. What was left of Byrd's body was dumped near a Black church in Jasper, TX.[429]

The news of this uniquely brutal lynching spread far and fast, but what made this event stand out among all the others was the aftermath.[430] Arrests were made relatively quickly, and at least one confession was offered up within days of the incident. The media swarmed as it had been well trained to do so coming out of the O.J. Simpson trial.[431]

---

[428] Dragging the victims through the streets was a part of the lynching ritual at times, as in the 1923 case of Mississippi sharecropper Joe Pullen. Pullen was confronted at his home by two White men over an alleged $50 debt which Pullen denied owing. An altercation ensued, and Pullen wound up shooting one of the assailants and killing him. Pullen immediately left his home, went to his parents' home and grabbed as many weapons and ammunition as possible; he made retreat to hold up in the woods and await the mob.

When the mob finally showed up an epic firefight ensued, by the end it took well over a hundred men to finally kill Pullen but not before he took the lives of nine Whites and wounded nine others; this gun battle raged for over seven-hours. Umoja discusses this event and how reinforcements had to show up from a neighboring town with an automatic weapon to get the better of Pullen. The enraged Whites tied Pullen's corpse to the back of an automobile and dragged it to a nearby town to terrorize other sharecroppers, cut his ear off and displayed it in a jar, and showed his shotgun; this tale of armed response and resistance electrified Africans all over the world to the point where a call for a raising of a monument in his honor were penned in Black newspapers like the *Richmond Planet* and the *Negro World* months later. See Umoja's We Will Shoot Back; pp. 19.

[429] Ibid. pp. 26-8.

[430] The outcome of this tragic event led to the passage of hate crimes legislation discussed *below*.
[431] Ibid. pp.102, Here Petersen deftly makes that point that King and Brewer's physical appearance, especially the tattoos, essentially made it easier for non-Africans to dismiss this event as relic of a bygone era committed by "real racists" and "evil lunatics" and not as a byproduct of a convulsion of the settler state due changing demographics, for example, or perceptions of loss of culture, job loss, desires to turn back the clock to simpler times, tired calls to "Make America Great Again", economic downturn, scapegoating, etc. pp.102.

Like the Emmett Till funeral forty-three years earlier in Chicago, Bryd's funeral was jam-packed, and paid for by native Texan and NBA star Dennis "The Worm" Rodman, and attended by high profile personalities.[432] The funeral itself became a flashpoint as members of the New Black Panthers and a Black Muslim group from Dallas, TX, and Houston, TX, respectively, were met by members of the Klan whom all decided to have armed-marches and protests at various points across Jasper.[433] Nothing happened during those stand-offs, but the media ate it up, just like the subsequent trials.

October 28, 2009 ceremony for the signing of the *Matthew Shepard and James Byrd Federal Hate Crimes Act of 2009*; White House, Washington, D.C. (Public Domain)

---

[432]<u>Murder, the Media, and the Politics of Public Feelings: Remembering Matthew Shepard and James Byrd, Jr.</u>, Op.Cit. pp.95. Petersen makes the point that it was critical for President Bill Clinton (43) to reach out to the family directly as he was wrapping his "racial reconciliation" tours which he tried to tout as a cornerstone of his election campaigns, and sent Transportation Secretary Rodney Slater as the rep of his administration representative, and who was joined by Congressional Black Caucus Chairwoman Maxine Waters (D-CA), Jesse L. Jackson, Rev. Al Sharpton, TX State Representative Kay Bailey Hutchinson, NAACP President Kweisi Mfume, and throngs of others.

[433]Ibid.

James Byrd's brutal lynching directly led to legislation, both state and federal hate crimes legislation a lot like the Freedom Summer lynchings led to the *Civil Rights Act of 1964* and *Voting Rights Act of 1965*.

Laws are important, those who make the laws are important, those who determine what the laws "are" are important, and as the last lynchings, we examine tells us how important those who "execute and enforce the law" (or take the law in their own hands) are equally important. As we have seen, the brutal practice of lynching has been weaponized and utilized by all the defenders of the settler state at one time or another; sometimes it's the bloodthirsty mob, other times it's a radicalized lone wolf, other times its disaffected law enforcement, and sometimes a mix or variation of all three.

As we entered into 2009 and the beginning of the presidency of Barack Obama (44), keen observers noticed and predicted that the responsibility for lynching the Africans would fall back into the lap of law enforcement, so much so that one of the new president's first official acts would be to get brow-beaten into hosting a "beer" summit on the campus of his alma mater, Harvard University, after a renowned professor, Henry Louis Gates got arrested by Cambridge, MA police sergeant James Crowley, so much for post-racial Shangri-La, E-40 was right, we almost always "fit the description" and any one of us can get it; professors and patriots alike.[434]

---

[434]Gates got arrested for no real discernable reason like so many of us have gone through since our arrival in the 1520's and Obama (44) caught the full measure of criticism from the reactionary settler state defense team when he appeared to even dare raise a half-hearted critique of any member of law enforcement, so much so that a lot of us felt that this doomed any chance of him taking a stand (strong, weak, or mild) to defend us in the face of the looming onslaught. This sentiment was precisely captured by Deborah Douglas in her column titled "Obama's Beer Summit Derailed Him on Race" posted to the USA Today website on July 20, 2016 and located at: https://www.usatoday.com/story/opinion/2016/07/20/obama-black-lives-matter-police-shootings-beer-summit-column/87310566/.

Obama (44) was particularly muted, on calling out White supremacy and *American Terrorism*, in the immediate aftermath of the "color of law" lynchings of Eric Garner, Sandra Bland, John Crawford, Sam DuBose, Terrance Crutcher, Mike Brown, Freddy Gray, Tamir Rice, Philando

$12,500.00 REWARD!

Rewards totaling $12,500.00 have been offered for information leading to the arrest and conviction of persons involved in the killing of 4 Negroes in Walton County on July 25, 1946.

All Information Will Be Kept Confidential

— CONTACT —
FEDERAL BUREAU OF INVESTIGATION
Telephone WAlnut 3605   Atlanta, Ga.
— OR —
GEORGIA BUREAU OF INVESTIGATION
Telephone WAlnut 5333   Atlanta, Ga.

1946 FBI Reward Posting for information on a lynching. This is a tactic that the feds would use from time to time when investigating lynchings. (Public Domain)

Castile, Alton Sterling, LaQuan McDonald, etc. Please see, Allen, Q., & Metcalf, H. (2019). "Up to No Good": The Intersection of Race, Gender, and Fear of Black Men in US Society. In Boyce T. & Chunnu W. (Eds.), *Historicizing Fear: Ignorance, Vilification, and Othering* (pp. 19-34). Louisville: University Press of Colorado. doi:10.2307/j.ctvwh8d12.4

Chapter 7

American Law and American Terrorism in the Twenty-First Century

Law Enforcement Excessive Use of Force Against African-Americans

"Crispus Attucks fit the description too. Black men, by and large, always fit the description."

> RAN away from his Master *William Brown* of *Framingham*, on the 30th of *Sept.* last, a Molatto Fellow, about 17 Years of Age, named *Crispas*, 6 Feet two Inches high, short curl'd Hair, his Knees nearer together than common; had on a light colour'd Bearskin Coat, plain brown Fustian Jacket, or brown all-Wool one, new Buckskin Breeches, blue Yarn Stockings, and a check'd woollen Shirt. Whoever shall take up said Run-away, and convey him to his aforesaid Master, shall have ten *Pounds*, old Tenor Reward, and all necessary Charges paid. And all Masters of Vessels and others, are hereby caution'd against concealing or carrying off said Servant on Penalty of the Law. *Boston*, *October* 2. 1750.

Escaped African, Crispus Attucks "Wanted" Poster, Boston Gazette October 2, 1750 (Public Domain)

The very first person to shed blood for the sake (and in the name) of the nascent settler project in its earliest days of revolt from the Crown, the patriot Crispus Attucks, was a lynched African whose name and likeness was meant to go viral on wanted posters in the hopes of tipping off the kidnappers and pattlerollers.[435] He fell

---

[435] David, C. (1924). The Fugitive Slave Law of 1793 and its Antecedents. *The Journal of Negro History*, 9(1), 18-25. doi:10.2307/2713433 Op Cit pp.18, as noted earlier the *Boston Gazette* circulated a fugitive slave notice for Attucks. According to David, Attucks returned to bondage on his own volition, eventually gained liberation, and then was gunned down in cold blood in the Boston Massacre in 1770. See also Felker Kantor, M. (2016) "The Coalition

at the hands of a British regiment who telegraphed the moves of the American Terrorists, lynching an African in the street because he "fit the description" and was probably "guilty of something."

So clearly, Africans on these shores have had to develop instincts, coping skills and mechanisms, and ways to control fight or flight impulses when confronted with law enforcement for centuries now. Ahmad Aubrey, like Emmett Till and Michael Donald, before him decided to stand and fight.

As discussed *above*, the pattlerollers were relentless, and their professional descendants are equally relentless. Sally Hedden connects the dots between enslaved patrols, the castle doctrine, and the fear of African insurrection in the waning days of the Civil Wars when she notes that as a Southern town was set to fall that "city officials (concerned about enslaved Africans leaving) might call upon every resident able to pull a trigger to keep the peace and defend it…such groups were called police and guard forces".[436]

One story Hedden recounted was of how things got so bad in King William County, VA. The pattlerollers would show up at church services and start whipping and beating both "free" and enslaved Africans alike, on sight. Church leaders had enough and started to convince the Black parishioners to commit the cardinal sins of 1) attending church meetings at night and 2) physically resisting arrest.[437]

---

against Police Abuse: CAPA's Resistance Struggle in 1970s Los Angeles" *Journal of Civil and Human Rights*, 2(1), 52-88. doi:10.5406/jcivihumarigh.2.1.52. See Hadden, Slave Patrol; pp.126-7.
[436] Hadden Slave Patrol; pp.187.

[437] Ibid.

It is no wonder that pattleroller language and imagery are still heavily influencing the language and imagery of their professional descendants. Cops today are still talking about "beats" and "patrols even now.[438]

To the Africans coming out of chattel enslavement, there was little difference between the pattlerollers, the Klan, and the police. [439]

Statue of Harriet and Dred Scott, St. Lois, MO next to the old Courthouse; during a Women's Rights March
By Eric - Dred & Harriet Scott (photo), CC BY 2.0,
https://commons.wikimedia.org/w/index.php?curid=55329805 January 21, 2017

The list of names of Africans who have been lynched by law enforcement, new breed pattlerollers, and those whom law enforcement tried to lynch like Rodney King and Jacob Blake, seems just to grow exponentially. We look at a sampling of

---

[438] Hadden, Slave Patrol; pp.216, 219. Hadden notes that through the White nationalist's beliefs that the Klan was the last defender of the Southern way of life, the White race, and Anglo-Saxon institutions that the "Klan was the true keepers of the peace, looking past all the terrorism, and that Law Enforcement (and racial dominance) rested in the hands of any White man who owned a gun and was willing to use it on the Klan's behalf".

[439] Please Sally Hadden Slave Patrols; Op.Cit. pp.212-13; where she lists the quotes from formerly enslaved Africans expressing this very sentiment especially a J.T. Tims who recalled that "There wasn't no difference between the patroles and the Klu Klux. If th'd they ketch you they would whip you".

those now-ancestors and the impacts of their lynchings on the law and the world we live in.[440]

Park Slope, Brooklyn, NY May 30, 2020
Credits: Rhododendrites - Own work, CC BY-SA 4.0, https://commons.wikimedia.org/w/index.php?curid=9081036

The Lynching of Berry Washington, July 27, 1919
- News_Coverage_of_Berry_Washington_Lynching_over_Milan_Map

- Albuquerque morning journal. July 26, 1919, CITY EDITION
- The Greeneville Daily Sun. July 25, 1919
- Phoenix Tribune, August 02, 1919
- Richmond times-dispatch. September 07, 1919
- File:1950 Census Enumeration District Maps - Milan Georgia.png

---

[440] The #SayAllTheirNames movement posts a running log and offers some vignettes on the lives and deaths of some of those ancestors. The link to the web posting is located here: https://sayevery.name/.

During the time of drafting, Jacob Blake was shot seven, times in the back, by members of the Kenosha Police Department who were responding to a call about a fight. Blake was apparently helping to break up the fight, but the police engaged with him, and as he was trying to walk away, he was shot in the back. Reports are still coming in, but it looks like Mr. Blake may survive but may be paralyzed; and his children will need counseling after having been on the scene and watching their father get lynched by cop. A link to the story can be located here: https://www.bbc.com/news/world-us-canada-53909766.

Ahmaud Arbery Lynching (2020)

"I honestly think that if we didn't get national attention to it, my son's death would have been a cover-up."
Wanda Cooper-Jones, Mother of Ahmaud Arbery 2020

Ahmaud Arbery, lynched by three defenders of the settler state and #MAGA warriors in Brunswick, GA, stood, fought, and paid a terrible price for that fateful decision.[441]

Mural of Ahmaud Arbery at 1621 Albany Street, Brunswick, GA. The building is scheduled to house the Brunswick African-American Cultural Center, and Marvin Meeks painted the Mural in May 2020. Photo Credit: Judson McCranie / CC BY-SA (https://creativecommons.org/licenses/by-sa/3.0)

The story is disgustingly similar to the story of an unnamed African that was lynched around 1912 near Hackleburg, AL.[442] Someone named C.P. Lunsford of Hackleburg, AL, actually sent a letter to Birmingham U.S. District Attorney O.D. Street to report the brutal murder and ask if there were any laws to prevent these happenings. The letter recounts that a week prior, a "negro man" was chased and "hounded" down while peacefully going down the railroad tracks, and "there was not anything against him, but a party of men got after him because his skin was Black and murdered

---

[441]The British Broadcast Corporation (BBC) posted an extensive timeline of events to its webpage on June 5, 2020. Please see https://www.bbc.com/news/world-us-canada-52623151.

[442] This story is recounted in Ginzburg's <u>100 Years of Lynchings</u>, Op. Cit. pp.77-8.

him.[443] Street planned to forward the letter to Governor Emmett O'Neal, but he published it in the *Montgomery Advertiser* beforehand.[444]

And just like his unnamed ancestor got lynched just for being African and walking around in public a hundred and eight years prior, Ahmaud Arbrey got lynched for being African and jogging around in public.[445]

Arbery was jogging on February 23, 2020, when he was stalked, trapped, and eventually shot to death by Travis McMichael. The latter was joined by his father, Greg McMichael, and their friend William "Roddie" Bryan. The killers claimed that they saw Arbery, and he "fit the description" of a robbery suspect they heard about. They grabbed a shotgun and a pistol and decided to follow him. The McMichael's are in one vehicle while Bryan is videotaping the incident and trailing in another vehicle.[446]

The video shows that Arbery is running along, and Bryan bumps into him and tries to pin him in. The younger McMichael jumps out of the car, a fight ensues, and Arbery gets the better of him, and shots ring out. Arbery dies on the scene, and in a report, it states that Travis McMichael calls him a "fucking nigger" as he stands over the body as it bleeds out on that asphalt road. Initial autopsy shows that Arbery had "two gunshot wounds in his chest, and a gunshot graze wound on the inside of one of his wrists."[447]

---

[443] Ibid.

[444] Ibid.

[445] BBC, June 5, 2020 https://www.bbc.com/news/world-us-canada-52623151

[446] Ibid.

[447] Ibid.

All of the authorities involved effectively swept this case under the rug; suspicions are because the McMichaels and Bryan were well connected in that part of the state; in fact, the elder McMichael is a retired investigator for the local District Attorney's office.[448]

The immediate aftermath of this case and initial investigation has been marred with the stench of cover-up and "color of law" allegations due to the connections and incestuous relationships between the cops, investigators, and multiple D.A.'s involved in this matter at one time or another. Seventy-four days passed, four D.A.'s were appointed after multiple recusals until charges were eventually filed, and the Grand Jury returned charges of malice murder, felony murder (4 counts), aggravated assault (2 counts), false imprisonment, and criminal attempt to commit false imprisonment for each killer.[449]

It's truly amazing to think that the only reason we, and the rest of the world, found out about this lynching was that an attorney released the Bryan video, which immediately went viral like those Crispus Attucks wanted posters. This video was released on behalf of the McMichael's, clearly thinking that if a "suspicious Black man" is running, then he must be guilty of something. The race warriors felt as if they were within their "rights" to confront him, and if he dies, so be it, and that the tape would ultimately be exculpatory, in other words, clear them.[450]

---

[448]Ibid.

[449]Ibid. The world is watching this case now, especially since interested parties have tried to smear Arbury's name by posting stories of a previous arrest and law enforcement claims that he had a baggie of marijuana on him and posting surveillance videos of Arbery inspecting an unfinished home in the community; no drugs were found on Arbery at the scene of the lynching, the post-mortem toxicology screen came back clean, and Arbery was unarmed when he got lynched.

[450]These #MAGA warriors, taking cues from the various *Fugitive Slave Acts*, thought the tape was going to give them just enough cover in the court of public opinion that they could get away with whatever was going to come down the pipe, probably realizing that the story was going to pick up steam as Arbery's family kept asking questions.

Less than three weeks later, Breonna Taylor got lynched by law enforcement gundown, and no one in that lynch party has been brought to "justice" at the time of drafting.

Breonna Taylor Lynching (2020)

"She had a whole plan on becoming a nurse and buying a house and then starting a family, Breonna had her head on straight, and she was a very decent person. She didn't deserve this. She wasn't that type of person".
Tamika Palmer, Breonna Taylor's mom

The lynching of Breonna Taylor is eerily reminiscent of the 1946 lynchings of Dorothy Malcolm, Mae Murray Dorsey, and their husbands Roger Malcolm and George Dorsey in Walton and Oconee, GA.[451] This tragic event involving these young Africans occurred due to a domestic violence incident between Malcolm's, who was known to have these types of altercations; in this case, Roger was drunk and was yelling and chasing Dorothy across the yard.[452]

They were tenant farmers and lived and worked for Loy Harrison. Harrison hired a supervisor named Barnette Hester, who also lived on the property, which tried to intervene in the altercation; needless to say, Roger, wound up stabbing Barnette Hester and almost killed him.[453] Roger got arrested and sat in the county jail for eleven days until Harrison came to bond him out; Harrison was joined on this trip to retrieve Roger by Dorothy and the Dorsey's.[454]

---

[451]Wexler, Laura <u>Fire In A Canebrake: The Last Mass Lynching in America</u> (New York: First Scribner, 2004) Wexler offers a detailed history of the events that led up to this multiple lynching and the aftermath.

[452]Ibid. 2-3; the role that domestic violence against African women and its role in the history and psychosis of lynching really needs to explored in depth.

[453]Ibid. The lynching is recounted in chapter 6, spanning from pp. 56-70.

[454]Ibid.

Hester survives, and his father, Bob Hester, was incensed. At the same time, Loy was at the county jail to pay Roger's $600 bond; Bob Hester was there checking in on Roger and to see if he could go free, got his answer, and left. Harrison went to collect Roger while the rest of the party stayed in town, enjoying themselves. All five individuals piled into Harrison's car and made their way back home but were ambushed at the Moore's Ford Bridge, which spans the Apalacbee River that separates Walton County and Oconee County.[455]

Harrison's car was surrounded by a White mob of about twenty men armed to the teeth with shotguns and pistols. One of the assailants held Harrison at gunpoint while the others dragged the other two men out first; Dorothy recognized one of the men, and then the women get dragged out. Harrison, who was giving this recount as a formal statement, said he heard a countdown and a fire order, then the booming shotgun blasts, over, and over, and over. When the lynching was over, Harrison was left to collect himself and allowed to drive off unharmed.[456]

Dorothy Malcolm was found lying on her side, staring at Roger Malcolm with shotgun wounds to her right jaw and a bullet wound behind her left ear, and a fractured left arm. Mae Murray Dorsey was found in a crouching position, facing the river, with a large caliber bullet wound through the top of her head, and a bullet wound and shotgun wound through her left shoulder. Roger Malcolm, the intended target, was lying on his back with a gunshot wound on the left side of his forehead. He had a through and through a shot that entered the left side of the chest and exited out of his back, and another bullet hit him in the hip. Malcolm had a noose around

---

[455]Ibid.

[456]Ibid. That incident all occurred within twenty minutes of Roger Malcolm bonding out of county jail.

his neck, and his wrists were tied to the same rope that George Dorsey was tied to on the other end. George Dorsey was lying on his side, with a bullet hole in the right side of his jaw, a bullet hole above his right ear, and another bullet hole in the left side of his gut.[457]

While evidence was presented to a grand jury, no charges were ever filed in the case. The FBI had opened and closed multiple investigations but to no avail. The tragedy of this case is that innocent African women lay dead because of bloodthirsty White men with guns, who were looking for somebody else, lynched them by shooting them multiple times, and no one had to ever answer for it (again, at least at the time of this drafting), just like Breonna Taylor.[458]

Breonna Taylor was lynched by shooting on March 13, 2020, around midnight in Louisville, KY.[459] Outside of the day, time, and manner of Taylor's death, critical facts of this killing are still fiercely contested. The general story is that members of Louisville Metro Police Department, while serving a "no-knock" warrant in a search for individuals believed to be selling drugs, violently burst into Taylor's apartment.

---

[457]Ibid. This brutal damage assessment is located on pp.65-6. This lynching had always been marked by theories of shady political involvement from former Governor Eugene Talmadge, The Klan, and a lazy FBI investigation. pp.192.

[458]Ibid.

[459]This traumatic event had become a *cause celebre* throughout the bulk of 2020 Taylor has become one of the latest martyrs of the #BLM movement and calls for justice for her family and loved ones have joined those of Ahmaud Arbery and George Floyd during the massive protests that kicked during the early Summer months of that year.

High-profile Blacks, like media mogul Oprah Winfrey, weighed in and amplified the case of Breonna Taylor in ways that they had not done before. *The New York Times* published an article which lays out Winfrey's assistance with highlighting the #Justice for Breonna campaign through her billboard buys across the City of Louisville and story placements across Winfrey's media platforms. Please see Richard Oppel, Jr. and Derrick Bryson Taylor, "Here's What you Need to Know About Breonna Taylor" *New York Times*, July 31, 2020 located here: https://www.nytimes.com/article/breonna-taylor-police.html

Simultaneously, she was asleep with her boyfriend Kenneth Walker, who awoke and grabbed a weapon as he heard the front door get rammed open.[460]

A gunfight erupted with the police firing multiple rounds, a police officer was wounded by Walker, Taylor was hit and killed in the melee, and Walker claims that the Police never announced their presence and Taylor was left to bleed out for over twenty minutes with no medical attention; the Police denied both of these claims.[461] No drugs were ever found, and one of the suspects being sought was an ex-boyfriend of Taylor's. She was lynched in 2020 because the bloodthirsty mob was out to get some guy she had a relationship with and didn't care one iota who was in their way, just like Dorothy Malcolm and Mae Murray Dorsey got lynched in 1946 for roughly the same reasons.[462]

While the Louisville Metro Police Department indeed lost a police chief and its ability to use "no-knock" warrants in the aftermath of the Breonna Taylor lynching, at the time of drafting, no charges have been filed against the killers despite public pressure to bring them to "justice."[463] At the time of drafting this manuscript, Breonna Taylor's family and the City of Louisville settled a wrongful death civil lawsuit.[464]

---

[460] *Hudson v. Michigan*, 547 U.S. 586 (2006), Here, the Court held that evidence gathered as a result of a violation of the 4th amendment knock requirement does not automatically mean that collected evidence has to be suppressed; but it is cited here for its recitation of the knock requirement, to highlight how dangerous these "no-knock" exceptions can really be.

[461] Oppel, Jr. "Here's What you Need to Know About Breonna Taylor" July 31, 2020. Op Cit.

[462] Ibid. I still contend that lynching of African women needs to be closely analyzed so that counter measures can be developed.
[463] Ibid.
[464] Please see Christina Carrega, et. al. and their report posted to the *CNN* website on September 15, 2020 entitled "Louisville Has Settled Breonna Taylor's Wrongful Death Lawsuit" located here: https://www.cnn.com/2020/09/15/us/breonna-taylor-louisville-settlement/index.html

Memorial for Breonna Taylor in Jefferson Square, Louisville, KY. August 16, 2020
FloNight / CC BY-SA (https://creativecommons.org/licenses/by-sa/4.0)

The lynching of Breonna Taylor, in Louisville, KY, went down just a couple of months before the earth-shattering lynching of George Floyd at the hands of law enforcement on the streets of Minneapolis, MN.

George Floyd Lynching (2020)

"Can't believe this, man. Mom I love you. Love you. Tell my kids I love them. I'm dead".
George Floyd's dying words, 2020

The record of unarmed Africans getting lynched by members of law enforcement, acting under the "color of law" is long, traumatic, soaked in blood, and scribed in death. According to the Genocide petition, on May 18, 1946, William Arthur was killed in Baltimore, MD, while allegedly resisting arrest by police officers. The following day, May 19, Wilbur Bundley was killed by an officer. Nine eye-witnesses state that the Bundley was shot in the back while running away. A few days later,

---

According to public reporting, the settlement details include cash payments to the family, mandatory drug and alcohol testing of officers involved in shootings, dissolution of no-knock warrants, etc.

Isaac Jackson was shot and killed by a policeman. Several organizations began a protest consistent police brutality in Baltimore.[465]

On May 25, 2020, George Floyd was lynched in Minneapolis, MN, while allegedly resisting arrest by police officers. A few officers held down Floyd, one, Officer Derrick Chauvin, held his knee on Floyd's neck for eight minutes and forty-six seconds, effectively suffocating him, while another one just stood there smugly watching the whole thing go down and merely asking if Floyd should be turned over.[466]

Chauvin, who worked at a bar as a part-time bouncer where Floyd also worked, responded to a call where fellow officers were investigating the attempted passing of a counterfeit bill, a misdemeanor charge at best.[467] Chauvin joined Officer Thomas Lang, who had drawn his weapon on Floyd in the moments before, Officer J. Alexander Keung, and Officer Tou Thao.[468]

---

[465] Patterson, William, <u>We Charge Genocide</u>; Op.Cit. pp.63.

[466] Please refer to a BBC uncredited post on its website dated July 16, 2020 located at: https://www.bbc.com/news/world-us-canada-52861726

[467] Ibid.

[468] Ibid.

Protest for the Lynching of George Floyd in Washington, DC June 6, 2020
tedeytan / CC BY-SA (https://creativecommons.org/licenses/by-sa/2.0)

At the beginning of the encounter, a minor scuffle broke out as Floyd was being moved in and out of the back of a squad car. Floyd was taken to the ground and lying on his stomach with his face in the concrete. Chauvin began his murderous neck restraint, by now, a crowd of horrified onlookers began to gather, and the camera phones broadcast video that would soon set the world, punch drunk from Covid-19 lockdowns, on absolute fire.

The pleas from the crowd for Chauvin to let Floyd up, or check his pulse, or Floyd's pleas that he couldn't breathe (a harrowing yet familiar refrain) and knowledge that he urinated on himself were not only ignored but met with the same steely-eyed rage other ancestral lynching victims were likely met with as well, that's the look captured in the faces of so many of those White onlookers that are forever captured in those iconic terror photos.[469] That look of ice-cold evil in Chauvin's eyes, the eight-plus minutes of terror that ended the life of Floyd, and Covid-19 lockdown fatigue sent hundreds of thousands of people, if not millions of people all over the world pouring into the streets at one point under the single banner Black Lives Matter or #BLM.[470]

---

[469] Ibid.

[470] Ibid.

A marked difference in this lynching aftermath, from all of the others, addressed so far is the presence of Minnesota State Attorney General Keith Ellison, a Black man, whose office assumed control of the investigation into the four former officers who have all been charged and are awaiting trial, after conflicting reports, lackluster autopsy, and foot-dragging.[471]

Those eight minutes and forty-six seconds sent an aftershock across the settler state and led to several weeks of protests, the likes of which hadn't been seen on these shores since the heyday of the Civil Rights Movement of the 1960s.

Photo of crowd protesting the lynching of George Floyd on the Tennessee State Capitol on May 30, 202Nick Shockey-Creative Concepts 4.0 / CC BY (https://creativecommons.org/licenses/by/4.0)

---

[471] Ibid. On June 3, 2020, the charge against Chauvin was upgraded to second-degree murder, and the three other officers were charged

Chapter 8

Confronting American Jurisprudence, American Law, and American Terrorism—Conclusion and Solutions

"We sang, and we moved, slowly at first, then increasingly faster...and faster, til' the sound of our voices was one voice, and we no longer had bodies to restrain us. We sang, and we moved until we were able to experience the spirit within in us...through our experience in these rituals, we became one. We became a community again. Each of us gained the strength necessary to deal with our incarceration. Sometimes, we prepared for rebellion".[472]
Mama Marimba Ani, 1970

Looking Back

American Terrorism is not some new, half-baked phenomena executed by a handful of miscreants. Instead, it is a systemic, unrelenting form of oppression that has adjusted tactics and swapped perpetrators in and out over the generations. Lynchers included enslaved owners, militias, pattlerollers, police forces, the Klan, and back and forth. American jurisprudence and American law, for its part, has a history of playing games with African people in this country, whether it's a see-saw, bait, and switch, or three-card monte.

The oppression of American Terrorism is reinforced at every step, even today, as the law enforcement lynch mob is finally starting to be held to as much account as their unions allow. Still, the law only lets the victims of these lynch mobs get "but so much justice."

---

[472] Ani, Marimba, <u>Let The Circle Be Unbroken: The Implications of African Spirituality in the Diaspora</u> (New York: Nkonimfo Productions, 1997) pp. 24-5. Ani's classic treatise is still as relevant and centering after all these years since its original publication in 1980. Indeed, it was that sense of spirituality that African people have been able to hold onto, it has been that "deep well" as Baba Jacob Carruthers (Djedi Shemsu Djehuti) would have called it that we have been able to draw from that has permitted our continued survival against all the odds that Whiteness, White supremacy, and anti-Blackness, have repeatedly placed in our way, over, and over, and over again. And it is that sense of spirituality that will keep us here, thriving and striving, in the future.

As we have covered, the entire African experience in America is based on oppression, resistance, and contradiction. The contradiction is ever-present, whether we look back to the case of John Bunch in 1640, who escaped bondage with his White cohorts but was caught and returned to a life sentence while the White men nearly got a "few more years," but all three committed the same crimes.

Or the fact that "true American hero" Crispus Attucks, heralded as the first patriot of the Republic, was a run-away African who "fit the description." Or the fact that so many "Founding Fathers" were Virginia enslaved "holders." The contradictions are felt across all walks of African life and in almost every conceivable situation, especially when it comes to the lynching of Africa's sons and daughters in this country.

The lynching of Rubin Stacy, Ft. Lauderdale, FL 1935
Loewenthall Collection of African-American Photography
Cornell University Library, Rare Collections Department

Gerald Horne, again who's multiple works were heavily and gratefully relied upon here, points out that in 1916, fifteen thousand Whites in Waco, TX joyously celebrated the brutal lynching of a seventeen-year-old African named Jesse Washington as he was "unsexed, his fingers cut off, nose and ears cut off, burned alive with his extracted teeth fetching up to five dollars each." At the exact same time, the NAACP was lamenting the fate of African "Buffalo Soldiers" sent by the White supremacist to "certain defeat" at Carrizal.[473] Black bodies sent off to meet a predetermined death in a foreign land, on behalf of a government that sits idly by and blindly lets them meet certain death at home.

That list goes on down the line, from the lynchings of yesteryear, where some were meted out against Black folk based on mistaken identity or after they had been sitting in jail awaiting arraignment on formal charges. Some of the lynchings occurred after Black folk was released on bail, acquitted, or no-billed (as the grand jury refused to indict). Some of the lynchings occurred after the Black victims were on their way out of jail.

The lynchings continue today when so many unarmed, unarmed Africans just get mowed down by trigger happy cops who figure, "Blacks are dangerous and guilty of something," even as they turn and run away. The lynchings happen when young African men, who get stalked by "wannabe" twenty-first-century patttlerollers living out their nineteenth-century *Fugitive Slave Act* cosplay fantasies.

---

[473]Horne, Gerald <u>Black and Brown: African-Americans and the Mexican Revolution, 1910-1920</u> (New York: New York University Press, 2005) Op.Cit. pp.74. Here Horne offers a detailed, expansive history of the various interactions African people had with the Mexico and its people during its upheaval. Pay particular focus on the blood soaked Chapter which showed the level of pure viciousness Texans would resort to show their anti-Blackness and dedication to White supremacy, and the powerful recruiting presence that professional boxing champ Jack Johnson played in convincing Africans to leave the settler state and give Mexico, its laws, its people, and the opportunities there a try. Carrizal is a small town in Chihuahua Mexico and was the site of a key battle in the Mexican Revolution.

The terrorism occurs during the unrelenting phenomena of Whites stopping us, questioning us, demanding us to "show our papers" and "prove" our rights to be wherever we are found in public, and then have the cops called on us. *American Terrorism* shows us that whether we are at cookouts in a public park, jogging down the street, entering our apartment complex, decorating our private property, playing in front of a relative's house, napping in a university common area, selling bottled water on the street, mowing the wrong lawn, or being the first President of the United States of America who just so happened to be "Black," being of African descent in America comes with a heavy, heavy price[474]

This battle against White supremacy, White fear, anti-Blackness, and the brutal practice of lynching, ebbs, and flows, true, but it never ceases.[475] Returning to Sally Hedden, she dedicates a significant portion of the fourth chapter of her book <u>Slave Patrols</u>, to the daily dehumanization enslaved Africans experienced during chattel slavery. Hedden tells this story through the granting of passes, papers, and tickets

---

[474]Make no mistake about it, all that "birtherism" nonsense directed at Obama (44) in the early days of his presidency was more than mere political gamesmanship but it actually hearkens back to the various *Fugitive Slave Acts*, *Slave Codes*, and *Black Codes* addressed at various times throughout this book. Control of the movement of African bodies and the assertion of White supremacy over those bodies, through whatever means necessary, are foundational co-pillars since the launch of this settler project as has been shown; also see Brandon Griggs, "Living While Black: Here are all the routine activities for which police were called on African-Americans this year" posted to the CNN website and updated on December 28, 2018 and found here: https://www.cnn.com/2018/12/20/us/living-while-black-police-calls-trnd/index.html.

[475]White fear has been a hallmark of life for the settlers, fear of the Indigenes, fear of colonial armies, fear of dragooned African rebellions, escape, and maroon societies, fear of Japanese-Americans during WWII, fear of integration, fear of encroached suburbs, fear of Multi-Culturalism, fear of an invading caravan of Brown and Black folk, fear of changing demographics, etc. It has often been a powerful political platform or impulse to galvanize around, sometimes it has deadly consequences.

by the White planters and overseers (in some instances) and the humiliation of having to show them on demand any time these Whites snapped their fingers.[476]

Beyond the Bison-Colin Kaepernick Kneeling Boycott during a professional American Football game/Knee Man's Tank

Top/https://www.clipartmax.com/download/m2i8d3A0G6G6K9Z5_beyond-the-bison-colin-kaepernick-kneeling-boycott-knee-mans-tank-top/

Brother Kaepernick's and Brother Eric Reid's courageous protest in the fall of 2016 inspired thousands, if not millions of people, to engage the history of the pattlerollers and their mistreatment of Black people.

---

[476]Hadden, Sally Slave Patrols; pp. 105-36; the nature of the control of African life was so invasively infuriating that the White pass granters would either do so as a form of manumission or refrain from issuing them as punishment, and sometimes passes could be ripped up and/or ignored by the pattlerollers themselves, who could sometimes be bribed. The passes were heavily scrutinized and the more specific the better for the ancestor.

The Whites were so comfortable in their control they could make jokes about and literally through the passes themselves; Hadden notes that an enslaved ancestor named John used to get a pass to see his wife on a neighboring death camp every weekend and while he was illiterate the pass used to read as follows: "To my man John, I give this pass, Pass an repass to Sally's Black...., Ef don't nobody like this pass, They can kiss..."; the Whites thought this was hilarious; Op.Cit. pp. 112.

Anti-Slavery Almanac depiction of old-school pattlerollers rousting an African man, 1839 (Public Domain)

African people in America, though, we get to points and places where enough is enough and decide to fight back; in the early summer of 2020, others joined us in that fight this time en mass. Non-Africans, at times, led those fights themselves,

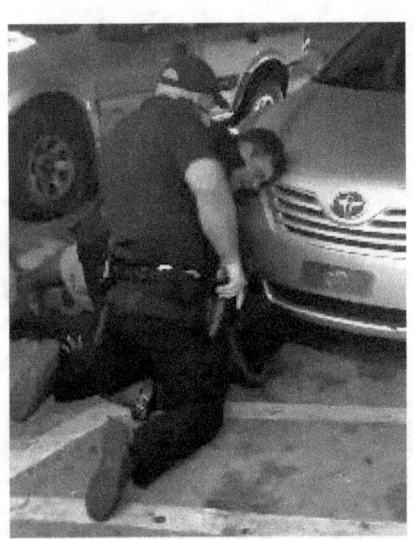

especially in places where we barely exist or exist in minuscule numbers. Folks of all stripes and from all over took to the streets under the banner #BLM, and while not all of the individual protestors had good intentions, the vast majority appeared to do so.[477]

Alton Sterling was reportedly selling CD's when these new-school pattlerollers held him at gunpoint and then lynched him. July 5, 2016; Bryn Stole / CC BY-SA (https://creativecommons.org/licenses/by-sa/4.0) (Public Domain)

---

[477]Please see the uncredited, undated report posted to the KBOI, news station in Boise, ID, website posted discussing the identity of the infamous "umbrella man" who was seen on video destroying property during the early stages of the George Floyd rebellions in Minneapolis, MN. The report notes that the authorities, while not releasing the suspects name believe he is a part of a White nationalist prison gang called the Aryan Cowboy Brotherhood. The link to the report can be found here: https://www.kboi.com/news/minneapolis-police-identify-umbrella-man-who-helped-incite-george-floyd-riots-warrant-says/.

The #BLM General Strike in its street action form has finally started to die down a bit (except for the flare-up in Kenosha, WI). While what went down in Portland, OR, show just how far how paid defenders of the settler state are willing to go to reassert themselves, after weeks of multi-racial, multi-generational marches, protests, and other forms of mobilization.[478]

Several weeks of direct street action protesters were met head-on with deployed chemical agents, tear gas, pepper-spray, buzzing helicopters, and repeated over aggressive police strongman tactics reminiscent of the types of responses seen from repressive and fascist regimes the settler state usually hypocritically condemns on the world stage and castigates. But like our ancestors faced similar challenges and obstacles that were far worse, the choice is ours whether we resist, rebel, and get rolling despite the opposing forces rolled out to defend the settler state and maintain the status quo or get rolled over.

Looking Ahead

The street heat has to transition to political organizing, policy, and legislative action (as far as lynching goes), including goals of finally passing Federal Anti-Lynching legislation, as highlighted earlier.

This legislation has to address the mandated use of "bad cop" databases, so officers like Betty Shelby (who was a part of the lynch mob that killed Terrance Crutcher) and Timothy Loehmann (the lone wolf, who was shielded by both the law and his cop union after lynching twelve-year-old Tamir Rice) are kept off the streets armed with guns, badges, and the ability to detain the public. The legislation must also

---

[478]Please see the uncredited BBC report posted to its website on July 18, 2020 which lays out some of the interplay between local law enforcement, marked and unmarked federal agents and contractors, and protestors located here: https://www.bbc.com/news/world-us-canada-53453077.

include removing qualified immunity protections for members of law enforcement involved in the murders of unarmed people and a change in law enforcement use of force standards from a "reasonable" standard to a "necessary standard" as well.[479]

If *American Terrorism* is to end, especially as it has been carried out against Black folk on these shores for centuries now, the truly driven organize goal-oriented, "comprehensive" campaigns geared towards changing the laws of the land. They must organize around changing the way communities of Black, Brown, and Red folks are "patrolled." Organize around how our bodies are "controlled" and to break the back of White supremacy finally and forever as an ordering principle.

Policy and organizing goals should focus on overturning crippling habitual offenders laws ("three strikes laws") on the federal and state levels, reducing law enforcement budgets, and redirecting funds to other public services (like mental health, drug, and family counseling).[480]

---

[479] Ali, Amir H. and Emily Clark, "Qualified Immunity Explained" posted to *The Appeal* website on June 20, 2019. Qualified Immunity is a legal construct, made to circumvent the spirit of the *Civil Rights Acts* and their overall attempts to level the playing field against the "color of law". Essentially it is based on the idea that public employees who are acting in "good faith" should not be held civilly accountable for their actions, regardless of how wrong or negligent those actions may be.

Amir H. Ali and Emily Clark, from *The Appeal*, posted an excellent, and thorough essay on the history and conceptualization of qualified immunity. Pay particular attention to the story of Mailaka Brooks and her handling by local law enforcement and the handling of her case by the courts. The report can be found here: https://theappeal.org/qualified-immunity-explained/#.Xy3p5dhyxHk.email.

[480] The August 2020 decision by the Louisiana Supreme Court to decline to overturn a life sentence for an African man, 62 year old Wayne Bryant, for stealing a pair of hedge clippers over 40 years ago was just the latest example (at the time of drafting) of the dual criminal disposition systems that, again as we have shown throughout this essay, have always existed in this settler state; there is a system for the rich and privileged and generally a system for everybody and the difference is really felt when it comes to Black and Brown people. The left leaning organization, Common Dreams, has posted an on-line petition which gives both an excellent review of the Bryant case and a call-to-action, located here: https://www.commondreams.org/news/2020/08/07/enraging-and-inexcusable-louisiana-supreme-court-rules-black-man-convicted-garden;

Policy and organizing goals should also focus on changing the Stand Your Ground and Castle Doctrines for civilian and police use of force regulations from a "reasonable use of force" standard to a "necessary use of force" standard. There needs to be a litigation strategy to pursue claims and haul responsible law enforcement parties into court. Those lawsuits seek to damages targeting lynching cops' pensions, real property holdings, children's college funds, and strike some fear of accountability in their hearts.[481]

See also Tana Geneva's report to *The Appeal* posted on August 6, 2020 which lays out some of the current calls from community and faith based organizations to overturn these utter crippling "habitual offender" and "three-strikes laws" especially for petty offenses like in the Bryant case; you can find the link to the report here: https://theappeal.org/as-decriminalization-drives-reforms-for-marijuana-convictions-activists-see-others-serving-time-left-behind/#.Xy3sUwGAraA.email;

And also see Bill Chappell's article posted to the NPR website noting that Colorado voters approved a ballot measure to remove the "crime" exception to the 13th Amendment discussed *above*; Chappel, Bill "Colorado Votes to Abolish Slavery 2 Years After Similar Amendment Failed" NPR, November 7, 2018 located here: https://www.npr.org/2018/11/07/665295736/colorado-votes-to-abolish-slavery-2-years-after-similar-amendment-failed.

Also see, Sarah Lustbader, "Joe Biden's Role in Mass Incarceration Was No Mistake: It Was Politics" *The Appeal*, April 25, 2019 original published as part of The Daily Appeal Newsletter located here: https://theappeal.org/politicalreport/joe-bidens-role-in-mass-incarceration-was-no-mistake-it-was-politics/#.Xy3rpGgb0us.email, here Lustbader offers a pointed critique of the Democratic presidential Nominee and his role, and underwhelming apology, for helping to craft the *1994 Federal Crime Bill* which promoted "three strikes laws", furthered already existing federal minimum sentencing laws, and disparate sentencing (again like we saw with John Punch) guidelines for defendants convicted of crack cocaine charges (possession and intent to sell) and powder cocaine charges (possession and intent to sell), etc.

[481] This is a strictly legal argument, but it is a critical one. Returning to the killing of Trayvon Martin, the suggested change in the law would have had the jury in the case of George Zimmerman decide if Zimmerman actually had to shoot Martin in the midst of the scuffle, taking all the various factors into consideration, as opposed to asking what a "reasonable person" would have done in a similar scuffle. This very important change in that law may have resulted in a different legal outcome for Zimmerman and perhaps he wouldn't be taking viral pictures signing bags of "Skittles" and auctioning off the gun he used to lynch Martin; see Wagner, Laura and Laura Domonoske, "George Zimmerman Auctions Off Gun He Used to Kill Travon Martin" NPR May 12, 2016 located here: https://www.npr.org/sections/thetwo-way/2016/05/12/477769731/george-zimmerman-auctioning-off-gun-with-which-he-killed-trayvon-martin.

The City of Louisville, KY, and Breonna Taylor's family settled the wrongful death suit filed in her case. The emotional, September 15, 2020 press conference announced some initial police reforms that the city may employ in addition to a twelve-million-dollar settlement. Any solid litigation strategy must have a built-in rapid response media component ready to publish the details of every settlement agreement. Showing taxpayers how much money their local governments are spending on settling police brutality cases must be part of the legal argument for "Defunding the Police."

The Marshall Project and the NAACP Legal Defense Fund's Thurgood Marshall Institute National Police Funding Database (NPFD) provides tremendous resources in tracking police brutality settlements. They should be amplified. For example, the City of Phoenix, AZ, paid over twenty-six million dollars to settle 191 police brutality cases between 2008 and 2018. This wave of *American Terrorism* costs taxpayers millions of dollars. If the calls to "Defund the Police" fail as ethical and moral arguments, perhaps the economic arguments may fare better.[482]

Policy and organizing goals should address the issue of consent decrees. Black's Online Dictionary defines a Consent Decree as the following: one entered by consent of the parties; it is not a judicial sentence but is like a solemn contract or agreement of the parties, made under the sanction of the court, and in effect, an admission by them that the decree is a just determination of their rights upon the real facts of the case if such facts had been proved.; similar to an "agreed judgment" used to settle a

---

[482] Please see The Marshall Project at: https://www.themarshallproject.org/records/1712-police-settlements and the NAACP Legal Defense Fund's Thurgood Marshall Institute National Police Funding Database website at https://policefundingdatabase.tminstituteldf.org/misconductsettlements

case in civil litigation.[483] These negotiated agreements are viewed as the most powerful ways to effect changes in local law enforcement departments short of federal legislation because they can include real teeth that result in actual accountability.[484]

These political platforms will have to transform into a multi-faceted, mature, and sophisticated complex campaign that addresses the needs of Black populations of this settler state seriously and produce concrete, tangible results. This campaign must involve participation in the electoral process on every level. If a stated goal is to change the law, it will also need to work hand in hand with the above-referenced litigation strategy and an effective and focused legislative action strategy. All we will be doing is looking for the next hashtag and viral video.

Black people, for their part, really need to support positive, independent Black and Black facing institutions like the American Holocaust Museum and the National Memorial and Museum for Peace and Justice, which are two prominent, independent memorials dedicated to the traumatic legacy of the lynching of Africans in America, frequently support Black-owned businesses, especially bookstore, resource centers, and Black facing media outlets, join or form local organizations and move the much-needed dialogue and programs forward, become politically active and amplify positive platforms, and get into the habit of critically reading as much information as you can; watching movies, videos, listening to podcasts, and taking virtual classes are fantastic, but they aren't substitutes for doing any of the work.[485]

---

[483]*Allen v. Richardson*, 9 Rich. Eq. (S. C.) 53; *Kelly v. Milan* (C. C.) 21 Fed. 842; *Schmidt v. Mining Co.*, 28 Or. 9. 40 Pac. 1014. 52 Am. St. Rep. 759.

[484]Please the U.S. Department of Justice's Civil Division's webpage on a power point primer on consent decrees and how they operate located here: https://www.justice.gov/crt/page/file/922456/download; also see

[485]The American Black Holocaust Museum website is located here: https://abhmuseum.org/ and the National Memorial for Peace and Justice website is located here: https://museumandmemorial.eji.org/memorial

Photo of a street mural at Black Lives Matter Plaza in Washington, DC June 7, 2020
Washington, DC June 7, 2020
Eytan / CC BY-SA (https://creativecommons.org/licenses/by-sa/2.0)

There was a time when our organizations, sometimes close allies and at other times, some opposed groups, all set their collective sights on stamping out the cruel practice of lynching. For example, the 1922 world convention of the Universal Negro Improvement Association and the ACL held a keynote session, chaired by Marcus Mosiah Garvey addressed as: "Lynching, How to Correct It?" Even the most vehement detractors of the UNIA, like A. Phillip Randolph, Richard B. Moore and Cyril Briggs, W.E.B. DuBois, and William Monroe Trotter, for example, would have understood (and hopefully) the focus on lynching, as they themselves fought against on it.[486]

So the modern-day movements and coalitions African people in America have found themselves building should spend the time rebuilding connections with other organizations across the African world family that are equally focused on stamping out the modern lynching of Black folk.

Another powerful organization that African people in this country should always support is the Institute of the Black World 21st Century and its numerous efforts to implement solutions to alleviate the current conditions we still find ourselves in. This

---

[486] Umoja, We Will Shoot Back; Op.Cit., Garvey held the session at the UNIA World Conference on November 12, 1922 in New York City.

organization is mainly committed to the eternal fight for reparations paid to Black folk in America; you can find more information on this link to their website: https://ibw21.org/initiative-posts/naarc-posts/naarc-rolls-out-preliminary-10-point-reparations-plan/.[487]

Hopefully, the readers find this information covered in this brief historical legal analysis harrowing, sobering, enraging, engaging, and ultimately armoring and can clearly, and easily find the evidence supporting the calls for a) reparations to be paid to descendants of Africans who were in bondage, disenfranchised, un and undereducated, lynched "legally" and or "off-the-books, redlined, thrown back into *de facto* enslavement through peonage, share-cropping, vagrancy, drug laws, poverty, and abject poverty, and or otherwise brutalized by *American Terrorism*, b) measures to redirect and redefine the roles and models of policing, especially in communities of Black, Brown, and Red folks and finally move away from the colonial code and Antebellum pattleroller models that have been in place for centuries, and c) calls for local hate crimes and federal anti-Lynching legislation.

If not nothing else, this book should hopefully provide a few historical, fact-based answers for the questions that will inevitably be asked after the next Elijah McClain gets lynched or the next Amy Cooper screams into a phone (channeling her ancestors like Carolyn Bryant, Sarah Page, and so many countless, nameless, faceless others) about being threatened by a random African somewhere, somehow "fitting description" and maybe setting up yet another lynching.[488]

---

[487] The IBW21 was founded in 2001 and has been working diligently to do its part for creating a vibrant, dynamic future for African people in this part of the Diaspora through organizing, programming, legislation advocacy, and intellectual contribution.

[488] Elijah McClain, self-proclaimed introvert and African man aged 23, was lynched by three police officers in Aurora, CO Nathan Woodyard, Jason Rosenblatt and Randy Roedema who were responding to a call of a "shady" character and approached McClain because "he fit the description". The brutal murder occurred on August 24, 2019 and McClain's killing stands out as these "color of law" killers actually roughed him up to the point where he got sick,

Hopefully, readers realize how important it is to weigh in on how the laws are made here, who makes the law, who enforces the law, and who ultimately says what the law "is" after engaging this, we know what's coming; way better to be prepared then to get caught slipping, again.

EMT's arrived and shot him up with 500mgs of the sedative Ketamin, he had a heart attack, and subsequently expired. There is a lot of finger pointing around the cause of McClain's heart attack, but what cannot be denied is that the scrawny, little guy was unarmed and posed no threat to anyone, let alone anyone in the lynch party posing as cops. And it took almost a year before the public even found out about the case. Please refer to story posted by Knez Walker, et.al, to the ABC News website on June 30, 2020 located at: https://abcnews.go.com/US/happened-elijah-mcclain-protests-bring-attention-death/story?id=71523476.

And on May 25, 2020 (the same day George Floyd got lynched) Amy Cooper, a White woman, was confronted by an African man and avid bird watcher named Christian Cooper (no relation or acquaintance) in Central Park in Manhattan, NY over her dog being off his leash. Becoming instantly irate, offended, and indignant, Amy Cooper whips out her cell phone and channels her inner Sarah Page and Carolyn Bryant, attempts to activate law enforcement, and used voice manipulation to manufacture an imminent threat; luckily for Christian Cooper no pattlerollers ever showed up and he was taping the whole event which his sister posted the video of online and went viral; as history shows this could have ended tragically different. This is a report on this incident can be found in a CNN article by Amir Vera and Lura Ly posted to its website on May 26, 2020 and can be found here: https://www.cnn.com/2020/05/26/us/central-park-video-dog-video-african-american-trnd/index.html.

Pattleroller badge, Georgetown County, South Carolina, 1858 (Public Domain)

This postcard was taken from death, lynching at Russellville, Logan County, Kentucky, at the Proctor Tree
By Unknown author - http://collections.carli.illinois.edu/cdm/singleitem/collection/nby_teich/id/4084, Public Domain, https://commons.wikimedia.org/w/index.php?curid=80774481

International Case

Somerset v. Stewart 98 ER 499 (1772)

Federal Cases

Marbury v. Madison 5 U.S. 137) (1803)

Cherokee Nation v. Georgia, 30 U.S. 1 (1831)

Prigg v. Pennsylvania 41 US 539 (1842)

Scott v. Sandford 60 US 393 (1857)

Slaughterhouse Cases 83 U.S. 36 (1873)

United States v. Cruikshank 92 U.S. 542 (1876)

United States v. Harris, 106 U.S. 629 (1883)

Plessy v. Ferguson 163 U.S. 537 (1896)

McCain v. Des Moines, 174 U. S. 108, 19 Sup. Ct. (H4, 43 L. Ed. 936) (1899)

Moore v. Dempsey, 261 U.S. 86 (1923)

Powell v. Alabama, 287 U.S. 45 (1932)

Norris v. Alabama, 294 U.S. 587 (1935)

Brown v. Mississippi 297 U.S. 278 (1936)

Korematsu v. United States, 323 U.S. 214 (1944)

Brown v. Board of Education of Topeka, 347 U.S. 483 (1954)

Gideon v. Wainwright, 372 U.S. 335 (1963)

United States v. Cecil Price, et al. 383 U.S. 787 (1966)

United States v. Sioux Nation of Indians, 488 U.S. 371 (1980)

Harlow v. Fitzgerald 457 U.S. 800 (1982)

Donald v. United Klans of America C.A. 84-0725 (S.D.Ala. Feb. 12, 1987)

Hudson v. Michigan, 547 U.S. 586 (2006)

In re *African-American Slave Descendants Litigation*, 375 F.Supp. 2d 721 (N.D. IL, 2005), 471 F.ed 754 (7th Cir. 2007)

Holder v. Shelby County 570 U.S. 579 (2013)

Ogala Sioux Tribe v. Van Hunnik, 100 F. Supp 3d.749 D. S.D. 2015); order vacated by *Ogalas Sioux Tribe v. Fleming*, 904 F.3d. 603 (8th Cir. 2018)

State Cases

Allen v. Richardson, 9 Rich. Eq. (S. C.) 53

Kelly v. Milan (C. C.) 21 Fed. 842

Schmidt v. Mining Co., 28 Or. 9. 40 Pac. 1014. 52 Am. St. Rep. 759

Snelling v. State, 49 Fla. 34 (1905)

Weiand v. State, 732 So.2d 1044 (1999)

Constitutional Articles, Amendments, Codes, and Acts

U.S. Const. art I §2.

U.S. Const. amend V

U.S. Const. amend VI

U.S. Const. amend XIII

U.S. Const. amend XIV

U.S. Const. amend XV

10 USC §§ 251-54 (1807)

P.L. 42-22 (1871)

1 Stat. 302 (1793)

Pub.L. 31–60 (1850)

P.L. 88-352 (1964)

P.L. 89-110 (1965)

P.L. 909-284 (1968)

42 U.S.C. § 1983 (1979)

P.L. 100–383 (1988)

H.R. 35 Emmet Till Anti-Lynching Act, 116th Congress H. Rept. 116-267 (2019-2020)

Works Cited

Allen, James <u>Without Sanctuary</u> (Sante Fe: Twin Palms Publishing 2000)

Allen, Q., & Metcalf, H. (2019). "Up to No Good: <u>The Intersection of Race, Gender, and Fear of Black Men in US Society</u>. In Boyce T. & Chunnu W. (Eds.), *Historicizing Fear: Ignorance, Vilification, and Othering* (pp. 19-34). Louisville: University Press of Colorado. doi:10.2307/j.ctvwh8d12.4

Alexander, Michelle <u>The New Jim Crow: Mass Incarceration in the Age of Colorblindness</u> (New York: The New Press, 2010) (E-Book)

Ani, Marimba, <u>Let The Circle Be Unbroken: The Implications of African Spirituality in the Diaspora</u> (New York: Nkonimfo Productions, 1997)

Anderson, Devery <u>Emmett Till: The Murder That Shocked the World and Propelled the Civil Rights Movement</u> (Jackson: University Press of Mississippi, 2015) (E-Book)

Apel, Dora, and Shawn Michelle Smith, <u>Lynching Photographs: Defining Moments in American Photography</u> (Berkeley: University of California Press, 2007).

Aptheker Herbert (ed.) <u>Afro-American History in The Modern Era: A Pioneering Chronicle of the Black People in Twentieth-Century America</u> (New York: Carol Publishing Group, 1971

- (ed.) <u>A Documentary History Of the Negro People in The United States, Vol. IV: From The New Deal to The End of World War II</u> (New York: Carol Publishing Group, 1992)

- To Be Free: Pioneering Studies in Afro-American History, (New York: Carol Publishing Group ed. 1991)

Barnett, Ida B. Wells Lynch Law in Georgia: a six-weeks' record in the center of southern civilization, as faithfully chronicled by the "Atlanta Journal" and the "Atlanta constitution": also the full report of Louis P. Le Vin, the Chicago detective sent to investigate the burning of Samuel Hose, the torture and hanging of Elijah Strickland, the colored preacher, and the lynching of nine men for alleged arson (Georgia, 1899) E449 .D16 vol. 16, no. 12
E449 .D16 vol. C, no. 4
HV6465.G4 W45 1899 Copy 1. https://www.loc.gov/item/91898209/

- Mob Rule in New Orleans with Southern Horrors: Lynch Laws in All Its Phases (Fairford Glos: The Echo Library 2005).

- The Red Record Revisited: African American Lynching Then and Now (ed. Destiny Coleman) (Topeka: International Consortium International, 2020)

- Southern Horrors: Lynch Law in All Its Phases (New Delhi: Alpha Editions and VJJ Books. 2018).

Arnesen, Eric. "The fugitive slave acts of 1793 and 1850".. *Cobblestone* 1 Feb. 2003: n. pag. Print.

Arnett, Autumn A. "Land Grant HBCU's Celebrating the 130th Anniversary of the 1890 Morrill Act" *Diverse Issues in Higher Education,* August 27, 2020. https://diverseeducation.com/article/188838/

Bascom, J. (1906). "The Three Amendments." *The Annals of the American Academy of Political and Social Science, 27,* 135-147. Retrieved July 29, 2020, from www.jstor.org/stable/1010516

Benbow, Mark (2010). "Birth of a Quotation: Woodrow Wilson and Like Writing History with Lightning." *The Journal of the Gilded Age and Progressive Era, 9*(4), 509-533. Retrieved August 3, 2020, from www.jstor.org/stable/20799409

Bibb, Henry Narrative of the Life and Adventures of Henry Bibb, An American Slave, Written by Himself: Electronic Edition. (1815)
Funding from the National Endowment for the Humanities supported the electronic publication of this title. Located here: https://docsouth.unc.edu/neh/bibb/bibb.html (Public Domain)

Bowers, Rick Spies of Mississippi (Washington, D.C.: The National Geographic Society, 2010)

Brawley, Benjamin A Social History of the American Negro (London: Collier Books Limited, 1970)

Breitman, George The Last Year of Malcolm X: The Evolution of a Revolutionary (Atlanta: Pathfinder Press, 21st. Edition 2011)

Bullitt, W. (1924). THE SUPREME COURT AND UNCONSTITUTIONAL LEGISLATION. *American Bar Association Journal, 10*(6), 419-425. Retrieved August 25, 2020, from http://www.jstor.org/stable/25711622

Cameron, James A Time for Terror: A Survivor's Story. (Wauwatosa: LifeWrightPress, 3rd Edition, 2016)

Carson, Claybourne, In Struggle (Cambridge: Harvard University Press, 1995)

Carruthers, Jacob H. Intellectual Warfare (Chicago: Third World Press, 1999)

Charles Rivers Editors, The Mississippi Burning Case: The History and Legacy of the Freedom Summer Murders at the Height of the Civil Rights Movement (San Bernardino: Charles Rivers Editors, 2020) (EBook)

Christian, M. (2002). An African-Centered Perspective on White Supremacy. *Journal of Black Studies, 33*(2), 179-198. Retrieved August 19, 2020, from www.jstor.org/stable/3180933

Cobb Jr., Charles E. This Nonviolent Stuff'll Get You Killed (Durham: Duke University Press, 2014)

Cokely, Robert The Role of Federal Military Forces in Domestic Disorders: 1789-1878 (Washington: Center of Military History, U.S. Army)

Conover, Jim and James Brecher, Lynch Law (Pekin: Lynch Law, 1992)

Cooper, Anna Julia A Voice From the South (ed. Janet Leary) (New York: Dover Publications, Inc., 2016)

Cooper, Afua The Hanging of Angelique: The Untold Story of Canadian Slavery and the Burning of Old Montreal (Athens: University of Georgia Press, 2006)

Corwin, E. (1914). "Marbury v. Madison and the Doctrine of Judicial Review." *Michigan Law Review, 12*(7), 538-572. doi:10.2307/1274986

Cronin, Edmund David Black Moses: The Story of Marcus Garvey and the Universal Negro Improvement Association (Madison: The University of Wisconsin Press, 1966)

Currier, D. (2003). (Rep.). Strategic Studies Institute, US Army War College. Retrieved July 28, 2020, from www.jstor.org/stable/resrep11801

David, C. (1924). "The Fugitive Slave Law of 1793 and its Antecedents". *The Journal of Negro History, 9*(1), 18-25. doi:10.2307/2713433

De Las Casas, Bartolome A Short Account of the Destruction of the Indies in 1552 (London: Penguin Publishing Group, 1992)

Du Bois, William Edward Burghardt (1898). The Study of the Negro Problems. *The Annals of the American Academy of Political and Social Science, 11*, 1-23. Retrieved July 28, 2020, from www.jstor.org/stable/1009474

Finding The Law ed. Robert C. Berring and an Elizabeth A. Edinger (St. Paul: West Group, Am. Casebook Series, 11th ed. 1999)

Fisher, Leslie, and Benjamin Quarles (eds.) The Negro American: A Documentary History (Glenview: Scott, Foresman, and Company 1967)

F. R. (1874). Circuit Court of the United States. District of Louisiana. *The United States v. Cruikshank et al. The American Law Register (1852-1891), 22*(10), 630-644. doi:10.2307/3303600.

Fairfax, Colita Nichols Black America Series: Hampton Virginia (Charleston: Arcadia Publishing 2005).

Favors, Jelani, Shelter In a Time of Storm: How Black Colleges Fostered Generations of Leadership and Activism (Chapel Hill: The University of North Carolina Press, 2019)

Felker-Kantor, M. (2016). "The Coalition against Police Abuse: CAPA's Resistance Struggle in 1970s Los Angeles". *Journal of Civil and Human Rights*, 2(1), 52-88. doi:10.5406/jcivihumarigh.2.1.52

Franklin, John Hope, "Propaganda as History" pp. 10–23 in *Race and History: Selected Essays 1938–1988* (Louisiana State University Press, 1989

Gines, Kathryn T., "Anna Julia Cooper," *The Stanford Encyclopedia of Philosophy* (Summer 2015 Edition), Edward N. Zalta (ed.), URL = <https://plato.stanford.edu/archives/sum2015/entries/anna-julia-cooper/>. https://plato.stanford.edu/entries/anna-julia-cooper/

Ginzburg, Ralph 100 Years of Lynchings (Baltimore: Black Classic Press, 1988 ed.)

Haas, Jeffrey The Assassination of Fred Hampton: How the FBI and the Chicago Police Murdered a Black Panther (Chicago: Lawrence Hill Books, 2010).

Hadden, Sally Slave Patrols: Law and Violence in Virginia and the Carolinas (Cambridge: First Harvard University Press, 2001).

Hamilton, Alexander, et al. The Federalist Papers (New York: Penguin Group and Signet Classic Printing, 2003)

Harlan, Louis Booker T. Washington: Wizard of Tuskegee from 1901-1915 (New York: Oxford University Press, 1983)

Henderson, L. (2004). "Brown v. Board of Education at 50: The Multiple Legacies for Policy and Administration". *Public Administration Review, 64*(3), 270-274. Retrieved July 28, 2020, from www.jstor.org/stable/3542592

Hixson, W. (1969). "Moorfield Storey and the Defense of the Dyer Anti-Lynching Bill." *The New England Quarterly, 42*(1), 65-81. doi:10.2307/363500

Horne, Gerald The Apocalypse of Settler Colonialism (New York: New York Monthly Review Press. 2018)

- Black and Brown: African-Americans and the Mexican Revolution, 1910-1920 (New York: New York University Press, 2005)

- Confronting Black Jacobins: The United States, the Haitian Revolution, And the Origins of the Dominican Republic (New York: Monthly Review Press, 2015)

- The Counter-Revolution of 1776, (New York: New York University Press, 2014)

- The Dawning of the Apocalypse (New York: Monthly Review Press, 2020)

- <u>The Rise and Fall of the Associated Negro Press: Claude Barnett's Pan-African News and the Jim Crow Paradox</u> (Champagne: University of Illinois Board of Trustees, 2017)

- <u>White Supremacy Confronted: U.S. Imperialism and Anti-Communism vs. the Liberation of Southern Africa, from Rhodes to Mandela</u> (New York: International Publishers, 2019)

Ifill, Sherrilyn, et al. <u>A Perilous Path: Talking Race, Inequality, and the Law</u> (New York: Center on Race, Inequality, and the Law, New York University School of Law (2018)

Jalonick, Mary Clarke, Michael Balsamo, Eric Tucker William *Barr Vigorously Defends Federal Law Enforcement Response to Protest During House Testimony*, Time July 28, 2020

James, Cyril Lionel Robert <u>The Black Jacobins</u> (New York: The Vintage Books ed. 1998) Georgia.

- <u>A History of Pan-African Revolt</u> (Oakland: PM Press, 2012)

Johnson, A. (1921). "The Constitutionality of the Fugitive Slave Acts" *The Yale Law Journal, 31*(2), 161-182. doi:10.2307/789306

Joseph, Peniel <u>Stokely: A Life</u> (New York: Basic*Civitas* Books, 2014)

Katagiri, Yasuhiro <u>The Mississippi State Sovereignty State Commission: Civil Rights and States Rights </u>(Jackson: University Press of Mississippi, 2001)

Kellogg, Charles Flint <u>History of the National Association of the Advancement of Colored People 1909-1920 (vol.1)</u> (Baltimore: The Johns Hopkins Press, 1967)

Kendi, Ibram X. Stamped From the Beginning: The Definitive History of Racist Ideas in America (New York: BoldType Books, 2017)

King, Jason Duty to Retreat: A Review of the Evolution of the Duty to Retreat, the Castle Doctrine, Florida Stand Your Ground Law and Relevant Court Cases (Coppell: 2015)

King, Joyce Hate Crime: The Story of Dragging in Jasper, TX (New York: Pantheon Books, 2002)

Kinyatti, Maina wa (ed.) Kenya's Freedom Struggle: The Dedan Kimathi Papers (www.BookSurge.com, 2009)

Klarman, Michael From Jim Crow to Civil Rights: The Supreme Court and the Struggle for Racial Equality (New York: Oxford University Press, 2004)

Krugler, David, 1919, The Year of Racial Violence: How African-Americans Fought Back (New York: Cambridge University Press, 2015) (EBook)

Landon, F. (1922). "The Anderson Fugitive Case." *The Journal of Negro History,* 7(3), 233-242. doi:10.2307/2713418

- (1920). "The Negro Migration to Canada after the Passing of the Fugitive Slave Act." *The Journal of Negro History,* 5(1), 22-36. doi:10.2307/2713499.

Leamer, Laurence The Lynching: The Epic Courtroom Battle that Brought Down the Klan (New York: Harper Collins, 2016)

Lee, John Michael, and Samaad Wes Keys <u>Land Grant but Unequal: State Match One to One Match Funding for 1890 Land Grant Universities</u>: https://www.aplu.org/library/land-grant-but-unequal-state-one-to-one-match-funding-for-1890-land-grant universities/file#:~:text=A%20second%20Morrill%20Act%20was, institution%20for%20persons%20of%20color

Lewis, David Levering, <u>W.E.B. DuBois: Biography of a Race 1868-1919</u> (New York: Owl Book Company Henry Holt and Company, LLC 1993) (EBook)

Logan, Rayford <u>Betrayal of the Negro</u> (New York: McMillan 1965)

- <u>Betrayal of the Negro: From Rutherford B. Hayes to Woodrow Wilson</u> (Cambridge: Da Capo Press, 1997)

Lynching Statistics. (1918). *Journal of the American Institute of Criminal Law and Criminology, 9*(1), 144-146. Retrieved July 28, 2020, from www.jstor.org/stable/1133750 pp. 144-45.

Madison, James H. <u>A Lynching in the Heartland: Race and Memory in America</u> (New York: Palgrave McMillan, 2001)

Madigan, Tim <u>Burning of Greenwood, The Burning: Massacre, Destruction, and the Tulsa Race Riots of 1921</u> (New York: St. Martin's Press, 2001)

Mallison, A. (1920). "THE POLITICAL THEORIES OF ROGER B. TANEY." *The Southwestern Political Science Quarterly, 1*(3), 219-240. Retrieved July 28, 2020, from www.jstor.org/stable/42882963

Markovitz, Jonathan Legacies of Lynching: Racial Violence and Memory (Minneapolis: University of Minnesota Press, 2004)

Martin, C. (1997). Internationalizing "The American Dilemma": The Civil Rights Congress and the 1951 Genocide Petition to the United Nations. *Journal of American Ethnic History,* 16(4), 35-61. Retrieved July 28, 2020, from www.jstor.org/stable/27502217

Martin Tony, Race First: The Ideological and Organizational Struggle of Marcus Garvey and the Universal Negro Improvement Association (Dover: Majority Press, 1976)

Martinez, Elizabeth B. "What is White Supremacy?" Philadelphia Yearly Meeting of the Religious Society of Friends (Quakers) annual meeting website posted here: http://www.pym.org/annual-sessions/wp-content/uploads/sites/7/2017/06/What_Is_White_Supremacy_Martinez.pdf

Matthews, Donald, At the Altar of Lynching: Burning Sam Hose in the American South (New York: Cambridge University Press, 2018)

Moore, Richard B. The Name Negro: Its Origin and Evil Use (Baltimore: Black Classic Press, 1992)

McKinstry, Carolyn Maul entitled While The World Watched (Carol Stream: Tyndale House Publishers, 2011)

McTaggart, U. (2014). "The Empty Noose: The Trouble With Removing Spectacle From Lynching Iconography" *Journal of Black Studies,* 45(8), 792-811. Retrieved August 1, 2020, from www.jstor.org/stable/24573594

Mitchell, Don Freedom Summer Murders (New York: Scholastic Press, 2014)

Natsu Taylor Saito's Settler Colonialism, Race, and the Law (New York: New York University Press. 2020)

Oklahoma Commission (published on February 28, 2001, as its Final Report, Oklahoma Commission to Study the Tulsa Race Riot of 1921, Tulsa Oklahoma (retrieved archive on July 29, 2020, and recalculated for 2020 equivalency).

Pakenham, Thomas, The Scramble for Africa: 1876-1912 (London: Abacus, 1992)

Parsons, Elaine Frantz, Ku Klux: The Birth of the Klan Reconstruction (Chapel Hill: University of North Carolina Press, 2015). (EBook)

Patterson, William, We Charge Genocide: The Crime of Government Against The Negro People (New York: International Publisher's Co. 4th Edition, 2017).

Petersen, Jennifer, Murder, the Media, and the Politics of Public Feelings: Remembering Matthew
Shepard and James Byrd, Jr. (Bloomington: University of Indiana Press, 2011)

Pillsbury, A. (1909). "A Brief Inquiry into a Federal Remedy for Lynching." *Harvard Law Review, 15*(9), 707-713. doi:10.2307/1323748 and Vernier, C. (1912). Local Sentiment and Lynching in Pennsylvania. *Journal of the American Institute of Criminal Law and Criminology, 3*(2), 171-173. Retrieved July 28, 2020, from www.jstor.org/stable/1133019

- "The War Amendments" *The North American Review,* 189(642), 740-751. Retrieved July 29, 2020, from www.jstor.org/stable/25106358

Quarles, Benjamin, Lord Dunmore as Liberator. *The William and Mary Quarterly,* 15(4), 494-507. (1958). doi:10.2307/2936904
- The Negro and the Making of America (London: Collier Books, 1969)

The Rand Corporation "Overview of the Posse Comitatus Act" Preparing the U.S. Army for Homeland Security: Concepts, Issues, and Opinions by Eric E. Larsen and John E. Peters (2001)

Rosser, L. (1921). "The Illegal Enforcement of Criminal Law." *The Virginia Law Register,* 7(8), 569-586. doi:10.2307/1107032

Rucker, Phillip, and Carol Leonnig Very Stable Genius: Donald Trump' Testing of America (New York: Penguin Press, 2020)

Schill, Michael H and Samantha Friedman, "The Fair Housing Act of 1988: The First Decade", Cityscape: A Journal of Policy Development and Research, Vol.4, No.3 (1999)

Sha, Kushbu "Textbook Voter Suppression: A Battle Years in the Making" *The Guardian* November 10, 2018, located here: https://www.theguardian.com/us-news/2018/nov/10/georgia-election-recount-stacey-abrams-brian-kemp

Seale, Bobby Seize The Time: The Story of the Black Panther Party and Huey P. Newton (Baltimore: Black Classic Press, 1991)

Sweet, Lynn "How Rand Paul Blocked the Emmett Till Anti-Lynching Bill while the nation mourned George Floyd" Chicago Sun-Times June 5, 2020

Stephenson, G. (1909). "The Separation of the Races in Public Conveyances." *The American Political Science Review, 3*(2), 180-204. doi:10.2307/1944727; see also Richardson, J. (1969). Florida Black Codes. *The Florida Historical Quarterly, 47*(4), 365-379. Retrieved July 29, 2020, from www.jstor.org/stable/30140241

Smith, David "Rand Paul stalls bill that would make lynching a federal hate crime." *The Guardian* June 11, 2020

Terrell, Mary Church *"Lynching from a Negro's Point of View." The North American Review, 178*(571), 853-868. Retrieved July 28, 2020, from www.jstor.org/stable/25150991

Thiongi, Ngogi wa and Micere Githae Mugo's <u>Trial of Dedan Kimathi</u> (Portsmouth: Heinemann Educational Books, 1976)

Trefousse, Hans L. <u>Andrew Johnson: A Biography</u> (New York: W.W. Norton, 1989)

Tucker, D. (1971). Miss Ida B. Wells and Memphis Lynching. *Phylon (1960), 32*(2), 112-122. doi:10.2307/273997.

Umoja, Akinyele Omawale in his excruciatingly detailed work <u>We Will Shoot Back: Armed Resistance in the Mississippi Freedom Movement</u> (New York: New York University Press, 2013)

Walters, Ronald Pan-Africanism in the African Diaspora: An Analysis of Modern Afrocentric Political Movements (Detroit: Wayne State University Press. 1998)

Weitzer, Ronald Transforming Settler States: Communal Conflict and Internal Security in Northern Ireland and Zimbabwe (Berkeley: University of California Press, 1990)

Welling, J. (1880). "The Emancipation Proclamation." *The North American Review, 130*(279), 163-185. Retrieved July 29, 2020, from www.jstor.org/stable/25100834

Wexler, Laura Fire In A Canebrake: The Last Mass Lynching in America (New York: First Scribner, 2004)

Williams, Robert Negroes With Guns (Mansfield Center: Martino Publishing, 2013 ed.)

White, Derrick Blood, Sweat, and Tears: Jake Gaither, Florida A & M, and the History of Black College Football (Chapel Hill: University of North Carolina Press, 2019)

Wiggins, W. (1988). "Boxing's Sambo Twins: Racial Stereotypes in Jack Johnson and Joe Louis Newspaper Cartoons, 1908 to 1938". *Journal of Sport History, 15*(3), 242-254. Retrieved August 1, 2020, from www.jstor.org/stable/43609224

Wood, Amy Louise Lynching and Spectacle: Witnessing Racial Violence in America, 1890-1940 (Chapel Hill: University of North Carolina Press, 2015)

Woodson, Carter Godwin, and Charles Harris Wesley The Negro in Our History (Washington, D.C.: The Associated Publishers, 1972)

--"What the Framers of the Federal Constitution Thought of the Negro". (1918). *The Journal of Negro History, 3*(4), 381-434. doi:10.2307/2713818

-- "The Negroes of Cincinnati Prior to the Civil War." *The Journal of Negro History, 1*(1), 1-22. doi:10.2307/2713512

Wyatt, Traci Steve Biko: The Radical Gospel of Black Consciousness (Meadville: Fulton Books, Inc., 2020)

X, Malcolm as told to Alex Haley; The Autobiography of Malcolm X (New York: Ballantine Books, 1999 ed.)
"The Jurisdiction of the Federal Courts in Cases of Conspiracy against Persons of African Descent." (1907). *The Yale Law Journal, 16*(3), 200-202. doi:10.2307/783978

Zangrando, R. (1965). "The NAACP and a Federal Antilynching Bill, 1934-1940". *The Journal of Negro History, 50*(2), 106-117. doi:10.2307/2715996

Media Cited

Ali, Amir H., and Emily Clark https://theappeal.org/qualified-immunity-explained/#.Xy3p5dhyxHk.email.
Common Dreams, https://www.commondreams.org/news/2020/08/07/enraging-and-inexcusable-louisiana-supreme-court-rules-black-man-convicted-garden

Vera, Amir, and Lura Ly: https://www.cnn.com/2020/05/26/us/central-park-video-dog-video-african-american-trnd/index.html

Barcella, Laura: https://www.aetv.com/real-crime/ted-bundy-execution

Booker, Brakkton "Oregon Governor Says Federal Officers Will Begin Phased Withdrawal From Portland" NPR July 29, 2020, located here: https://www.npr.org/2020/896840086/oregon-governor-on-federal-agents-leaving-portland07/29/

Chappel, Bill "Colorado Votes to Abolish Slavery 2 Years After Similar Amendment Failed" NPR, November 7, 2018, located here: https://www.npr.org/2018/11/07/665295736/colorado-votes-to-abolish-slavery-2-years-after-similar-amendment-failed

Fulton, Sybrina and Tracy Martin *Rest In Power: The Enduring Life of Trayvon Martin* (New York: Spiegel and Grau, 2017)

Griggs, Brandon https://www.cnn.com/2018/12/20/us/living-while-black-police-calls-trnd/index.html

Geneva, Tana https://theappeal.org/as-decriminalization-drives-reforms-for-marijuana-convictions-activists-see-others-serving-time-left-behind/#.Xy3sUwGAraA.email

Householder, Mike, and Scott Bauer "Lawyer: Blake Not Likely to Walk Again After Shot by Police" August 25, 2020, Associated Press website link: https://www.bbc.com/news/world-us-canada-53909766

Heisig, Eric "Tamir Rice Shooting: A Breakdown of the Events that lead to the 12-year Old's Death", *Cleveland.com* January 13, 2017

Lustbader, Sarah "Joe Biden's Role in Mass Incarceration Was No Mistake: It Was Politics" *The Appeal*, April 25, 2019, originally published as part of The Daily Appeal Newsletter located here: https://theappeal.org/politicalreport/joe-bidens-role-in-mass-incarceration-was-no-mistake-it-was-politics/#.Xy3rpGgb0us.email

McCullough, Jolie April 24, 2019, *Texas Tribune* website: https://www.texastribune.org/2019/04/24/texas-execution-john-william-king-james-byrd/

Montanaro, Domenico "What is the Insurrection Act that Trump is Threatening to Invoke" *NPR* June 1, 2020, located here:

Naughtie, Andrew "Former KKK leader endorses Trump for President Again and Tucker Carlson for VP" July 9, 2020, *The Independent* located on the link to their website here: https://www.independent.co.uk/news/world/americas/kkk-trump-david-duke-tucker-carlson-election-2020-a9609491.html

https://www.npr.org/2020/06/01/867467714/what-is-the-insurrection-act-that-trump-is-threatening-to-invoke

Oppel, Jr., Richard, and Derrick Bryson Taylor, "Here's What you Need to Know About Breonna Taylor" *New York Times*, July 31, 2020. https://www.nytimes.com/article/breonna-taylor-police.html

Turner, Allen to *The Houston Chronicle* September 22, 2011: https://www.chron.com/news/houston-texas/article/Hate-crime-killer-executed-2182684.php.

University of Arkansas Libraries, Special Collections Department has archived a copy of the speech in a document and made it available on this link: https://libraries.uark.edu/specialcollections/research/lessonplans/FaubusSpeechLessonPlan.pdf (2008)

Wagner, Laura, and Laura Domonoske, "George Zimmerman Auctions Off Gun He Used to Kill Travon Martin" *NPR* May 12, 2016, located here: https://www.npr.org/sections/thetwo-way/2016/05/12/477769731/george-zimmerman-auctioning-off-gun-with-which-he-killed-trayvon-martin.

Walker, Knez et al., https://abcnews.go.com/US/happened-elijah-mcclain-protests-bring-attention-death/story?id=71523476

Ward, Alex https://www.vox.com/2020/6/5/21281604/lafayette-square-White-house-tear-gas-protest

https://digital.library.cornell.edu/?f%5Bsubject_tesim%5D%5B%5D=Lynching&page=1&per_page=20

https://ibw21.org/initiative-posts/naarc-posts/naarc-rolls-out-preliminary-10-point-reparations-plan/

https://www.ada.gov/ada_voting/ada_voting_ta.htm

https://www.wapt.com/article/civil-rights-activist-r-l-bolden-dies/2079420

http://www.oopau.org/2.html

https://blacklivesmatter.com/

https://www.fbi.gov/investigate/terrorism

https: www.vault.fbi.gov

https://www.change.org/p/department-of-counterterrorism-change-kkk-status-into-terrorist-organization.

https://www.adl.org/resources/profiles/al-qaeda

https://sayevery.name/say-their-names-list

https://policefundingdatabase.tminstituteldf.org/misconductsettlements

https://www.themarshallproject.org/records/1712-police-settlements

http://law2.umkc.edu/faculty/projects/ftrials/shipp/lynchingsstate.html

http://law2.umkc.edu/faculty/projects/ftrials/zimmerman1/zimcalls.html

https://govtrackus.s3.amazonaws.com/legislink/pdf/stat/9/STATUTE-9-Pg462.pdf

https://www.merriam-webster.com/dictionary/nadir?src=search-dict-box

https://abhmuseum.org/

https://www.britannica.com/topic/lynching

https://www.naacp.org/naacp-history-dyer-anti-lynching-bill/

https://www.washingtonfootball.com/news/redskins-announce-franchise-will-be-called-washington-football-team-pending-adop.

https://www.bia.gov/bia

https://joebiden.com/

H.R. 35 Emmet Till Anti-Lynching Act, 116th Congress H. Rept. 116-267 (2019-2020).
https://www.congress.gov/bill/116th-congress/house-bill/35/text.

https://www.archives.gov/exhibits/featured-documents/emancipation-proclamation#:~:text=President%20Abraham%20Lincoln%20issued%twentiethe,and%20henceforward%20shall%20be%20free.%22;

https://pgdigs.tumblr.com/image/3086908730

https://www.greenwoodreparations.com/about-us;

https://ktul.com/news/local/betty-shelby-talks-about-starting-over-one-year-after-her-acquittal.

https://www.splcenter.org/20110228/ku-klux-klan-history-racism.

https://www.pbs.org/wgbh/americanexperience/features/till-killers-confession/.

https://www.emmett-till.org/visit-the-museumhttps://www.cnn.com/2019/10/20/us/emmett-till-memorial-bulletproof-trnd/index.html

https://www.splcenter.org/fighting-hate/extremist-files/group/aryan-brotherhood-texas.

https://senate.texas.gov/press.php?id=23-20010521a; https://www.justice.gov/crt/matthew-shepard-and-james-byrd-jr-hate-crimes-prevention-act-2009-0.

https://www.usatoday.com/story/opinion/2016/07/20/obama-black-lives-matter-police-shootings-beer-summit-column/87310566/.

https://www.bbc.com/news/world-us-canada-52623151.

https://www.bbc.com/news/world-us-canada-52623151

https://www.bbc.com/news/world-us-canada-52861726

https://www.kboi.com/news/minneapolis-police-identify-umbrella-man-who-helped-incite-george-floyd-riots-warrant-says/.

https://www.bbc.com/news/world-us-canada-53453077.

https://www.justice.gov/crt/page/file/922456/download

https://museumandmemorial.eji.org/memorial

Film

Birth of a Nation (1915) directed by David W. Griffith

Enter the Dragon (1973) directed Robert Clouse

Rosewood (1997) directed by John Singleton

The Untold Story of Emmett Till (2005) directed by Keith Beauchamp

Spies of Mississippi (2014) directed by Dawn Porter

Rest in Power: The Story of Trayvon Martin (2018) directed Jennifer Furst and Julia Willoughby Nason

Who Put the Klan into Klu Klux Klan (2018) directed by Ian Lilley and Neil Oliver

Modern Day Slavery (2019) directed by Edwin Freeman

Music

Meeropol, Abel and Milt Gabler (1939) Strange Fruit, Recorded by Eleanor Fagan (Billie Holiday) New York: Commodore

Stevens, Earl G., et al. (1993) Anybody Can Get It on: Breakin' News [cassette] New York: Sic' Wit It/Jive

Parker, Lawrence "Kris" (1989) Bo Bo Bo: Ghetto Music: The Blueprint of Hip-Hop [cassette] New York: Jive
- (1989) Who Protects Us From You: The Blueprint of Hip-Hop [cassette] New York: Jive
- (1993) Black Cop: The Boom Bap [cassette] New York: Jive

   Ridenhour, Carlton D., et al. (1991) Can't Truss' It: Apocalypse 91' The Enemy Strikes Black [cassette] New York: Def Jam/Columbia
   - o (1991) By The Time I Get to Arizona: Apocalpyse 91' The Enemy Strikes Black [cassette] New York: Def Jam/Columbia
   - o (1989) Fight The Power: *Do The Right Thing* Official Movie Soundtrack [cassette] Detroit: Motown

   Jackson, O'Shea, et al. (1990) Endangered Species Tales From the Darkside: Amerikkka's Most Wanted [cassette] New York: Lench Mob/Priority
   - o (1990) Endangered Species Remix: Kill At Will [cassette] New York: Lench Mob/Priority

- (1990) The Product: Kill At Will [cassette] New York: Lench Mob/Priority
- (1991) A Bird in the Hand: Death Certificate [cassette] New York: Lench Mob/Priority

Shakur, Tupac A. (1993) Keep Ya Head Up: Strictly For My N.I.G.G.A.Z. [cassette] Santa Monica: Interscope